ALSO BY HARRY G. SUMMERS, JR.

On Strategy: A Critical Analysis of
the Vietnam War

On Strategy II: A Critical Analysis
of the Gulf War

The New World Strategy

A Military Policy for America's Future

Colonel Harry G. Summers, Jr.

A Touchstone Book
Published by Simon & Schuster
NEW YORK LONDON TORONTO
SYDNEY TOKYO SINGAPORE

TOUCHSTONE
ROCKEFELLER CENTER
1230 AVENUE OF THE AMERICAS
NEW YORK, NY 10020

DESIGNED BY LEVAVI & LEVAVI

MANUFACTURED IN THE UNITED STATES OF AMERICA

10   9   8   7   6   5   4   3   2   1

LIBRARY OF CONGRESS CATALOGING-IN-PUBLICATION DATA

SUMMERS, HARRY G.
THE NEW WORLD STRATEGY : A MILITARY POLICY FOR AMERICA'S FU-
TURE / HARRY G. SUMMERS, JR.
P.   CM.
"A TOUCHSTONE BOOK."
INCLUDES BIBLIOGRAPHICAL REFERENCES AND INDEX.
1. UNITED STATES—MILITARY POLICY. 2. UNITED STATES—ARMED
FORCES—ORGANIZATION. 3. INTERNATIONAL POLICE. 4. WORLD
POLITICS—1989—   I. TITLE.
UA23.S926 1995
355'.033573—DC20   95-32868
                                                      CIP

ISBN 0-684-81208-8

permissions continued on p. 272

IN HONOR OF
MY WIFE
ELOISE CUNNINGHAM SUMMERS,
WHOSE ENCOURAGEMENT AND SUPPORT
MADE IT ALL POSSIBLE

‖ Acknowledgments

This work is an outgrowth of a series of lectures given throughout the military establishment since the end of the Cold War on the future direction of the U.S. Armed Forces, as well as participation in a number of conferences and symposiums on peacekeeping and the nature of conflict into the twenty-first century.

Thanks to Lieutenant General Paul G. Cerjan, USA, for his invitation to serve as moderator/rapporteur for the National Defense University's 1992 symposium on "Non-Traditional Roles for the U.S. Military in the post–Cold War Era." And thanks also to General Carl E. Munday, Jr., USMC, the Commandant of the Marine Corps, and Lieutenant General C. C. Krulak, USMC, the Commanding General, Marine Corps Combat Development Command, for their kind invitation to participate in the 1993 Policy and Strategy War Game VII, "The Balkan Dilemma" at the Marine Corps Research Center at Quantico, Virginia.

Especially valuable were the insights provided by my fellow participants, including Marine Major Generals Charles E. Wilhelm and A. C. Zinni, both of whom had taken part in U.S. military operations in Somalia. General Wilhelm also later shared in the invitation by Rear Admiral Joseph C. Strasser, USN, the President of the Naval War College, to take part in a panel discussion on "The Ethical Use of Force and the Responsibility to Intervene" at the 1993 Professional Ethics Conference at Newport, Rhode Island.

Thanks also to Lieutenant General Bradley C. Hosmer, USAF, Superintendent of the U.S. Air Force Academy, for inviting me to participate in the panel on "Peacekeeping,

Peacemaking and Peace-Enforcement" as part of the 1994 Ira C. Eaker Distinguished Lecture on National Defense Policy.

Fellow panelist Brigadier General Ian Douglas of the Canadian Army, a longtime veteran of United Nations peacekeeping operations now stationed in Liberia, gave a unique perspective to the symposium and provided valuable background papers on the practical details of peacekeeping operations.

Also providing personal insights into peacekeeping operations was Sir Brian Urquart, who had served with the United Nations since 1945 and had taken part in peacekeeping operations in the Congo, Cyprus, Jammu and Kashmir, and the Middle East. In September 1993, thanks to Representative Tom Lantos, chairman of the Subcommittee on International Security, International Organizations, and Human Rights of the House Committee on Foreign Affairs, Sir Brian and I were both able to testify before the Congress on the issue of "U.S. Participation in UN Peacekeeping Activities."

When it comes to warfighting, retired Navy Captain James A. Barber, Jr., Executive Director of the U.S. Naval Institute, provided a special vantage point by naming me moderator of the 1992 panel on "Joint Operations in the New World Order," the "Pacific Basin Joint Strategy" panel in January 1993, and then of a joint war game, "Operation Precision Strike," in April 1993.

A joint perspective was also provided by my thrice yearly lectures to the Joint Flag Officer War Fighting Course at the Air University, Maxwell Air Force Base, Alabama. The interchange with the Army, Air Force, and Marine generals, and Navy admirals, provided a sounding board for current strategic concerns.

Also especially helpful were the interactions with students during my continuing series of lectures at the National Defense University, the Army War College, the Armed Forces Staff College, and the Inter-American Defense College, as well as the General Omar Bradley Lectures at the Army Command and General Staff College.

Giving additional perspective were the periodic lectures

and seminars at such institutions as the State Department's Foreign Service Institute, the Defense Intelligence College, the Air War College, the Armor School, Army Intelligence School, and the Air Force Special Operations School. Talks with Reserve and National Guard forces were most valuable, including lectures to the annual Reserve Components National Issue Seminar.

Equally valuable was the chance to talk with the planners at the Naval Doctrine Command at Norfolk, Virginia, and at the Army's National Simulation Center and Battle Command Battle Labs. General Frederick Franks, Commander of the Army's Training and Doctrine Command (TRADOC), provided valuable insights as well as an opportunity to discuss the future direction of the Army with his school commanders during the 1992 TRADOC "Strategy for the Future" senior leaders conference.

An enormous debt is owed to the United States Marine Corps University for my appointment to the 1993–94 Brigadier General H. L. Oppenheimer Chair of Warfighting Strategy, and subsequently to the 1994–95 Marine War College Chair of Military Affairs. Involved were a series of lectures at the Marine War College, Command and Staff College, Amphibious Warfare School, Communications Officer School, and the Basic School, as well as visits to Marines at Camp Pendleton, 29 Palms, and at the Recruit Depot at San Diego, California.

Thanks to Major General William M. Steele, I had the chance to talk with the senior officers and NCOs of the 82d Airborne Division about future military operations. And through the good offices of Lieutenant General Johnnie Corns, U.S. Army Pacific Commander, I was able to meet with his soldiers as well.

Named the Honorary Colonel of the 21st Infantry Regiment, part of the Army's 25th Infantry Division in Hawaii, in 1994, I saw at firsthand the fighting forces that man our defenses. A different view was provided by the American Bar Association's invitation to take part in a 1993 panel on women in the military, and by the United States Information Agency's invitation to address several visiting foreign delegations on the American way of war.

Special thanks to House Armed Services Committee Chairman (later Secretary of Defense) Les Aspin and committee members Ike Skelton, Robert Dornan, and Floyd Spence for background papers on national defense issues. And thanks as well to Aspin's successor, Congressman Ron Dellums, and the members of the Armed Services Committee for their October 1994 invitation to testify on U.S. intervention in Haiti and peacekeeping operations in general. And special thanks as well to Senators Strom Thurmond and Sam Nunn for the opportunity to testify before their Senate Armed Services Committee in July 1995 on U.S. policy in Bosnia.

I am grateful to Army Colonel Larry Icenogel, Office of the Chairman, Joint Chiefs of Staff; Air Force Colonel Charles J. Dunlap, Jr., U.S. Central Command; Mr. Bill Nixon of the Army's Training and Doctrine Command; and retired Army Colonel F. William Smullen III for their assistance in providing reference material and for their advice.

A final word of thanks to Simon & Schuster's Mitch Horowitz, who provided the initial inspiration for this work, and to Carlo DeVito and Caroline Sutton, who saw it through to completion; to my wife, Eloise Cunningham Summers, whose support made this work possible; to our two sons, Army Majors Harry G. Summers III and David C. Summers, who may have to carry the military policy for America's future into execution; and to our daughter-in-law, retired Chief Warrant Officer Kathy Summers, a veteran of the Gulf War, who provided personal insights into the role of women in the military.

In expressing my thanks to all those who provided comments and advice, I must add that the conclusions and such errors as this book contains are solely my responsibility.

H.G.S.
Bowie, Maryland
July 1995

‖ Contents

Part III
OPERATIONS OTHER THAN WAR

Part IV
A MILITARY POLICY FOR AMERICA'S FUTURE

Introduction

Our purpose was not to assign, in passing, a handful of principles of warfare to each period. We wanted to show how every age had its own kind of war, its own limiting conditions, and its own peculiar preconceptions. . . . It follows that the events of every age must be judged in the light of its own peculiarities.

—CARL VON CLAUSEWITZ, *On War,* P. 593

Although the "new world order" proclaimed by President George Bush in his January 1991 State of the Union address has become something of a cliché, when it comes to the world's strategic military environment a new world is unquestionably at hand. For the first time since the days of the Roman Empire, there is a single dominant world power. And unlike the Roman Empire, which dominated only Europe and the Mediterranean basin, America has the military power to dominate the entire world.

As a senior Lithuanian government official said at a recent U.S. Information Agency seminar, the most important strategic question today is, will the U.S. turn imperialistic and use that power to dominate the world, or, even worse, will the country ignore the world and retreat back into Fortress America? The answer did not lie so much in an analysis of the physical aspects of American military power as in an appreciation of the American character, the peculiarities of our unique civil-military relations, and the American way of war.

Overlooked by futurologists in the current rage for information-age computer-generated scenarios, such unquantifiable factors have always been the key to understanding war. As Carl von Clausewitz, the great Prussian philosopher of war, observed in 1832, every age has its own kind of war, with "its own limiting conditions and its own peculiar preconceptions."

It also had its own *policy*, defined as "the interaction of peoples and their governments," what Clausewitz called war's "guiding intelligence." That policy in turn provides the basis for the formulation of military strategy, simply defined as the use of military means to achieve the political ends of the state.

The first step in policy formulation, wrote Navy Lieutenant Commander (later Commodore) Dudley W. Knox in 1915, is "to determine whether our strategic and tactical operations will be offensive or defensive in character and whether they will be introduced by 'secondary warfare' . . . or by 'primary warfare' etc.

"The determination of such matters as these," Knox said eighty years ago, "produces a 'conception of war' which furnishes a point of origin, without which we are as uncertain of our bearings as a ship in a fog."

In both World War I and World War II, the United States had a clearcut conception of war: adopt the strategic defensive temporarily to buy time to prepare, then go on the strategic offensive to destroy the enemy armed forces and achieve victory.

During the Cold War with the Soviet Union, the conception of war was also relatively well understood. At the strategic level in Washington, D.C., pursuant to the national policy of containment, the United States waged "secondary warfare" on the strategic defensive against the Soviet Union while carefully avoiding any direct military showdown. To that end, in its wars with Soviet client states in Korea and Vietnam, at the battlefield level the United States adopted the operational (i.e., theater-level) defensive in order to stalemate the conflicts, rather than go on the offensive to achieve victory and thereby risk a superpower confrontation.

With the collapse of the Soviet Union in 1989, the national policy of containment was overtaken by events, and the U.S. conception of war reverted back to the strategic offensive. During the Persian Gulf War in 1990–91, the United States defeated the Iraqi military on the battlefield and forced Saddam Hussein to evacuate Kuwait and beg for a cessation of hostilities.

When it comes to the warfighting dimension of U.S. military policy, that conception of war remains in effect, as President Bill Clinton demonstrated in October 1994 when he quickly moved U.S. combat forces into attack positions in Kuwait when Saddam Hussein began a military buildup on the border there. And the Clinton administration has been quite forceful in using military power to reaffirm America's commitment to protecting the vital U.S. national interests in Western Europe, Northeast Asia, and the Middle East that have remained constant since World War II.

By its continued forward deployment of U.S. forces in those areas, the Clinton administration has guaranteed U.S. involvement in any crisis arising in them. And with the Defense Department's 1993 *Bottom-Up Review*, the United States gave its imprimatur to a small but powerful and highly mobile conventional military force capable of protecting those worldwide vital interests.

Unfortunately, the Clinton administration has also unwittingly subverted that warfighting stance and, some claim, undermined military subordination to civilian control, by insisting that military policy should have a peacekeeping dimension as well.

One of the purposes of this book is to explore how the peculiarities of the American way of war, combined with the dynamics of warfighting and peacekeeping dimensions in current policy, have caused the United States military to lose its way.

What emerges is an almost Hegelian dialectic, in which the early peacekeeping *thesis* rooted in humanitarian concerns provoked a public and congressional *antithesis* fueled by concerns over the costs of such actions in U.S. lives and treasure.

The result is a new *synthesis,* stating that national interests should determine U.S. involvement abroad.

Drawing on that analysis, *The New World Strategy* concludes with ten commandments that should govern a new military policy for the post–Cold War world. The intent is not to provide a "manual for action," but rather, as Clausewitz put it, "to provide a thinking man with a frame of reference."

Part I

The Strategic Environment

Policy is the guiding intelligence and war only the instrument, not vice versa . . . the supreme standard for the conduct of war, the point of view that determines its main lines of action, can only be that of policy. . . .

It might be thought that policy could make demands on war which war could not fulfill; but that hypothesis would challenge the natural and unavoidable assumption that policy knows the instrument it means to use.

—CARL VON CLAUSEWITZ,
On War, P. 607

Chapter 1

The Peculiar Relationship

Vietnam was a reaffirmation of the peculiar relationship between the American Army and the American people. The American Army really is a people's army in the sense that it belongs to the American people who take a jealous and proprietary interest in its involvement. . . . The Army, therefore, cannot be committed lightly.

—GENERAL FRED C. WEYAND,
CHIEF OF STAFF, U.S. ARMY, 1976

People's Military

As Carl von Clausewitz warned in 1832, the effectiveness of policy rests on the "natural and unavoidable assumption that policy knows the instrument it means to use." That is especially true in the United States, where military policy must be founded on a clear understanding of the unique relationship between the American military and the American people. This relationship is a key factor in determining how the U.S. military may be committed to action.

That fact is anathema to foreign and military policy elitists, who would arrogate to themselves alone the authority to decide what is best for America. When Secretary of Defense Caspar Weinberger announced the so-called Weinberger Doctrine in 1984, the fifth of his "six major tests to be applied when we are weighing the use of U.S. combat forces abroad" stated that "before the U.S. commits combat forces abroad, there must be some reasonable assurance we will have the support of the American people and their elected representatives in the Congress."

That formulation drew immediate fire from those who would deny such constraints by the hoi polloi on the commitment of military power. *New York Times* columnist William Safire complained, "Secretary Weinberger's stunning doctrine suggests that we take a poll before we pull a trigger. No more unpopular wars—if the public won't hold a big parade to send us off, we're not going." Secretary Weinberger's purpose in enunciating the doctrine of "only-fun-wars," Safire continued, was "to undermine Secretary of State George Shultz [who has been] putting forward the more traditional, less simplistic theory that power and diplomacy must be used in tandem if we are to stop the erosion of our national interests."

Calling the requirement for public support "highly questionable," the *National Review* editorialized that "In his fifth test . . . Weinberger gets into trouble." Seeing "the long Tet Offensive of the homefront" as the genesis of that test, the editorial noted that the loss of public support "was not the military's fault; strictly speaking it was none of their business. . . . The rallying of public support," it emphasized, "is the task of the political leadership."

Weinberger had set "an impossible standard," said the editors. "The sine qua non of popular support is success. But if the mission is indeed 'vital,' then it has to be carried out, even at the risk of failure. . . . Not all wars are Grenada. If the Bolsheviks had thought so, they wouldn't be where they are today."

A decade later the irony of that remark is obvious. Perhaps if the "Bolsheviks" had not ignored the importance of public support, they would indeed "not be where they are today." And while all wars include the risk of failure, it is foolhardy indeed to include risks that can be avoided.

The critics' frustrations with the constraints imposed by

the need to gain public and congressional support as a prereq-uisite for military action are understandable, yet the notion that such support can be ignored flies in the face not only of history but the realities of American political-military tradi-tion as well.

The need for public and congressional support for military operations has far deeper roots than Vietnam, going back to the War for Independence and the founding of the Republic. But, as I have discussed at length elsewhere, the Vietnam de-bacle was the most powerful example in our history of the perils of failing to factor in that fundamental consideration.

The error began at a time in the 1960s when military policy was in a state of flux. Echoing the limited-war theorists of the time, Secretary of Defense Robert S. McNamara was quoted as saying in 1965 that "The greatest contribution Vietnam is making—right or wrong is beside the point—is that it is de-veloping an ability in the United States to fight a limited war, to go to war without arousing the public ire."

In a supreme demonstration of intellectual arrogance, the noted political scientist Robert Osgood "concluded that even though the American people will be hostile, because of their traditions and ideology, to the kind of strategy he [Osgood] proposes, that strategy must still be adopted." It is a persistent fallacy, for such public-be-damned arguments have been re-peated thirty years later by those who favor intervention in Bosnia.

If the war in Vietnam proved nothing else, it proved the American people could not be excluded from the strategic equation. The tragedy was that we should have known better, for as General Fred Weyand, the last U.S. commander there, said in 1976, that war merely *reaffirmed* the peculiar relation-ship between the American Army and the American people.

That relationship was forged during the Revolutionary War, a bitter and divisive eight-year struggle where public sup-port was by no means assured. It became clear then that there had to be legal sanctions against giving aid and comfort to the enemy if the war effort was not to be undermined from within.

As the historian Dave R. Palmer observed, "the British stay in [Philadelphia in 1777–78] had been most pleasant, their idle hours filled with entertainment. Indeed in some ways the natives might have been overly warm, for it seems the occupying army suffered more than was usual from intimate encounters. Apothecaries did a brisk business in such medicines as Dr. Yeldall's Anti-venereal Essence which both prevented and cured."

The framers of the Constitution, most of whom were veterans of that war, were determined never again to fight without the full backing and support of the American people. As the discussion of the proposed Constitution in *The Federalist* reveals, one way was to make the military an instrument of the people rather than of the government.

On December 19, 1797, Alexander Hamilton noted that in "the plan reported by the [Constitutional] Convention . . . the whole power of raising armies was lodged in the *legislature*, not in the *executive;* that this legislature was to be a popular body, consisting of the representatives of the people, periodically elected; and that . . . there was to be found . . . an important qualification even of the legislative discretion, which forbids the appropriation of money for the support of an army for any longer period than two years. . . ."

Elaborating on that theme on March 14, 1788, Hamilton pointed out that the power of the President would be

nominally the same with that of the King of Great Britain, but in substance much inferior to it.

It would amount to nothing more than the supreme command and direction of the military and the naval forces, as first General and Admiral of the confederacy; while that of the British King extends to the *declaring* of war and the *raising* and *regulating* of fleets and armies; all of which by the Constitution under consideration would appertain to the Legislature.

Thus, while Article II of the Constitution appoints the President as the Commander in Chief of the Armed Forces, Article I gives the Congress (the "representatives of the People, periodically elected") the sole power to raise the military, provide rules for its regulation and government, and declare war.

Secretary Weinberger's insistence that there must be some reasonable assurance of "the support of the American people and their elected representatives in the Congress" before U.S. forces are committed to action is clearly in line with the intent of the framers of the Constitution. As James Madison emphasized in *The Federalist* on January 19, 1788, a cornerstone of the American Constitution was "that the ultimate authority, wherever the derivative may be found, resides in the people alone." Thus there is a moral imperative that those American citizens whose sons' and daughters' lives are put in jeopardy ought to have some say in their commitment.

But if the moral argument does not persuade, the practical argument is even more compelling. If the Congress does not approve, who then pays for the war? Article I, Section 8, of the Constitution gives to the Congress alone the power to "pay the debts and provide for the common defense and general welfare of the United States." The President does not have a red cent that is not appropriated by the Congress, a powerful constraint on his warmaking powers.

As we shall see shortly, it was precisely this constitutional provision that forced the withdrawal of U.S. military forces from Somalia in 1994.

Unlike most world militaries, which are answerable primarily to a president or chief executive, the U.S. military belongs to the American people. This has a profound effect on the military policy of the nation, for it shapes, constrains, and determines how that military can be employed. Three aspects of the American character in particular—idealism, pragmatism, and non-interventionism—have a particularly strong influence.

Idealism

Idealism is a defining aspect of the American character. When it comes to military policy, idealism tends to push the nation into involvement abroad in pursuit of democratic and humanitarian ends. Now defined in terms of "human rights," it appeared, for example, in March 1994 with America's insistence that China reform its human rights policies as a precondition for continued U.S. most-favored-nation (MFN) trade status.

Indeed, one of America's first military interventions abroad began on just such an idealistic note. "In one of the most singular explanations for the formulation of a foreign policy ever devised by an American president," writes Stanley Karnow in his historical account of U.S. involvement in the Philippines, President William McKinley said publicly that his decision to send American troops to the Philippines in 1898 was based on divine guidance. "He had paced the floor of the White House nightly, even pausing to beg 'Almighty God for light and guidance.' Then suddenly one night a list of options appeared. . . . His only choice . . . was to take the archipelago and 'to educate the Filipinos, and uplift and Christianize them, and by God's grace do the very best we could by them, as our fellow men for whom Christ had died.'"

This must have come as some surprise to the Filipinos, who had been "Christianized" by Roman Catholic missionaries beginning more than three centuries earlier. Be that as it may, this idealistic rationale was popular with the American people.

McKinley was not the only idealist in the White House. President Woodrow Wilson was its very exemplar. With his "Peace Without Victory" speech in January 1917, his "Fourteen Points" for ending World War I a year later, and his advocacy of the League of Nations, Wilson sought to inject American idealism into world politics. But another character trait, non-interventionism, was a powerful counter to these idealistic impulses.

Even with the caveat that "The United States assumes no obligation to preserve the territorial integrity or political independence of any other country by the employment of its military or naval forces, its resources, or any form of economic discrimination," the League of Nations Treaty still failed to receive the necessary two-thirds vote for ratification in the Senate in March 1920, and the United States opted out of the League.

Non-interventionism—or, more properly, isolationism—replaced idealism as the guiding light for the next two decades. But with the outbreak of World War II, idealism returned to the fore. In his annual address to the Congress on January 6, 1941, President Franklin D. Roosevelt stated that the "historic truth" was that the United States "has at all times maintained opposition to any attempt to lock us in behind an ancient Chinese wall."

Calling such attempts "the very antithesis of the so-called new order of tyranny which the dictators seek to create with the crash of a bomb," Roosevelt proposed a world founded upon four essential freedoms. "The first," he said, "is freedom of speech and expression—everywhere in the world. The second is freedom of every person to worship God in his own way—everywhere in the world. The third is freedom from want . . . everywhere in the world. The fourth is freedom from fear . . . everywhere in the world. . . .

"Freedom means the supremacy of human rights everywhere," FDR went on. This new "moral order is no vision of a distant millennium. It is a definite basis for a kind of world attainable in our own time and generation." Presaging by half a century President Clinton's call for U.S. "engagement" in the "enlargement" of democracy and free market economies, Roosevelt stated: "The world order which we seek is the cooperation of free countries, working together in a friendly, civilized society."

Idealism reached its highest point after World War II, with President John F. Kennedy's pledge in 1961 to "bear any burden, meet any hardship, support any friend, oppose any foe to assure the survival and success of liberty." While the Vietnam War cast a cloud over these high-flown promises, idealism still remains a powerful factor in U.S. foreign and military policy.

Although idealism tends to push the nation toward military involvement, it also imposes severe limits on how military operations can be conducted. During the Philippine Insurrection, an American rifle company was massacred and terribly mutilated at Balangiga on the island of Samar. "The press rated it with the Alamo and Custer's defeat as one of the worst tragedies in American military annals," notes Karnow in his history of U.S.-Philippine relations. The local military commander, Brigadier General Jacob "Hell-Roaring Jake" Smith, was ordered "to end the resistance on Samar once and for all.

"'I want no prisoners,'" Smith told his subordinates. "'I wish you to kill and burn, the more you kill and burn the better it will please me. I want all persons killed who are capable of bearing arms in actual hostilities against the United States. . . . Samar 'must be made a howling wilderness.'"

When news of Smith's order became public, the American public recoiled in horror at this offense to their idealism. Smith was recalled from the Philippines by President Theodore Roosevelt himself, court-martialed for conduct prejudicial to good military order and discipline, and—"disgraced in the eyes of the American public"—forced into retirement.

"Hell-Roaring Jake" was an extreme case, but there are always limits to what the American people will tolerate. During the Korean War, the age-old military policy of attrition (wearing down an enemy by imposing unacceptable casualties) was condemned by the Senate in 1951 during what came to be known as the "Great Debate" on the conduct of the war in Korea.

The policy of "destroying the effective core of the Communist Chinese armies by killing that government's trained soldiers, in the hope that someone will negotiate . . . is essentially immoral," said the Senate report, "not likely to produce either victory in Korea or an end to aggression. At the same time such a policy tends to destroy the moral stature of the United States as a leader in the family of nations."

And idealism has been a major constraint on nuclear war as well. I was in Hanoi in April 1975, a week before the fall of Saigon, to negotiate the terms for the withdrawal of the U.S. Embassy and the Defense Attaché Office. My North Vietnamese Army counterpart said, "This just goes to show you cannot stamp out a revolutionary idea with force."

"That's nonsense and you know it," I replied. "When the Muslims declared a jihad against Genghis Khan and his Mongols in Central Asia in the thirteenth century, he killed most of the population and turned the area into a howling desert. That took the starch out of the revolution. And you'll find few people in southern France who can repeat the Albigensian Creed.

"When that heresy was suppressed in 1250, the military commander asked the bishop, 'How can you tell the heretics from the true believers?' The terrible answer was, 'Kill them all! God will know His own.'

"You know," I continued, "we had the means to totally destroy North Vietnam with nuclear weapons at any time of our choosing."

"We knew that," he replied. "We also knew you'd never do it."

He was absolutely right. It was not because the United States lacked the means to do it. We had the nuclear capability many times over. It was because the American people would never permit such an action to be done in their name. That moral constraint was as real, and as binding, as any physical constraint might be.

Today, a new factor in the role of idealism in U.S. foreign and military policy is the role of television. As will be discussed in more depth below, there are those who believe that television may become the arbiter of U.S. intervention.

Its power was demonstrated during the Persian Gulf War, when televised pictures of the terrible carnage on the "Highway of Death" leading north from Kuwait City were reportedly a factor in the decision to end the war. According to *The Washington Post*'s Rick Atkinson, Chairman of the Joint Chiefs of Staff General Colin Powell "anticipated that Americans and allies alike would soon see televised images of the carnage . . . and react with outrage. To blight the dazzling performance of the U.S. military with images of a 'turkey shoot' was both unnecessary and foolish."

But the role of idealism as a constraint on war is by no

means absolute. Violence deemed disproportionate certainly evokes revulsion among the American public—the television pictures of U.S. Marines setting fire to the thatched roofs of Vietnamese huts while wailing babies clutched at their mothers' skirts in the foreground is a classic case in point.

However, as the 1994–95 public reaction against attempts by the Smithsonian Institution to turn the exhibit of the *Enola Gay,* the aircraft that dropped the atomic bomb on Hiroshima, into a condemnation of American cruelty and racism makes clear, violence seen as necessary to the war effort, and especially violence that saves American lives, is accepted by most with equanimity.

As Atkinson noted, "Powell's sentiments were defensible and cogent and even magnanimous. But some of his premises, as he surely knew, were open to question. The belief that Americans would recoil from the Highway of Death may have misread a popular culture steeped in violence. [America] had endured one of the bloodiest civil wars in history and two world wars in this century. . . . And the issue was still theoretical: no pictures of the Highway of Death had yet appeared on American TV networks, nor would they until after the war was over."

What may at first glance appear to be idealism could in fact be something quite different. The Vietnam War is a case in point. Often forgotten is that it was idealism that propelled our initial involvement there. "Vietnam represents the cornerstone of the Free World in Southeast Asia, the keystone to the arch, the finger in the dike," said Senator John F. Kennedy in a speech to the American Friends of Vietnam in June 1956.

But once the war turned bloody, the idealists did an about-face and became the war's most vociferous critics. "Not only are the rats leaving the sinking ship," said political scientist Hans Morgenthau, himself an early opponent of the war, during a 1968 seminar at the Army Command and General Staff College; "they are now standing on the shore claiming they were never on the ship to start with."

Part of the mythology of that war is that it was the idealists, in the form of the anti-war movement, who got America out of Vietnam. Ironically, as Professor John Mueller of the University of Rochester found, the Vietnam protest movement "actually was somewhat counterproductive in its efforts to influence public opinion—that is, the war might have been somewhat more unpopular had the protest not existed."

The Vietnam protest movement, Mueller goes on, "generated negative feelings among the American people to an all but unprecedented degree. . . . Opposition to the war came to be associated with violent disruption, stink bombs, desecration of the flag, profanity and contempt for American values. Not only would those associations tend to affect public opinion in a negative way, they also would tend to frighten away more 'respectable' would-be war opponents from joining the cause."

Pragmatism

What ultimately turned the American people against the Vietnam War was not "idealism," it was *pragmatism,* the second powerful determining force in the American character. Pragmatism can and often does override purely idealistic concerns. For example, in May 1994, pragmatic concerns over U.S. economic interests caused President Clinton to grant China the MFN trade status he had called into question only two months earlier.

But pragmatism can reinforce idealistic concerns as well. In November 1967, some thirty-one months after the start of U.S. involvement in the ground war in Vietnam in March 1965 (notably a period identical to that of the ground war in Europe in World War II from the landing in North Africa in November 1942 until V-E Day in May 1945), public opinion turned against the war.

This shift was reflected in the New Hampshire primaries in March 1968 when the "peace" candidate, Senator Eugene McCarthy, came within several hundred votes of defeating

President Lyndon Johnson. "The election was widely her-alded as a repudiation by the voters of the administration and its Vietnam policies," said analyst Herbert Y. Schandler, "but among the McCarthy voters, those who were dissatisfied with Johnson for not pursuing a *harder* line in Vietnam outnum-bered those who wanted a withdrawal by a margin of three to two." The mood of the McCarthy voters, and of the American public in general, was either "win the damn thing or get out," and when the government seemed incapable of doing either, they lost their patience.

Pragmatism is a powerful determinant of military policy. In his treatise on war, Clausewitz emphasized that "Since war is not an act of senseless passion but is controlled by its political object, the value of this object must determine the sacrifices to be made in pursuit of it in *magnitude* and also in *duration*. Once the expenditure of effort exceeds the value of the politi-cal object, the object must be renounced. . . ."

That's precisely what happened in Vietnam, and what hap-pened again almost twenty years later in Somalia and Bosnia. There is a simple equation involved. Ask a War College audi-ence what they will go to war for, and as professional soldiers they say they'll go when ordered by their political leaders. But ask them what they'll send their sons and daughters to war for, and the composite answer is: "Not much! The reasons must be clear and the stakes high." That's exactly what the larger American public says as well.

The public said that in 1994 about U.S. military involve-ment in Bosnia. Although bombarded for months by TV pic-tures and news articles about the terrible suffering of the Bosnian Muslims and the perfidy of the Bosnian Serbs, they, and their representatives in the Congress, were still opposed to intervention there. Responding to that sentiment, in No-vember 1994, Secretary of Defense William J. Perry eloquently stated the pragmatic foundations of American military policy:

In Bosnia . . . it would take hundreds of thousands of troops and probably significant casualties to impose the outcome we want—peace. That's a level of blood and treasure that is not commensurate with our national interests . . . we're not about to enter the war as a combatant. . . .

Our interests should dictate where we get involved and the extent of our military involvement. Our level of military involvement must reflect our stakes. At the extreme end of the spectrum, where our vital national interests are at stake we will use overwhelming force and go it alone if necessary. But where the interest is less we will be more selective in using force.

Non-Interventionism

In charge of the landing zone at the American Embassy during the evacuation of Saigon on April 30, 1975, a South Vietnamese officer plaintively asked, "How can you do this? How can you abandon an ally at its time of greatest need?"

"You don't understand America," I cynically replied. "I'm from Ohio, and not only don't Ohioans give a damn about Vietnam, they're not too keen on New York or San Francisco either!"

Said in bitter frustration, there was more than a little truth in those remarks. Yet another major constraint on military policy imposed by the American character is *non-interventionism*—or isolationism in its more extreme form.

Its roots were planted by President George Washington in his Farewell Address on September 17, 1796:

> It is our true policy to steer clear of permanent alliances with any portion of the foreign world. Taking care always to keep ourselves by suitable establishments on a respectable defensive posture, we may safely trust to temporary alliances or extraordinary emergencies. . . .
>
> The nation which indulges toward another an habitual hatred or an habitual fondness is in some degree a slave. It is a slave to its animosity or to its affections, either of which is sufficient to lead it astray from its duty and its interests. . . .
>
> A passionate attachment of one nation for another produces a variety of evils. Sympathy for the favored nation, facilitating the illusion of an imaginary common interest in cases where no real

common interest exists . . . betrays the former into a participation in the quarrels and wars of the latter without adequate inducement or justification.

"Against the insidious wiles of foreign influence (I conjure you to believe me, fellow-citizens)," Washington concluded, "the jealousy of a free people ought to be *constantly* awake." Those admonitions were put to the test twenty-five years later when American idealism threatened to drag the United States into the Greek struggle for independence from the Turkish Ottoman Empire. In 1821, presaging similar efforts in the 1990s to involve the United States in yet another civil war in the Balkans, the popular press and interventionists like Daniel Webster in the Congress "assailed the Monroe Administration for its apparent indifference to human suffering in other parts of the world," and demanded the intervention of the U.S. Navy's Mediterranean Squadron.

But Secretary of State John Quincy Adams would have no part of it. In a speech on July 4, 1821, Adams began with a nod to American idealism: "Wherever the standard of freedom and independence has been or shall be unfurled, there will her heart, her benedictions, and her prayers be." But then he turned to the American countervailing principle of non-involvement:

> But she goes not abroad in search of monsters to destroy. She is the well-wisher to the freedom and independence of all. She is the champion and vindicator only of her own. . . .
> She knows well that by once enlisting under other banners than her own, were they even the banners of foreign independence, she would involve herself beyond the power of extraction, in all the wars of interest and intrigue, of individual avarice, envy and ambition, which assumes the colors and usurp the standards of freedom.

"She might," Adams concluded in words even more applicable today, "become the dictatress of the world." Although there were some notable exceptions, especially in this hemisphere, non-interventionism was the dominant theme in

American foreign and military policy for the first century and a half of the nation's existence. After World War I, writes historian Robert Leckie, "isololationism became so firmly imbedded in the public mind that no other attitude seemed possible." When World War II began with the Nazi invasion of Poland on September 1, 1939, "only 2.5 percent of the nation favored intervention."

After the fall of France in 1940, Leckie continues, "America Firsters maintained that the nation could best defend herself on her own shores and should make herself so strong as to discourage invasion, while their opponents argued that now was the time to intervene while Britain still held out as a free world bastion and the British fleet still controlled the seas. . . . At no time up until Pearl Harbor was this debate ever resolved." Leckie goes on to note that "America remained hesitant, indecisive. A poll taken at this time showed only 7.7 percent favoring intervention."

The common belief today is that campus dissent over American involvement abroad began with the Vietnam War. When Army Chief of Staff General Fred C. Weyand, who was the last U.S. commander in Vietnam, was named "Man of the Year" by the University of California at Berkeley in 1976, many expressed amazement, given the fervor of anti-military dissent there.

But Weyand himself was not surprised. Anti-military dissent at Berkeley was nothing new, he said. Opposition to U.S. involvement in the war then brewing in Europe was one of the big issues during his senior year in 1939. As in the Vietnam War a quarter century later, that opposition manifested itself in student protests to kick the ROTC (Reserve Officer Training Corps) off campus.

Most of those protesters, he went on to say, were in uniform after the attack on Pearl Harbor two years later, for with America's entrance into World War II, internationalism replaced isolationism as the dominant theme in U.S. foreign policy.

But the isolationist impulse in American society was not entirely dead. The cry at the end of the war was "Bring the Boys

Home," and U.S. military strength in Europe fell from 3,500,000 men in 1945 to some 81,000 on the eve of the founding of the North Atlantic Treaty Organization (NATO) in 1949.

And even then, NATO was sold as what George Washington would have described as a temporary alliance to meet an extraordinary situation, i.e., the Soviet buildup in Central Europe. Will the United States "be expected to send substantial numbers of troops [to Europe] as a more or less permanent contribution to the development of [Western Europe's] capacity to resist?" asked Senator Bourne Hickenlooper of Iowa during the Senate hearings to ratify the treaty.

"The answer to that question," said Secretary of State Dean Acheson, "is a clear and absolute 'No.'" Ten years later, in his autobiography, Acheson admitted that "even as a short-range prediction [the] answer was deplorably wrong." Almost a half century later, a substantial number of U.S. troops remain in Europe, and plans are to maintain at least 100,000 troops there for the foreseeable future.

Internationalism regained its strength with the U.S. reaction to the North Korean attack on South Korea in June 1950, and reached its apogee with President Kennedy's call to arms in 1961. But it began to decline once again during the Vietnam War, when "non-interventionism" made a significant domestic political shift.

The New Isolationists

Traditionally, isolationism was a province of the political right, who opined that America was so pure and unsullied that, as Adams had said, it should not taint itself by becoming involved with the corrupt and evil world beyond its shores. But during the Vietnam War that isolationistic mind-set shifted across the political spectrum. In a mirror image of the political right, the political left argued that America had become so evil and corrupt that it should not infect the innocent world around by interfering in other nations' domestic political affairs.

"From the cutoff of aid to Saigon and the Clark Amendment (banning U.S. intervention in Angola) to the retreat from Beirut and the Boland amendment (restricting aid to the Nicaraguan *contras*)," *The New Republic*'s Charles Krauthammer noted a decade ago,

> the United States has selectively . . . sought to reduce its international commitments. . . . Although as explicit an isolationist vision as George McGovern's "Come Home America" is still a rarity, a new isolationism has clearly emerged, picking up the strands of a tradition 200 years old.
>
> We tend to think of that tradition as a property of the right [and] tend to forget the pre-war tradition of left isolationism. . . . With World War II, both left and right isolationism went into eclipse, not to reemerge until Vietnam.
>
> Today isolationism has regained its voice. . . . It has reconstituted itself in both parties, finding, as in the pre-war era, two distinct forms of expression.

Krauthammer saw the reemergence of rightist isolationism reflected in the 1984 Weinberger Doctrine discussed above, which narrowly defined intervention to a defense of our own vital interests.

Although his belief that Weinberger's insistence on not going to war without public and congressional support was "almost a prescription for 'no wars'" was belied by the war in the Persian Gulf, where such support was indeed forthcoming, Krauthammer's larger point is more enduring.

The sentiment animating isolationists of the right, he argues, is that "America has let itself be drawn into commitments that serve not its interests but that of others. From Washington's farewell address on, that sentiment has always animated classic isolationism [and] its nationalist-unilateralist ideology."

"Left isolationism," on the other hand, "is the isolationism of means." While its ends remain "truly internationalist," and there is "no retreat from the grand Wilsonian commitment to the spread of values," now called human rights, isolationists of the left traditionally abhorred the use of military force, preferring economic assistance, economic and political reform, and support for democratic values. Their reliance was on "multilateralism: collective action by peace-loving countries against international malefactors."

Those left-isolationistic tenets became the foreign policy core of Bill Clinton's 1992 election campaign and, as will be discussed in Part III, central for a time to his national security policies. At the same time, right-isolationistic sentiment among the American people and in the Congress placed severe limits on his plans to put major reliance on multilateralism. But "multilateralism" means different things to different people.

"For the strong, multilateralism is a cover for unilateralism," Krauthammer noted presciently in 1985. That was certainly true for President Harry Truman in 1950, who used the United Nations as a cloak for his military intervention in the Korean War. It was true to a lesser degree of President Lyndon Johnson, who used the so-called Free World Military Forces to provide a veneer of multilateralism in Vietnam. And it was true of President George Bush in the Persian Gulf, who used both the United Nations and the allied coalition as the justification for U.S. intervention.

"For the rest," Krauthammer went on to say, "it is a cover for inaction." And that observation too was confirmed by events, as first President Bush and then President Clinton used lack of multilateral agreement to avoid intervention in the Bosnian civil war. "The irony," Krauthammer pointed out, "is that classic isolationism opposed multilateral entanglement for fear it would draw America into foreign conflicts. Modern isolationism embraces multilateralism because it keeps America out of foreign conflicts."

For a while the same dynamic applied to U.S. military intervention in Haiti, as President Clinton went first to the Organization of American States, the Caribbean Community, and then to the United Nations in what appeared to be attempts to evade making a decision whether or not to intervene. But in the end, unlike Bosnia, the United States did intervene.

What made Haiti different from Bosnia, said Defense Secretary Perry, was the degree to which U.S. interests were involved. "In Haiti we were prepared to use force because we have interests in protecting democracy in this hemisphere, preventing the flow of refugees and putting a halt to the systematic reign of terror over the Haitian people.

"When we had exhausted all other alternatives," Perry went on, "the United States and its allies threatened to use force to remove the junta from power. In Haiti this turned out to be sufficient. . . . Because of our demonstrated resolve to use military power, our armed forces entered Haiti without the loss of Haitian or American lives."

Deus ex machina

Perhaps one of the most peculiar manifestations of the American character has been the post–Cold War emergence of interventionist doves. "Left isolationists" had always taken it as a matter of faith that the military was the cause of all evil and that Senator Daniel Moynihan (D-NY) had been absolutely right when he said about Grenada: "You don't bring in democracy at the point of a bayonet."

But Bosnia changed all that. Suddenly the more fervent doves became the most ardent advocates of U.S. military intervention against the Serbs. Air strikes in particular became their foreign policy initiative of choice.

The anomaly was that the less they knew about the military, and the less they knew about military weaponry and its effects, the more convinced they were that military action could in itself be decisive. This new interventionism, argues Johns Hopkins University Professor Stephen John Stedman, "has its roots in long-standing tendencies of American foreign policy—missionary zeal, bewilderment when the world refuses to conform to American expectations and a belief that for every problem there is a quick and easy solution."

The interventionist doves see the military as a kind of *deus ex machina*, literally, "God from a machine," the ancient Greco-Roman dramatic device of lowering "God" by stage machinery down at the end of a play to sort out complications in the plot. Military force, they believe, can resolve all the problems of the post–Cold War world. Today, instead of promoting the use of military power, the Pentagon has to explain its limitations.

Conclusion

"In war," said Napoleon, "the moral is to the material as three to one." And in the formulation of military policy, that axiom also holds true. It is especially true in the United States, where the people have the final say on whether such a policy will endure. As General Weyand pointed out of U.S. military policy in Vietnam, when the American people lose their commitment, "the Army . . . cannot be committed lightly."

Three American character traits especially shape and constrain the parameters of U.S. military policy. The strongest is idealism, which both propels the nation into involvement and at the same time constrains the military means and methods that can be used. Serving as a counterweight is a second character trait, pragmatism, which places limits on America's idealistic impulses and demands that military actions be in consonance with tangible national interests.

The third character trait, non-interventionism, has ebbed and flowed throughout our history. Quiescent during World War II and the Cold War, what has been called the "new isolationism" is now reemerging as a major factor to be considered in building a military policy for America's future.

Chapter 2

The American Way of War

In the eighteenth century . . . war was still an affair for governments alone, and the people's role was simply that of an instrument. . . . This was the state of affairs at the outbreak of the French Revolution. . . .

Suddenly war again became the business of the people. . . . Since Bonaparte, then, war . . . became the concern of the people as a whole [and] took on an entirely different character.

—CARL VON CLAUSEWITZ, *On War,* PP. 583, 591–93

The Philosophical Basis

Concentrating his attention on European affairs, Clausewitz credited Napoleon Bonaparte and the 1789 French Revolution with changing the fundamental nature of war. But that transformation had actually taken place fourteen years earlier, in 1775, with the American Revolution. In 1787, long before Clausewitz had even begun formulating his theories, the tenets of people's war had been incorporated into the U.S. Constitution.

But Clausewitz, without knowing it, formalized a theoretical and philosophical basis for the American way of war by drawing from the French Revolution the same conclusions the framers of the Constitution had earlier drawn from the American Revolution.

With the "back to basics" movement after the Vietnam War, his 1832 treatise, *On War* (*Vom Kriege*) was adopted as the foundation for the strategic policies and warfighting doctrines of the military and naval forces of the United States.

Fortuitously, the first truly readable English version had just become available with the publication of the 1976 Princeton University edition, translated from the original texts by Oxford University's Michael Howard and Stanford University's Peter Paret. The book also included a reader's guide by the University of California's Bernard Brodie. Its adoption as a teaching text by the Naval War College, Air War College, Army War College, and the National War College played a major role in the military's post-Vietnam renaissance that led to victory in the Gulf.

Trinitarian War

When it comes to formulating U.S. foreign and military policy, one of Clausewitz's most important insights is on what he called the "remarkable trinity," now known as *trinitarian war*. "As a total phenomenon," he wrote, "its dominant tendencies always make war a remarkable trinity. . . . The first of these three aspects mainly concerns the people; the second the commander and his army; the third the government" (p. 89).

While the military fights wars, it is the passions of the people that are war's very engine, Clausewitz noted, corroborating the role of idealism in U.S. foreign intervention discussed earlier. But "the political aims are the business of government alone," which has the task of transforming the sometimes inflamed passions of the people into pragmatic "instruments of policy."

"These three tendencies are . . . deep-rooted in their subject and yet variable in their relationship with one another," Clausewitz wrote. "A theory that ignores any one of them or seeks to fix an arbitrary relationship between them would conflict with reality to such an extent that for this reason alone it would be totally useless" (p. 89).

The United States learned precisely how useless they could be when the limited-war theories that deliberately excluded the American people from the strategic equation were put to the test in Vietnam. But the academic theorists who dominated U.S. military thinking since the end of World War II refuse to admit that they have been deposed by a long-dead Prussian theorist.

Harking back to the social scientists' counterinsurgency theories of the 1960s, which also rejected the role of conventional war, they seek to reverse the Clausewitzian renaissance, claiming that he has no relevance in the post–Cold War world. Some, like military historian John Keegan, are simply anti-Clausewitzian in the grand British tradition.

Early in his *History of Warfare* (1993), Keegan writes that "culture is as powerful a force as politics in the choice of military means and often more likely to prevail than political or military logic," thereby reinforcing the thesis advanced in the preceding chapter. But he confuses the issue by drawing a false distinction between "culture" and "politics."

Clausewitz defined "politics" as the interaction of governments and their peoples, a definition that surely includes "culture." Others would agree. In "The Clash of Civilizations?", Harvard's Samuel P. Huntington argues that "the fundamental source of conflict in the new world . . . and the dominating source of conflict will be cultural." Yet he goes on to say that "nation states will remain the most powerful actors in world affairs."

Keegan, on the other hand, sees "politics" as only the machinations of politicians. Thus he argues that "to perceive war as the continuation of politics [is] incomplete, parochial and ultimately misleading." Even using his narrower definition of "politics," however, his arguments still fail to persuade.

But at least Keegan does not claim, as do many futurologists, that the end of interstate war is at hand. The most outspoken has been Israeli historian Martin Van Creveld. His *The Transformation of War* (1991) argued that trinitarian war was a thing of the past. Ignoring Clausewitz's warning not to be overcome by the *"vividness* of transient impressions," Van Creveld was so mesmerized by the *intifada* in Israel between the Palestine Liberation Organization (PLO) and the Jewish settlers that he transposed that experience onto the entire world.

"Contemporary 'strategic' thought," Van Creveld argues, "is fundamentally flawed; and, in addition, is rooted in a Clauzewitzian world-picture that is either obsolete or wrong. We are entering an era . . . of warfare between ethnic and religious groups. . . . Already today the military power fielded by the principle developed societies in both 'West' and 'East' is hardly relevant to the task at hand; in other words it is more illusion than substance."

Using the Vietnam War to bolster his arguments, Van Creveld maintains that "there are solid military reasons why modern regular forces are all but useless for fighting what is fast becoming the dominant form of war in our age." As a historian, Van Creveld is on shaky ground. It was precisely the "modern regular forces" of the North Vietnamese Army (NVA) that proved to be the decisive factor in the Vietnam War.

Their guerrilla forces having been decisively defeated in the 1968 Tet Offensive and its aftermath, the NVA waged the last seven years of the war primarily with conventional forces. As the NVA commander of the final assault, Senior General Van Tien Dung, makes clear, his spring 1975 offensive, which brought the war to a close, had almost nothing to do with guerrilla tactics. The assault was a multidivision cross-border blitzkrieg supported by heavy tanks and artillery that had more in common with the fall of France in 1940 than with Van Creveld's low-intensity conflict.

It was an NVA tank that broke down the gates of the Presidential Palace in Saigon, observed former CIA director William S. Colby. "The people's war was over, not by the work of a barefoot guerrilla but by the most conventional of military forces.

"The ultimate irony," Colby concluded, "was that the people's war launched in 1959 had been defeated, but the soldier's war, which the United States had insisted on fighting during the 1960s with massive military force, was finally won by the enemy."

Centers of Gravity

Van Creveld had fallen into the same error as his fellow academic war theorists and the U.S. military counterinsurgency school who preached that the "center of gravity" in the Vietnam War was the "hearts and minds" of the South Vietnamese people, rather than those prescribed by traditional military theory.

Those traditional centers of gravity, wrote Clausewitz, ranged from such tangibles as the destruction of the enemy army, the seizure of the enemy capital, or the defeat of the army of the enemy's protector to such intangibles as the community of interests among coalition partners, the personalities of the leaders, and public opinion. "That is the point," Clausewitz emphasized, "against which all our energies should be directed" (p. 596).

But the United States thought it was fighting a whole new kind of war where the old rules did not apply. These notions were exemplified in the 1968 edition of the Army's operations manual. Abandoning its previous emphasis on warfighting, the new manual stated that "The fundamental purpose of U.S. military forces is to preserve, restore or create an environment of order or stability within which the instrumentalities of government can function effectively under a code of laws."

Unfortunately, the North Vietnamese were playing by the old rules. They were the ones who in the end correctly identified the centers of gravity of the war, "the hub of all power and movement," as Clausewitz said, "on which everything depends."

They correctly identified their first task as forcing the United States from the battlefield, thereby eliminating the army of South Vietnam's protector, which they could not hope to defeat by purely military means. To do so, they concentrated instead on such intangible centers of gravity as U.S. public opinion and the personalities of the American leaders.

Public support for the war collapsed by the fall of 1967; and President Lyndon Johnson, psychologically defeated by the Tet Offensive of 1968, chose not to run for reelection. With the demise of the community of interest between the United States and South Vietnam, the "army of their protector" began to withdraw in 1969; and with the signing of the Paris "Peace" Accords in January 1973, all U.S. military forces were withdrawn.

Although South Vietnam would continue to resist for another two years, the end was inevitable. Once the United States withdrew, the NVA could focus on the tangible centers of gravity, the destruction of the South Vietnamese military and the seizure of its capital. "Like us," Stuart Herrington noted in his account of the war in the villages, "Hanoi failed to win the 'hearts and minds' of the South Vietnamese peasantry. Unlike us, Hanoi's leaders were able to compensate for this failure by playing their trump card—they overwhelmed South Vietnam with a 22-division force."

Paradoxically, while counterinsurgency theory preached that the "hearts and minds" of the South Vietnamese people were the target at which the United States should be aiming, it turned out that *American* "hearts and minds" were really the key center of gravity, a fact we were well aware of in World War II. As the poet Archibald MacLeish, who was with the Office of War Information during that war, noted: "The principal battleground of the war is not the South Pacific. It is not the Middle East. It is not England, or Norway or the Russian Steppes. It is American opinion."

But by the Vietnam War, that truth had been forgotten. From July 1965 to January 1969, "there was not once a significant organized effort by the Executive Branch . . . to put across its side of a major policy issue or a major controversy to the American public," said former Assistant Secretary of Defense for Public Affairs Phil Goulding.

By misreading Vietnam, Van Creveld failed to appreciate that that war was a reaffirmation, not a refutation, of Clausewitzian principles of trinitarian war. But as far off the mark he was as a military historian, he was even farther wrong as a prognosticator. Examining the "Clausewitzian Universe" and "trinitarian war," Van Creveld concluded: "Considering the present and trying to look into the future, I suggest that the Clausewitzian Universe is rapidly becoming out of date and can no longer provide us with a proper framework for understanding war."

The Persian Gulf War

Completed in April 1990, *The Transformation of War* was subtitled "The most radical reinterpretation of armed conflict since Clausewitz." By a cruel twist of fate the book was published in the wake of the Persian Gulf War, which refuted almost all of Van Creveld's ruminations on the future of warfare.

There is "serious doubt," he had written, "concerning the ability of developed states . . . to use armed forces as an instrument for attaining meaningful political ends." Yet Saddam Hussein had harbored no such doubts in August 1990 when he ordered his armed forces to overrun Kuwait. And George Bush and the other coalition leaders also expressed little doubt when they ordered their armed forces to turn back that Iraqi aggression.

For the United States, the Persian Gulf War was a *return* to the trinitarian war model it had followed from its beginnings in the Revolutionary War through World War II. Although there was no formal declaration of war, the war in the Gulf was very much a shared effort of the American people, their government, and their military. The passions of the American people fueled the war. The government solidified those passions by formulating clearcut and attainable political objectives; and the armed forces achieved those objectives through rapid and decisive military action.

"For the first time since World War II" was the leitmotif of the Gulf War, for it was the first time since that war that American military policy was back on its traditional track. During the Korean War, for the first time in its history, the United States went to war without seeking a declaration of war from the Congress. And U.S. military policy became derailed completely in Vietnam with a reversion to what Clausewitz had called "eighteenth-century war," where war was a matter for governments alone and the people's role was merely that of an instrument.

Even worse, the U.S. government itself was split, with the executive and the legislative branches at loggerheads over the conduct of the war. The military was caught in the middle, leading to a lack of clearcut battlefield objectives and confusion on the battlefield.

The need to avoid such future catastrophes was one of the major lessons learned from the Vietnam War. As Weinberger had said in November 1984, when he made public and congressional support a prerequisite for the commitment of U.S. military forces abroad, "We cannot fight a battle with the Congress at home while asking our troops to win a war overseas."

During the Persian Gulf War there was an initial temptation again to follow the Korean War precedent. "War is in the grey area," Deputy Attorney General William P. Barr told President Bush on January 8, 1991. "The war power is a shared power with Congress; the Constitution intends it to be shared. . . .

"The situation most closely resembling the current crisis was the Korean War," Barr concluded, "when Truman acted without Congress under a United Nations resolution somewhat similar to the current one."

Bush wisely refused to repeat that terrible error, which had led the United States so far astray. Instead, returning to the American warmaking tradition, Bush asked the Congress for permission to wage war against Iraq. After three days of debate, on January 12, 1991, the Congress voted President Bush authority to go to war.

The "Authorization for Use of Military Force Against Iraq

Resolution" passed in the Senate by a vote of 52–47 and in the House by 250–183. America was back on the trinitarian war track.

And that is key to future American military policies. For even though, as Van Creveld and others argue, the nature of the threat may not be "trinitarian," the nature of the U.S. response must be in accord with the trinitarian realities of the American defense establishment.

Rules for the Government and Regulation . . .

The basic reality is that the American military is a people's military. During the opening months of his administration, President Clinton was reminded of that fact time and again.

Although not widely seen in that context, the first reminder was over his plan to remove the ban on homosexuals serving in the armed forces. The media, overwhelmingly in favor of lifting the prohibition, has advanced the notion that this move was frustrated by opposition within the military—especially by General Colin L. Powell, then the Chairman of the Joint Chiefs of Staff, and his fellow members on the Staff.

While they were unquestionably opposed to lifting the restriction on homosexuals serving in the military, their opposition was not decisive for the simple reason that they did not have it within their power to kill it.

It is axiomatic within the military that staff officers have not only the responsibility but the duty to speak up on pending policy issues with which they disagree. For the Clinton-era Joint Chiefs of Staff, including General Powell, this responsibility was keenly felt, for as junior officers during the Vietnam War they saw the Joint Chiefs sit on their hands and do nothing, even though they knew that there was no strategy worthy of the name, that all of the principles of war were being violated, and that American soldiers were being killed needlessly.

As General Bruce Palmer, himself (as the Army's Deputy Chief of Staff for Military Operations and Plans) a member of the Vietnam-era Joint Chiefs of Staff, ruefully noted, "The only explanation of this failure [to inform the President of their misgivings] is that the chiefs were imbued with the 'can do' spirit and could not bring themselves to make such a negative statement or appear to be disloyal."

General Powell and other senior commanders would not repeat that mistake. They spoke out loudly on their opposition to lifting the ban on homosexuals. But they knew that President Clinton could have silenced them with a word, for it is also axiomatic within the military that once a decision has been made, the responsibility then is to loyally execute that decision. Resignation is the only alternative, for to subvert the decision from within would be dishonorable, a violation of every principle a military officer has taken a solemn oath to uphold.

Although President Richard Nixon had given just such a gag order when he ordered the end of the draft in 1973, forbidding any public discussion by the military as to the rights and wrongs of that decision, for reasons not explained President Clinton never gave such an order.

What ultimately stayed Clinton's hand in issuing an Executive Order lifting the ban was not the opposition within the military. It was the unexpected opposition of the American people. They did not want to see homosexuals mistreated or abused, but they were not yet ready to agree with those who would lift the ban and say that homosexuality was an acceptable alternative lifestyle.

The role of the media was instructive. Almost all TV news anchors and commentators, as well as most newspaper columnists and editorial writers, were in favor of lifting the ban. "To judge from the [New York] Times' recent coverage of military affairs," wrote The New York Post's Hilton Kramer on October 5, 1993, "you would think that the gravest threat to our current position as a military power is the muddle that the White House has created over the gays-in-the-military issue."

Major newspapers and news magazines followed suit. Most editorials blasted the military as bigoted and reactionary, and New York Times editorial writers even ignored the retirement of General Colin Powell, the Chairman of the

Joint Chiefs of Staff. As Kramer surmised, they "could not bring themselves to forgive Gen. Powell for his opposition to gays in the military."

If the press was indeed as powerful in shaping opinion as many believe, the ban would have been quickly lifted. But in fact the precise opposite happened.

The beginning of the end of the attempts to lift the ban came when Democratic Congressman Barney Frank of Massachusetts, an open homosexual, said publicly that the votes just weren't there to lift the ban. The result was the July 1993 "don't ask, don't tell" compromise. Later, reacting to the wishes of their constituents, both the House and the Senate would pass resolutions by wide margins stating that homosexuality was incompatible with military service.

The people–government–military interaction on the homosexual issue reaffirmed the trinitarian nature of the U.S. Armed Forces as established by the Constitution. Although it did not formally do so, the Congress in effect had reaffirmed the provisions of Article I, Section 8, that the Congress, not the President, would be the one "to make rules for the government and regulation of the land and naval forces."

A Jealous and Proprietary Interest

The American people, through their elected representatives in the Congress, would have their say not only on the internal makeup of their armed forces; they would have their say on its commitment abroad as well.

The defining moment came in October 1993, when the U.S. Senate approved an amendment by Democratic Senator Robert C. Byrd of West Virginia which narrowed the mission of U.S. military forces, then on a "peacekeeping" assignment in Somalia, and forced their withdrawal by cutting off the funds for their deployment as of March 31, 1994.

"It was one of the few such direct congressional interventions in foreign policy since the Vietnam War," noted *The Washington Post* at the time, "and this from a Democratic

Congress asked to support a Democratic president in his first foreign policy crisis." In fact, it was much more severe than in Vietnam.

This time the Congress, for the first time in history, cut off the funds for U.S. military forces engaged in combat operations in the field. By comparison, even after opposition became almost total, Congress continued to appropriate funds for the Vietnam War as long as U.S. military forces were committed to battle. Only in June 1973, three months after all U.S. military forces were withdrawn from Vietnam following the signing of the Paris Peace Accords, did the Senate pass the Case-Church amendment cutting off the funds for all U.S. combat operations in Indochina. In December 1973, President Nixon accepted that restriction by signing a foreign aid authorization bill that contained a ban on the use of any funds for U.S. military operations in or over Vietnam, Laos, or Cambodia.

Senator Byrd had tried to warn the President of growing congressional opposition to U.S. peacekeeping operations, but he had been ignored by the Clinton White House. "I think there needs to be a serious reality check in certain quarters," Byrd said then. "Their basic problem has been that they forgot the high school civics lesson that there are three branches of government and that Congress controls the purse strings."

At the time of that vote, Senator Patrick J. Leahy (D-VT) cautioned that Clinton faced more intervention from Congress unless he got his foreign policy together.

True to that warning, congressional opposition to U.S. ground combat forces in Somalia was followed by its opposition to deployment of U.S ground forces to Bosnia. As a result, the administration specifically denied any plans for the involvement of U.S. ground forces there.

Behind that congressional opposition was the pragmatic opposition of its constituents. President Clinton had failed—some would say not even tried—to convince the electorate that such interventions were in their best interests.

Following the November 1994 elections, one of the first acts of Senator Robert Dole (R-KS), the new Senate Majority

Leader, was to introduce the "Peace Powers Act of 1995" restricting commitment of U.S. troops to UN peacekeeping operations. As we shall see in Part III, such restrictions will have a major impact on future U.S. military policy for the new world order.

The Media and the American Way of War

Although often maligned, the news media is an important part of the American way of war. By providing the trinitarian linkages among the military in the field, the American people, and the government, the media serves a crucial role in the formulation, interpretation, and execution of U.S. military policy.

Often overlooked, especially by the military, is the media linkage between the military and the American public. "A Gallup public opinion poll in early 1991 showed 85% of the public had a high level of confidence in the military as an institution after Desert Storm, the highest public confidence rating in our history," stated Rear Admiral Brent Baker, the Navy's Chief of Information, in 1991. "Where did the public get its perception of the military's professionalism? They got it from news media reports."

"Invariably if you allow the media to look at what you are doing and put them with the soldiers, it comes out fine," commented Major General Paul E. Funk, commander of the U.S. 3d Armored Division, on returning from Operation Desert Storm. And when you do not, the message gets distorted. "I was upset to find that people did not know that the 3d Armored Division and VII Corps had been in a very heavy fight under great contact with some of the enemy's first-rate units," Funk said. "The story was not told well enough about the people who did the fighting—the companies, platoons and task forces."

That story is essential, for it is precisely this kind of front-line reporting that ensures the U.S. Armed Forces remains a people's military. There are those foreign policy elitists who would prefer the U.S. military to be instead faceless automatons, a kind of American Foreign Legion that could be committed to battle at their whim, without concern for public opinion.

Some analysts believed that with the end of the draft in 1973, the emerging all-volunteer military would be precisely that type of force. But such notions were shattered by the public reaction to the deaths of 241 U.S. servicemen in the bombing of the Marine barracks in Beirut on October 23, 1983.

With their graphic reporting of the carnage the news media put a human face in those casualties, interviewing not only the survivors but also the families of the victims. No one asked whether they were draftees or enlistees. They were Americans, killed in the service of their country. As General Weyand had warned, the U.S. military cannot be committed lightly, for as a result of media coverage, the American people took a jealous and proprietary interest in what happened in Beirut.

The resulting furor forced a change in U.S. policy and the withdrawal of U.S. military forces from Lebanon. That scenario would be repeated almost exactly ten years later when on October 3, 1993, two U.S. helicopters were shot down in Mogadishu, Somalia, and eighteen U.S. servicemen were killed in the ensuing gun battle.

The American people were outraged when pictures of an American soldier's body being dragged through the streets were shown on television and published in their local newspapers. Again the incident forced a change in U.S. policy. The pictures, said national security adviser Anthony Lake, made President Clinton "very angry." He was not alone. Senator Byrd's amendment to cut off funds for U.S. military deployments to Somalia was a direct result of that reporting.

The elitists were indignant. "What sort of policy making is it to have Washington's actions decided, even in part, on the latest affecting pictures on the evening news?" asked Walter Goodman, television critic for *The New York Times*. But, said *Newsday*'s war correspondent Patrick Sloyan, the pictures "brought home to everybody in this country that something was wrong with the American policy."

Ironically, having bragged earlier that it was the U.S. news media that was responsible for the U.S. intervention in Somalia, no American photographer was available to shoot the scene. Fearing for their safety, U.S. news organizations had taken their reporters and photographers out of Mogadishu weeks before. The picture was in fact taken by a *Toronto Star* photographer, Canadian Paul Watson. He took it, he said, because "if they were my soldiers and I were back home, I'd sure as hell want to know about it so I could do something about it.

"I think it is important for the people who elect the politicians," Watson went on, in words that describe perfectly the role of the media in the American way of war, "and who should decide where their troops go, to know what happens to them." CNN's Ed Turner echoed those sentiments on CNN's "Reliable Sources" on October 10, 1993. The people, he said, "have a right to see what their foreign policy is, how their tax dollars are being spent, what's happening to their troops. It's fair and proper that they should understand what this kind of warfare is all about."

The Costs of War

"It is conventional wisdom now to say that instant television drives policy," editorialized *TV Guide* in its special D-Day anniversary edition on May 28, 1994.

What then if the carnage, confusion and uncertain outcome of D-Day's first battle—when nearly 3,000 American soldiers died on Omaha Beach alone—had been beamed into the world's living rooms? Would public revulsion have changed the course of the war? . . .

Yet most observers *TV Guide* talked to about TV on D-Day agreed that even the worst bloodletting would not have undermined public support of the campaign to defeat Hitler. Patriotism was at a fever pitch in 1944. . . . "I can't believe it would have affected the public's attitude," says former CBS anchor Walter Cronkite, who covered the invasion as a young wire-service reporter.

Cronkite was right. The news media is very effective in showing the costs of war, a fact that has led to the conventional wisdom that casualties per se are the limiting factor in the American ability to wage war. But cost does not stand alone. The cost of anything, be it a new car, a new home, or a new war, can only be evaluated in terms of value.

This value, as Clausewitz pointed out, is determined by the intensity of the war's political objective. In World War II, the political objective was survival of the nation. Its value was so high that the United States paid over a million casualties in pursuit of it. With patriotism at a fever pitch, TV coverage of the dead and wounded would be more likely to further inflame passions rather than to smother them.

In Vietnam, the reverse was true. With the war's objectives, and hence its value, never established, it's not surprising that the cost became unacceptable. What is surprising is that it took thirty-one months to do so. For almost three years the American people supported that war on faith. Their trust having once been betrayed, however, they were not about to do so again.

Vietnam exhausted the American patience with ill-defined military operations abroad, as evidenced by their quick reaction to the disaster in Somalia. The number of casualties per se did not force the change in U.S. policy following the disaster there. It was not the fault of the media for showing the cost; it was the fault of the government for not fixing the value.

As veteran newsman Bernard Kalb, now the director of Harvard's Center on the Press, Politics and Public Policy, emphasized, the picture was "not just an American body being dragged through the streets of Mogadishu," but "a symbol of American power being dragged through the Third World, unable to master the challenges of the post–Cold War era."

The Passions of the People

The common belief is that the one thing the media is definitely good at is stirring up the passions of the people. If so, that would be critical in the formulation and execution of U.S. military policy, for the passions of the people are war's very engine. Sometimes that is true. The classic case of jingo journalism was William Randolph Hearst's famous cable to illustrator Frederic Remington in Cuba in March 1898, on the eve of the Spanish-American War. "You furnish the pictures," said Hearst, the head of a nationwide newspaper chain, "and I'll furnish the war."

The U.S. intervention in Somalia almost a century later has been hailed as the latest case in point. NBC television commentator Jane Pauley credited the horrendous television pictures of the civilian suffering there as being instrumental in forcing the United States to intervene, a judgment corroborated by *TV Guide*.

"Somalia is an American foreign policy first," it editorialized, "a military operation launched by the evening news." After the involvement turned into a debacle, the government was only too glad to agree with that assessment. "American foreign policy," said Anthony Lake bitterly, "is increasingly driven by where CNN points its cameras."

But sometimes that common belief is wrong. Writing on the Op-Ed pages of the October 14, 1993, *New York Times* in response to an earlier article by the renowned former ambassador George F. Kennan, the father of containment policy, CBS news anchor Dan Rather refuted Kennan's claim that the media was responsible for Somalia. "Mr. Kennan blames television—'above all television'—for congressional and public support for President Bush's deployment of U.S. troops to Somalia," Rather wrote.

> To give television credit for so powerful an influence is to flatter those of us who toil there—but it's wrong.
> If Mr. Kennan were right, there would be U.S. Marines on the ramparts of Sarajevo right now, defending the Bosnian

Muslims. . . . Reporters sometimes feel strongly about the stories they cover, and some may wish for the power to direct public opinion and to guide American policy—but they don't have it.

As with the homosexual issue discussed earlier, the Somalia incident and the later media rush to judgment in favor of U.S. intervention in Bosnia, which was also rejected by the American people, is a telling rebuttal of the idea that the media are so powerful they can dictate government policy.

And it is also a powerful indicator of how far the mainline media have strayed from their role as a sounding board for the American public. "We have . . . distanced ourselves to a remarkable degree from the people we are writing for," said the *Washington Post*'s David Broder, "and have become much, much closer to the people [experts and politicians] we are writing about."

In any event, there is more to military policy formulation than the raw "passions of the people." Clausewitz emphasized that it is the "business of government"—and by this he meant the head of state—to transform these passions into an "instrument of policy . . . subject to reason alone."

As CNN's Ed Turner pointed out, "It's up to the president and the State Department to conceive policy and execute it, and if somehow we [the news media] are driving them, then maybe we need some new officials in Washington."

The Commander in Chief

Turner's comment leads to yet another dimension of the American way of war. It is exceptionally dependent on the leadership of the President. This has been true from the start, as Alexis de Tocqueville observed in 1835 in *Democracy in America*, following his earlier visit to the United States:

The propensity that induces democracies to obey impulses rather than prudence was seen clearly in America on the breaking out of the French Revolution. . . . The sympathies of the people declared themselves with such violence in favor of France that nothing but the inflexible character of [President George] Washington and the immense popularity which he enjoyed could have prevented the Americans from declaring war against England. . . .

If the Constitution and the favor of the public had not entrusted the direction of the foreign affairs of the country to [President] Washington, it is certain that the American nation would at that time have adopted the very measures which it now condemns.

This is precisely what President George Bush allowed to happen when he allowed public passions over the suffering in Somalia to push him into intervention there. And while Clinton bucked public passions against intervention by sending U.S. troops into Haiti, these passions seemed to have forestalled any attempts to intervene in Bosnia, and, if Dole's Peace Powers Act of 1995 has its way, to intervene anywhere else either.

Paradoxically, although the liberal *Washington Post* gave its qualified endorsement to Dole's proposal to restrict the authority of the President to commit U.S. troops to the United Nations, the conservative *Washington Times* labeled it "bad politics." "The power to deploy American forces has to rest in one hand, not 535," it editorialized.

Among the nine classic military Principles of War is the principle of unity of command: "For every objective, there should be unity of effort under one responsible commander." And that's the very reason why Article II, Section 2, of the Constitution appoints the President as the nation's Commander in Chief.

Conclusion

One of the anomalies of the American military is that its philosophical basis was formulated by a Prussian military theorist, Carl von Clausewitz, who knew little or nothing about America. But in his 1832 treatise *On War,* he drew from his experiences in the French Revolution the same lesson that the founding fathers had drawn from the American Revolution.

That lesson was that henceforth war would no longer be the province of the head of state, but a matter for the "remarkable trinity" of the people, the government, and the military. This trinitarian concept is the U.S. military's foundation stone.

It shapes and determines the American way of war, and when that fact is forgotten, as it was after World War II, the effect is felt directly on the battlefield. In the Vietnam War, for example, it was American public opinion, not the battlefield actions of the Viet Cong or the North Vietnamese Army, that proved to be the decisive center of gravity in that conflict.

In the Gulf War it was the reapplication of the trinitarian concept that made victory there possible. And during the post–Cold War world, the concept continues to shape and define the nature of U.S. military involvement, particularly in UN peacekeeping.

In ways little appreciated by itself or by the military, the U.S. media plays an important role in reinforcing the trinitarian concept, especially by putting a human face on the cost in terms of casualties of U.S. military operations abroad.

But the media is not a determinant of such actions. While influenced by the media, the American people make their own decisions as to the worth of such actions. And that places a premium on presidential leadership, most recently evidenced by President George Bush in the Gulf War, in setting the national agenda and calling the American people to action.

Chapter 3

The New World Disorder

The Cold War's end "lifted the lid from a cauldron of long-simmering hatreds. Now, the entire global terrain is bloody with such conflicts . . . instability, even abject chaos, rooted in the economic dislocations that are inherent in the change from communist to market economies, rooted in religious and ethnic battles long covered over by authoritarian regimes now gone, rooted in tribal slaughters, aggravated by environmental disaster, by abject hunger, by mass migration. . . ."

—PRESIDENT BILL CLINTON, U.S. NAVAL ACADEMY, MAY 25, 1994

Foreign Danger

"Security against foreign danger is one of the primitive objects of civil society. It is an avowed and essential object of the American Union," wrote James Madison in 1788 in *The Federalist.* "The means of security can only be regulated by the means and dangers of attack. They will in fact be ever determined by these rules and by no others. . . ."

Over two hundred years later, his arguments still shape the formulation of U.S. military policy. They were incorporated into the Constitution and, more recently, enacted into law by the National Security Act of 1947, as amended, which charges the armed forces of the United States with four specific missions:

—Support and defend the Constitution of the United States against all enemies, foreign and domestic.
—Insure, by timely and effective military action, the security of the United States, its possessions, and areas vital to its interests.
—Uphold and advance the national policies and interests of the United States.
—Safeguard the internal security of the United States.

The objective of U.S. military policy is clear enough. The difficulty lies in assessing the explicit nature of the "foreign danger." As President Clinton's remarks in the epigraph to this chapter make clear, this is especially true today. For the first time in sixty years we lack a clearcut and defining threat by which to shape that policy.

Beginning with Japan's seizure of Manchuria in 1931 and its invasion of China in 1937, concomitant with the rise of Adolf Hitler and his National Socialist (Nazi) Party in Germany in 1933 and his later abrogation of the Versailles Treaty that had ended World War I, the nature of the "foreign danger" prior to World War II became apparent. That threat shaped and defined prewar U.S. military policy as well as the wartime military strategies that led to the defeat of the Axis powers in 1945.

The beginning of the Cold War with the Soviet Union in 1947, followed by the Communist takeover of China in 1949, served the same purpose, defining the nature of the threat for the next forty-five years. That "conception of war" began to break down with President Nixon's visit to China in 1972, driving yet another wedge in the Sino-Soviet split that divided the Communist world.

Beginning with the collapse of the Berlin Wall in 1989 and the dissolution of the Soviet Union on December 26, 1991, the Cold War was over. For over four decades the watchwords at the Army War College, as elsewhere throughout the U.S. military, had been: "The Russians are coming! The Russians are coming!"

Sure enough, when I returned there in 1993 to lecture on strategy formulation, there sitting in the audience were the Russians . . . not as invaders but as students. The watchwords had changed to "The World Turned Upside Down."

Predicting the Future

In 1974, as the Vietnam War drew to a close, General Creighton Abrams, then Army Chief of Staff, set up a strategic study group to determine the need for military force in the postwar world. To do so required an assessment of likely threats.

Turning to the Joint Chiefs of Staff's official fifteen-year threat projections, it was found that over the years their projections has consistently missed the mark. No one had forecast the Korean War in 1950, for which we were singularly unprepared, and no one had forecast Vietnam either. And if in 1974 analysts had forecast that fifteen years later the Berlin Wall would fall and communism would collapse, they would have been taken away in straitjackets.

Although futurologists like Alvin and Heidi Toffler make their livings in claiming to predict coming events, their 1993 effort, *War and Anti-War: Survival At the Dawn of the 21st Century,* like other such works, is at best an exercise in scientific wild-ass guessing. Unless taken to heart and acted upon, most such attempts are harmless, and may even offer some minor insights. But the future is and will remain uncertain.

Collective Security

One way the United States hedged against such uncertainty during the Cold War was through a system of worldwide collective security alliances. Except for NATO, which, on the

Central European front at least, evolved into a genuine military warfighting alliance, most were at best psychological security blankets.

They assuaged the fears of our allies and satisfied the American public's desire for multilateral as opposed to unilateral military action. A prime example was the UN force during the Korean War. Although touted as an example of collective action, it was in reality only a veneer.

At peak strength in July 1953, United Nations ground forces totaled some 932,539 soldiers and Marines—590,911 from the Republic of Korea, 302,483 from the United States, and 39,145 from other UN countries. This multilateral UN action was in reality a cloak for U.S. unilateral action to protect its security interests, in Northeast Asia and Japan in particular.

But veneer or no, as *The New Republic*'s Charles Krauthammer argued in 1985, both the "left-isolationists" and "right-isolationists" continued to demand a multilateral approach to national security. From the North Atlantic Treaty Organization in Europe, to the bi-lateral treaties with Japan and South Korea in East Asia, to other such treaties around the world, collective security (what the military calls "combined operations") became the basis for U.S. military policy.

That military policy carried over to the post–Cold War world. The Persian Gulf War in 1991–92 was a classic combined operation. In all some forty nations, including former Warsaw Pact members Czechoslovakia, Hungary, and Romania, joined together to form the largest allied coalition since World War II, contributing some 200,000 friendly forces to the war.

Although it committed no troops, one of the most important coalition partners was the Soviet Union. The Soviets' cooperation was essential to UN Security Council approval for the war, enabling the United States to pull its VII Corps out of Europe, where it had guarded against a Soviet attack for some thirty years, and move it to the Gulf, where its armored divisions formed the main attack.

Still, the 500,000-strong U.S. contingent provided the bulk of allied forces in the war, leading Krauthammer after the war to denounce the Gulf War as yet another example of pseudo-multilateralism.

Having said that, he went on to point out that "Americans insist on the multilateral pretense. A large segment of American public opinion doubts the legitimacy of unilateral American action but accepts action taken under the rubric of the 'world community.'" Krauthammer overstates his case, for the war literally could not have been fought without the Arab coalition in particular. And it would have been much more difficult without the acquiescence of the Soviets and the help of our NATO allies.

But his attack on the "myth" of multilateralism carries an important message when it comes to the formulation of future U.S. military policy. "Multilateralism is fine," he says. "It provides cover for what are essentially unilateral American actions." The danger is "that we will mistake the illusions—world opinion, U.S. resolutions, professions of solidarity—for the real thing, which is American power. . . . The ultimate problem with multilateralism is that if you take it seriously you gratuitously forfeit American freedom of action."

Forfeiting "freedom of action" is always the price to be paid for multilateralism. The political and military objectives of World War II, for example, were not set by the United States alone. Rather, they were shaped through constant consultation, first with Great Britain and then with the Soviet Union as well. As with the Yalta Conference and the resulting Soviet dominance of Eastern Europe, the results were not always what the United States might have wished had it been free to set its own goals.

The Persian Gulf War is the most recent case in point. President Bush has been criticized for ending the war when he did, for not seizing Baghdad, and for not deposing Saddam Hussein and bringing him to trial. But those World War II–type "total war" objectives were never in the cards. Neither the U.S. "silent partner," the Soviet Union, nor our Arab coalition allies would have permitted the United States to be the kingmaker in the Gulf. And neither wanted a political vacuum created in Iraq.

The result was an attenuation of the war's objectives, which were specifically limited to one long-term and two short-term goals. The long-term goal was providing for peace and security in the area—an objective still being pursued with the continuation of UN sanctions against Iraq, reaffirmed most recently by the Security Council in January 1995; by the UN-mandated "no-fly" zones over northern and southern Iraq; and, in October 1994, by the reintroduction of U.S. and British ground combat forces into the area to counter an Iraqi buildup along the Kuwaiti border.

The more immediate short-term goals were the ejection of the Iraqi forces from Kuwait and the restoration of the Kuwaiti government to power. When these were attained with the liberation of Kuwait, the war was called to a halt. Though the result may not have been what many Americans, with their penchant for "total victory," desired, it was in accord with the limitations imposed by the coalition partners.

Thus, even when using multilateralism as a cloak for unilateral U.S. action, there is a price to be paid in terms of U.S. freedom of action. And that is even more true when "we mistake the illusions . . . for the real thing." Those formulating Clinton administration foreign policy seemed initially to see multilateralism as a way to slough off responsibility for world problems on the United Nations and thereby avoid unilateral U.S. actions.

But, as they found out in Somalia, that too came at a price. What had begun as an impartial humanitarian relief effort in 1992 changed when the UN Security Council voted in March 1993 to alter the mission to "political reconciliation" and helping Somalia rebuild its "national and regional institutions and civil administration." Called "peace building" by the United Nations and "nation building" by the United States, this change in mission led to disaster.

As will be discussed in Part III, the result has been a reexamination of the early Clinton administration attitudes toward multilateral UN peacekeeping operations. As *The Washington Post* editorialized in support of Senator Dole's 1995 Peace Powers Act, when the Cold War ended, peacekeeping "became a popular idea. Now, despite some successes, the wrecks—especially those in Bosnia and Somalia—have stirred a general disillusionment and a round of recriminations. The powerful United States has its own capacity to care for the interests it deems vital, as in Iraq, and in that sense it can do better than most without international peace-keeping."

Mutual Defense Treaties

"Treaties are like roses and young girls," said French President Charles de Gaulle in 1963. "They last while they last." The United States entered into a number of formal and informal mutual defense agreements during the Cold War, but when they outlived their usefulness they were quietly abandoned.

A case in point was the mutual defense treaty with the Republic of China (ROC) on Taiwan. Useful when "Red China" was seen as our main enemy in Asia, it was unilaterally abrogated when the United States decided to normalize relations with the People's Republic of China (PRC) on the mainland.

After the Sino-Soviet split, China had become a useful strategic counterweight to the Soviet Union and, with its more than a billion people, an enormous potential trading partner. Any compromise was ruled out by the insistence of both the ROC and PRC that they represented the legitimate government of all of China, a China that both agreed included the island of Taiwan.

More shameful was our abandonment of our South Vietnamese ally in 1975. The United States had promised, as a precondition for South Vietnamese agreement to the 1973 Paris Peace Accords (officially the Agreement on Ending the War and Restoring Peace in Vietnam), that it would militarily intervene if North Vietnam renewed its aggression. But when two years later, in a flagrant violation of those accords, North Vietnam launched its multidivision cross-border invasion of the South, the United States primly averted its eyes.

The reason was as simple as it was cynical. "Treaties at best are but complied with so long as interest requires their fulfill-ment," wrote Washington Irving in 1809. South Vietnam was no longer in the U.S. interest.

What was in the U.S. interest? General Creighton Abrams's post–Vietnam War strategic study group found that the United States was in a position of relative advantage—allied with the two most economically powerful regions in the world, West Europe and East Asia.

The primary utility of U.S. military forces, the group ar-gued, was to maintain that advantage. Especially after the United States abandonment of its Vietnam ally, it was impor-tant to assure our West European and East Asian allies they could rely on U.S. security guarantees. One way was through the continued forward deployment of U.S. ground forces in those areas.

Short of war, the study found, stationing American ground forces in harm's way on foreign soil is the strongest possible indicator that vital U.S. interests are involved. While air and naval forces also signal a degree of U.S. commitment, they can be quickly removed when tensions increase. But ground forces are less easily disengaged, forming a kind of "trip-wire" that almost guarantees U.S. involvement in developing crises.

Twenty years later, those findings remain valid. West Eu-rope and East Asia are still world power centers. In the post–Cold War world these, along with the oil-producing Gulf Cooperation Council states in the Middle East, are the only areas certified by the Clinton administration as being so vital to U.S. interests as to warrant continued stationing of U.S. combat forces abroad.

The North Atlantic Treaty Organization

The first, and most enduring, of U.S. mutual security al-liances, NATO, was formed in 1949. During the 1950–53 Ko-rean War, even though NATO itself was not formally involved, the solidarity of the alliance was so strong that most of the twelve NATO nations of the time sent troops to Korea. In addition to air and naval forces, Britain dispatched two brigades of infantry and Canada sent one brigade to fight the war there. Turkey also sent an infantry brigade, and infantry battalions were sent by Belgium, France, Greece, and the Netherlands. Italy and Norway sent medical teams, and even Luxembourg sent an infantry platoon.

British Commonwealth forces alone (which in addition to Britain and Canada included Australian, New Zealand, and South African forces) suffered 1,263 soldiers killed in action and another 4,817 wounded. While their numbers were not large compared to the South Korean and U.S. forces involved, they were concrete evidence of the strength of the alliance.

Meanwhile, even as it was actively waging war in Korea, the United States rapidly built up its forces committed to NATO. Several active-army divisions and two National Guard divisions were deployed to West Europe, along with most of the Air Force's newest aircraft. From 81,200 soldiers in 1950, troop levels increased to 260,800 in 1952, slightly more than the 238,600 soldiers then engaged in combat in Korea.

Driving this buildup was the belief that Korea was a diversion, and that the main attack would come in Europe. The conventional wisdom—incorrect, as it turned out—was that Korea was part of a worldwide attempt by "monolithic" world communism, directed by Moscow, to expand its empire by "armed invasion and war." Thus it was very much in NATO-Europe's self-interest to support the United States in Korea as a quid pro quo for U.S. support in Europe.

But fifteen years later, with the U.S. NATO buildup complete, no NATO nation furnished troops to support the U.S. involvement in Vietnam. Again, national interests were the key. America's concern with blocking the expansion of China, one of the main stated reasons for U.S. involvement in Indochina, was not shared by Europe. While the United States saw China as a threat to its Asian interests, Europe saw China as a counterweight in containing the Soviet Union. It was not until 1971, with his opening to China, that President Richard Nixon would reconcile those opposing views and, in effect, make China one of NATO's most important allies, abandoning our erstwhile ally on Taiwan in the process.

In 1991, self-interest would again propel NATO's European nations to support U.S. military operations in the field, this time in the Persian Gulf War. In addition to air and sea forces, Britain furnished its 1st Armoured Division and France dispatched its 6th Armored Division. The Netherlands sent ships and a field hospital. Belgium, Canada, Denmark, Greece, Italy, Norway, and Spain sent naval ships, and Canada and Italy sent aircraft.

Further, Britain, France, Germany, Italy, Spain, and Turkey provided bases and airfields for coalition use. Again, as in Korea, though NATO itself was not formally involved, its individual members made a major contribution to the war. In so doing, they may have given the alliance a new lease on life.

Prior to the Gulf War, there was some question of NATO's raison d'être in the post–Cold War world. Its original mission had been overtaken by events, and its reluctance to participate in out-of-area operations limited its usefulness. There was talk of the West European Union (WEU) supplanting NATO as West Europe's primary defense alliance, and the United States was rapidly drawing down its units in Europe as part of its worldwide reduction in force.

Reassessing U.S. participation, one observer said the United States ought to stay involved for the simple reason that every time the United States withdraws from the continent, the Europeans screw it up. Besides, the practical reality is that the only time you can deploy troops, short of war, is when they're not needed. Once withdrawn, it would be almost impossible to reinforce in time of crisis, for the very act of reinforcing would heighten the crisis. But troops already on the ground solve that paradox.

The Gulf War provided more tangible reasons. Not only was there the matter of the additional combat power that NATO provided; equally important were the airfields and depots necessary for resupply, as well as the in-being communications and command-and-control networks essential to combat operations.

In February 1993, soon after he took office, President Clinton's administration announced that U.S. force levels in Europe would be capped at a "level of approximately 100,000 by the end of Fiscal Year 1996," allaying fears of a total U.S. withdrawal.

U.S. military policy in Europe had moved from its original purpose of "forward defense" to a post–Cold War mission of "forward engagement." As the Association of the U.S. Army's Colonel Wolf-Dietrich Kutter explained, "forward engagement forces are intended to focus on the synergy of maintaining coalition stability and enhancing cooperative relationships."

Maintaining a substantial U.S. force presence forward-deployed in Europe "as an insurance policy," he argued, "constitutes less an insurance matter and more the glue that binds together the democratic nations of Europe and the emerging U.S. grand strategy for peace through collective security and cooperative economics."

For most of this century, a central tenet of U.S. foreign policy has been to oppose the domination of Europe by any one power or combination of powers. That foreign policy led to U.S. military involvement in World War I and World War II to prevent German domination, and to the formation of NATO in 1949 to oppose Soviet hegemony. But with the dissolution of the Soviet Union and the Warsaw Pact, that danger is now in abeyance.

NATO is in the process of redefining its reason for being. One main area of cooperation between the United States and its NATO partners has been in peacekeeping operations in Bosnia. Overriding its longtime opposition to out-of-area operations, in December 1992, NATO foreign ministers agreed that NATO could conduct UN peacekeeping or peace enforcement missions.

It is notable that NATO's first combat action as an alliance was not in repelling a Soviet Union/Warsaw Pact attack in Central Europe, the reason for which it had been initially created. Instead, it was its February 28, 1994, shootdown of four Serb aircraft in the airspace over central Bosnia in support of UN "peacekeeping" actions there.

But the old NATO concern with Eastern Europe and Russia has not entirely faded away. And here NATO is impaled on the horns of a dilemma. The main Eastern Europe attraction for NATO is as protection from its Russian neighbor. But the cost of providing such protection would be NATO alienation of Russia, still one of the most formidable military powers in the world. And to extend the shield to Russia as well would render NATO meaningless.

An attempt to alleviate that situation was made at the 1991 Rome summit of NATO heads of state and government, with the creation of a North Atlantic Cooperation Council (NACC) for "consultation and cooperation on political and security issues" with the former Warsaw Pact countries of Eastern and Central Europe, the former Soviet Union, and the independent states of Lithuania, Latvia, and Estonia.

Another initiative was proposed by President Clinton in December 1993. Called the "partnership for peace," its purpose was outlined by then Secretary of Defense Les Aspin. It was based on several assumptions, among them that "NATO remains our chief avenue of involvement in Europe [and] NATO should be at the heart of any new Euro-Atlantic security system."

The nations of the partnership would eventually participate with NATO in a range of military activities. "These activities could include joint military planning, training, exercises. They could even include operations such as search and rescue missions, disaster relief, peacekeeping and crisis management."

The partnership, however, would not provide the NATO security guarantee that requires each member to regard an attack on one as an attack on all, and would not provide for automatic membership in NATO. Seen by some West European commentators as a stopgap solution designed to allow the new democracies to "mature" while the West gets a better fix on Russian intentions, the "partnership for peace" proposal was approved at the NATO summit in January 1994.

Most Eastern European nations soon signed up, for, as the *Washington Times*'s Andrew Borowiec noted at the time, "The countries of Central and Eastern Europe are convinced that Moscow's imperialism did not end with communism's demise, and are looking to NATO for protection against Russia's possible territorial ambitions." This fear only increased with the bloodbath in Chechnya in 1994–95 as the Russian military sought to quell the uprising there.

That's good reason for East Europe to support NATO, but is it sufficient reason for the United States to remain involved as well? The North Atlantic Treaty, for all its almost half-century yeoman service to American national security interests, is still subject to Washington Irving's litmus test. Do U.S. interests still require its fulfillment? The answer to that question still lies with the original reason for NATO's existence—the threat to U.S. security posed by the Soviet Union's successor state.

Russia

On the one hand, there is no question that Russia does not constitute the military threat formerly posed by the Soviet Union. The Cold War has ended, the Warsaw Pact has disintegrated, and the Red Army that once occupied Eastern Europe is now back within its borders with its physical strength and—if Chechnya is any indication—its combat power dramatically reduced.

As with the American military, that combat power is a function of its arms, equipment, and other material factors, as well as the intangible moral factors of morale, dedication, and commitment. With the collapse of communism, one of the major moral foundations of the Red Army, Marxist-Leninist ideology, has been repudiated. For the Russian Army today, that sense of mission as the vanguard for the spread of communism worldwide is no more.

And there are indications that Russia has lost some of its

imperialistic designs. When the "partnership for peace" was initially proposed, Russia at first demanded "special status" within the NATO Partnership, based on the fact that it was a nuclear-armed great power. But NATO held firm, and in June 1994 Russia became a Partner for Peace without preconditions.

But, on the other hand, there is much that has not changed. Russia, with its enormous nuclear arsenal, still remains the only country capable of destroying the United States within minutes. And that fact, Defense Secretary William J. Perry has emphasized, leads to several realities:

> Reality number one is that even with the best possible outcome imaginable in Russia today, which is a fully democratic and market-oriented Russia, the new Russia will have interests different from our interests. . . . Reality number two is [that] a worst case outcome is possible, and we must be prepared for it. It is possible that Russia will emerge from her turbulence as an authoritarian, militaristic, imperialistic nation, hostile to the West. In such a situation, we could indeed see a renewal of some new version of the Cold War. . . . Reality number three is we in the United States cannot control the outcome of the struggle underway in Russia. Only the Russians can control that.
>
> Given those realities, the continued U.S. participation in NATO appears to be a wise investment. And so does continued U.S. involvement in the Partnership for Peace and the initiatives with Russia to lessen the threat of nuclear war. Among such initiatives is the Defense Department's Nunn-Lugar program.

Named after its authors, Senator Sam Nunn (D-GA) and Senator Richard G. Lugar (R-IN), this billion-dollar program works to reduce the threat of nuclear weapons by dismantling Russian weapons and their infrastructure—the hundreds of military and industrial facilities, and the thousands of people who used to make and operate nuclear weapons. As Perry emphasized, although we cannot control the outcome of Russia's evolution, "we can influence it through a program of constructive engagement."

East Asia

The Clinton administration has certified only three areas in the world as so vital to U.S. interests as to warrant stationing troops in harm's way. One is West Europe, where U.S. force levels have been capped at 100,000. The second is East Asia, where 100,000 U.S. military forces are also deployed.

As President Clinton told the Korean National Assembly in July 1993, "The Korean peninsula remains a vital American interest. . . . Here in Korea we have frozen American troop withdrawals and are modernizing Korean and American forces on the peninsula. We have deployed to Japan the [U.S. Navy/Marine Corps] *Belleau Wood* amphibious group and the U.S.S. *Independence* battlegroup, the largest and most modern in the world. These are not signs of disengagement. These are signs that America intends to stay."

It might appear from Clinton's remarks that South Korea is the reason for U.S. forward deployments in East Asia. Not so. The real focus is Japan, one of the world's major economic giants. But sensitivities still lingering from the days of Imperial Japan's Greater East Asia Co-Prosperity Sphere prior to and during World War II prevent that from being said publicly.

South Korea per se has no great strategic value to the United States. That is why in 1949 U.S. troops stationed there after World War II to disarm the Japanese, who had annexed Korea as a colony in 1910, were withdrawn.

And that's why in January 1950, Secretary of State Dean Acheson said publicly that Korea had been excluded from the U.S. defense perimeter in East Asia. But when North Korea launched its June 1950 invasion of South Korea, it was quickly realized that the fall of South Korea would place U.S. interests in Japan in jeopardy.

The received wisdom at the time was that North Korea's invasion of South Korea was part of a larger plot by the Communist "monolith," directed by Moscow, to extend its sway throughout the world by force of arms. With that logic, the notion then advanced that "Korea was a dagger pointed at the heart of Japan" made perfect sense.

Thus it was not the nation of Korea as such but Korea's important geographic location that prompted America to intervene in June 1950 and fight the Korean War. And, despite the fact that it has since been learned that the Korean War was instigated by North Korea's Kim Il Sung and not by Moscow, that is why during the Cold War U.S. forces remained there.

Today, with the Communist "monolith" no more, they remain stationed there to maintain stability in East Asia. By continuing to provide for Japanese security, they obviate the need for Japanese revanchism. For centuries Korea has been the flash point for East Asian instability, for it is where the major powers—China, Russia, Japan, and, most recently, the United States—come together.

Stability on the Korean peninsula, therefore, is essential to stability in East Asia. Failing to realize that fundamental strategic fact, in 1976 Jimmy Carter campaigned on a pledge to withdraw all U.S. forces from South Korea as a protest against its then authoritarian military government. But when he attempted to make good on that pledge, he met with remonstrances not only from Japan but from the Soviet Union and China as well that a U.S. withdrawal would create a power vacuum and destabilize the entire region.

As they had in the nineteenth and early twentieth centuries, it was feared these powers would be tempted to take advantage of the instability thus created. It was just such instability that led to the Sino-Japanese War of 1894–95, the Russo-Japanese War of 1904–05, and the thirty-five-year Japanese occupation that began in 1910.

Although he would reduce U.S. force levels there, Carter as President quietly abandoned his ill-considered plans. That had major strategic significance, for unlike NATO, East Asia is not a geographic or political entity. There is no equivalent to the North Atlantic Treaty that binds all the nations of the region together. Instead, there are some five bilateral treaties.

In his July 1993 speech to the Korean National Assembly, President Clinton affirmed these U.S. bilateral treaties with Korea, with Japan, with Australia and the Philippines, and with Thailand. "Those agreements work because they serve the interests of each of the states," he said.

"They enable U.S. armed forces to maintain a substantial forward presence [and] our commitment to an active military presence remains."

East Asia is important to the United States for the same reasons Western Europe is important, for the United States is a Pacific as well as an Atlantic power, and we have substantial economic interests in both areas. Evidence of how important East Asia is to American national interests is the fact that we have fought three major wars there this century. And, as in Europe, the deployment of some 100,000 troops there is a signal that the United States is prepared to do so again if our interests are seriously threatened.

China

For much of the Cold War, China was perceived to be the primary threat to those interests. That threat became a reality in November 1950, when it intervened in the Korean War, preventing the impending North Korean defeat, and prolonging the war for another three years. China was then seen as part of the world Communist "monolith" directed by Moscow, and for the next two decades China and the Soviet Union were lumped together as a common enemy. But that monolith never existed, as became increasingly apparent with the Sino-Soviet split, which began to develop in the early 1960s. With President Nixon's opening to China in 1971 and his visit there in 1972, China was no longer seen as an adversary.

Liaison offices were opened in Washington and Beijing in 1973 and formal diplomatic relations were established in 1979. By the late 1970s and early 1980s, notes the Brookings Institution's Harry Harding, "China had come to be regarded as a quasi-ally of the U.S. in the struggle against an expansionist Soviet Union." But in the late 1980s and early 1990s, with the disintegration of the Soviet Union, "China was viewed as a strategic irrelevancy, no longer able to tip the balance between the two superpowers and lacking its own weight in strategic affairs."

Especially after the televised bloodshed in Tiananmen Square in June 1989, says Harding, when an estimated five thousand anti-government protestors were killed by Chinese Army troops, and another ten thousand injured, "the principal preoccupation of U.S. China policy has been Beijing's violation of human rights." As a result, a more antagonistic view is beginning to emerge. "Today . . . some see China as an emerging threat to the U.S. because of its size, rapid economic growth, military modernization and authoritarian political system."

The specter of a "Pax Sinica" in East Asia has been raised, where China dominates East Asia as it did during the reign of the great Chinese dynasties such as the Han (206 B.C.–A.D. 220) that expanded China to its present borders, the T'ang (618–907), the Sung (960–1279), and the Ming (1368–1644), where China ruled supreme and the other nations of East Asia recognized the authority of and paid tribute to the Chinese emperors.

While the chances for such a "Pax Sinica" are ambiguous at best, the fact is that until the Communist takeover in 1949, the only China the West had ever known was a China in decline under their Manchu conquerors, whose Ch'ing Dynasty ruled China from 1644 to 1912. Even the Communist government has not begun to match the influence and power of dynastic China in East Asia.

But the Chinese themselves would claim that this latest version of the "yellow peril" is arrant nonsense. In 1968, I was the Army Command and General Staff College's principal instructor on "Red China." Reflecting the temper of the times, my lecture opened with an illustration of a Chinese dragon about to engulf the world. To my surprise, the Chinese Nationalist officers from Taiwan in the class took violent exception. "China in all its history has never been expansionist," they said. "China has never committed aggression beyond its borders!"

"How about Tibet?" I asked. "Everyone knows Tibet is part of China," they said. "Then how about Vietnam and Korea?" I countered; "China has invaded them often enough." Again they had the answer. "In ancient times Korea and Vietnam were vassal states of the Chinese Empire. And in 1950 it was Chinese People's *Volunteers,* not China, that intervened in Korea."

Their logic might have been strained, but it was remarkable that even the sworn enemies of the Communist government in Beijing agreed that China was not bent on foreign aggression.

If China poses a threat to the United States, it is one far more profound than military aggression. In 1884, a Chinese philosopher, K'ang Yu-wei, wrote a treatise that had widespread influence throughout East Asia and was even hailed by Mao Zedong when he took power in 1949. Called *Ta T'ung Shu* (The Great Utopia), it laid out a blueprint for the future which forecast NATO and the OAS almost exactly, and included a grand alliance between China and Japan.

Such an alliance, combining the more than 1 billion people of China with the industrial and technological capabilities of Japan, would create a power bloc of enormous magnitude that would directly challenge U.S. interests in East Asia. Fortuitously, K'ang Yu-wei believed that such developments might take "a thousand or several hundred years." But, having said that, his ideas do not seem nearly so farfetched now as when they were written over a century ago.

The Middle East

Apart from threats to the economic power centers of West Europe and East Asia, the only other criterion warranting forward deployment of U.S. military forces is access to the energy resources of the Middle East. President Clinton has continued deployment of U.S. warships in the Persian Gulf region to enforce the UN-mandated economic sanctions against Iraq, as well as combat aircraft to enforce the "no-fly" zones over northern and southern Iraq to protect the Kurds and Shi'ite "Marsh Arab" rebels.

Six months after taking office, Clinton ordered the firing of twenty-three TOMAHAWK cruise missiles at the Iraqi intelligence headquarters in Baghdad in retaliation for an Iraqi attempt to assassinate former President Bush during his visit to Kuwait. And in October 1994, he ordered U.S. air, ground, and naval forces into the area to counter an Iraqi military buildup along the Kuwaiti border.

In sending U.S. forces into the area, Clinton was following long-established precedents. Although no ground combat troops have been permanently stationed in the Middle East, warships of the U.S Navy's Joint Task Force Middle East have been operating in the Persian Gulf since 1949. In 1953, the "Eisenhower Doctrine" was announced, whereby U.S. help was pledged to any Middle East country in defending against outside aggression. To that end, President Eisenhower sent 14,000 U.S. troops into Lebanon in 1958 to defend against what he called Iraqi-sponsored aggression and, by some accounts, even threatened the use of nuclear weapons against Iraq.

In 1969, under the "Nixon Doctrine," President Nixon established Iran and Saudi Arabia as the "twin pillars" of U.S. security interests in the Middle East. The Iranian "pillar" collapsed in 1979 after the Shah of Iran was deposed and the country taken over the Ayatollah Ruhollah Khomeini and his radical Islamic fundamentalist mullahs.

In December 1979, with U.S. influence in the area at a low ebb, the Soviet Union invaded Afghanistan. This led to the announcement of the "Carter Doctrine" in January 1980. "An attempt by any outside force to gain control of the Persian Gulf region," said President Carter, "will be regarded as an assault on the vital interests of the United States." To implement this doctrine, the Rapid Deployment Joint Task Force (RDJTF) was formed to coordinate, command, and control any military action required.

In 1983, President Ronald Reagan redesignated the RDJTF as the U.S. Central Command (CENTCOM), on a par with the

European Command (EUCOM) and the Pacific Command (PACOM) as one of the several geographic commands under which the U.S. military is organized. Although originally formed to contain the Soviet Union, CENTCOM would be ordered into action by President George Bush in August 1990 to turn back the Iraqi invasion of Kuwait. Forming the bulk of the allied coalition that fought the Persian Gulf War, CENTCOM's ground forces were withdrawn from the area following the cease-fire on February 28, 1991, only to be temporarily reintroduced in October 1994 as a show of force when an Iraqi buildup once again threatened Kuwaiti security.

A longtime pillar of U.S. interests in the Middle East has been the nation of Israel. Except for some PATRIOT anti-missile batteries during the Gulf War, the United States had not stationed troops there, but it had provided major military arms and equipment during Israel's several wars with its Arab neighbors.

While at one time this posed the threat of drawing the United States into a conflict with one of Israel's Soviet-backed Arab enemies, that threat has disappeared with the end of the Cold War.

A 1994 *New York Times* poll found that "people in the United States . . . say the Middle East poses the biggest threat to world peace." A reflection of that concern was President Clinton's action to retain U.S. air and naval forces on station in the Middle East, and his willingness to use military force to enforce the UN Security Council resolutions upon which the Persian Gulf War cease-fire was based.

The Third World

From Clinton's campaign rhetoric, it appeared that the main focus of his administration's foreign and military policy would be the so-called Third World, a term coined during the Cold War. The "First World" was comprised of the world's rich, industrialized democracies, such as the United States, Canada, West Europe, Japan, Australia, New Zealand, and the like. The "Second World" included the state socialist countries of Eastern Europe, the Soviet Union, Cuba, China, Vietnam, and North Korea, all of which then had centrally planned economies.

The "Third World" lumped together the nations of Asia, Africa, and Latin America, often with colonial pasts, which in the main were marked by underdeveloped economies and low per capita incomes.

With the collapse of communism in Europe and the demise of the Soviet Union, the "Second World" has ceased to exist. Except for Cuba and North Korea, even the surviving Communist powers, China and Vietnam, are moving toward free market economies.

But the phrase "Third World" survives nonetheless. "With the end of the cold war," states a 1994 Army War College study, "the Third World became the centerpiece of American national security strategy." Echoing President Clinton's remarks at the Naval Academy graduation in May 1994, the study notes that "the thorniest security issues—U.S. peace operations, Haiti, Somalia, Iraq, North Korea, proliferation, are Third World problems." It is a road well traveled.

Seeking a counter to U.S. nuclear superiority at the time, in January 1961 Soviet Premier Nikita Khrushchev shifted the venue to the Third World and announced Soviet support for "Wars of National Liberation." President Kennedy bought the challenge. "It is clear that this struggle in this area of the new and poorer nations will be a continuing crisis of this decade," he said.

Kennedy selected Vietnam as the test case, but it was not the only Third World area where great power rivalries were played out. In Angola and Ethiopia, the United States and the USSR competed for influence, and the Soviets even deployed surrogate Cuban troops to aid their African allies. Insurgencies flourished throughout Latin America, especially in Nicaragua and El Salvador where, in both cases, democracy ultimately prevailed.

During the Cold War it was the Soviet use of insurgencies to spread the ideology of communism, not the unrest itself, that was the real threat. That game is now over. But while the Third World no longer poses a systemic threat, the turmoil there persists. A 1994 study found some sixty-three ongoing armed conflicts, most in Sub-Saharan Africa, the Middle East, South Asia/Pacific Rim, and South and Central America. The difference is that despite President Clinton's early rhetoric, in most cases the United States no longer cares.

Conclusion

James Madison was right that "the means of security can only be regulated by the means and dangers of attack." But it is also true, as Defense Secretary William Perry said in November 1994, that "most of the current and foreseeable threats to our interests do not threaten the survival of the United States."

Russia is a special case because of its nuclear capability. And the United States has made it clear, by the stationing of U.S. forces in the areas, that it considers its interests in West Europe, East Asia, and the Middle East so vital that it will go to war to protect them. A threat falls into the category of a vital interest, Perry said, "if it threatens the survival of the United States or key allies, if it threatens critical U.S. economic interests or if it poses the danger of nuclear threat."

In other areas, where what Perry called important but not vital national interests are at stake, "our use of force will be selective and limited, reflecting the relative importance of the outcome to our interests." In a particularly blunt statement of that selectivity, Perry went on to say that "Generally the military is not the right tool to meet humanitarian concerns . . . because of the need to focus on its war-fighting missions. We field an army, not a Salvation Army."

Part II

Warfighting

Combat is the only effective force in war. . . . That holds good even if no actual fighting occurs, because the outcome rests on the assumption that if it came to fighting, the enemy would be destroyed. . . .

Consequently, all action is undertaken in the belief that if the ultimate test of arms should actually occur, the outcome would be *favorable*. . . .

—CARL VON CLAUSEWITZ
On War, P. 97

Chapter 4

The Spectrum of Conflict

Let me begin by giving a little bit of a tutorial about what an armed force is all about. Notwithstanding all of the changes that have taken place in the world, notwithstanding the new emphasis on peacekeeping, peace enforcement, peace engagement, preventive diplomacy, we have a value system and a culture system within the Armed Forces of the United States. We have this mission: to fight and win this nation's wars.

—GENERAL COLIN L. POWELL,
CHAIRMAN, JOINT CHIEFS OF STAFF,
SEPTEMBER 1, 1993

Escalation Dominance

"We're warriors," declared General Colin Powell during his September 1993 press conference on the Defense Department's *Bottom-Up Review*. "We never want to lose sight of this basic underlying principle. That's why you have armed forces within the United States structure." It was a reiteration of a Clausewitzian dictum laid down over 160 years earlier. "The end for which a soldier is recruited, clothed, armed and trained," Clausewitz emphasized, "the whole object of his sleeping, eating, drinking and marching *is simply that he should fight at the right place and the right time*" (p. 95).

That holds true, Clausewitz said, even if it never comes to fighting, "for all action is undertaken in the belief that if the ultimate test of arms should actually occur, the outcome would be *favorable*" (p. 97).

As with many of Clausewitz's insights, this is simple common sense. If the belief was that the outcome would be *unfavorable*, i.e., that you would lose, the enemy would be encouraged rather than deterred. As British Admiral of the Fleet Sir Peter Hill-Norton once put it, the essence of deterrence is to "raise the fearful doubt in the mind of any potential aggressor that any possible gain is not worth the inevitable risk."

Anyone even thinking about attacking the United States or its interests must be convinced that such an attack will fail, for as the Australian military historian Geoffrey Blainey found, the one constant variable in every war in history is that at least one side believes it can win by force of arms. Blainey wryly observes, "defeat . . . is unintended."

Deterrence thus requires that the U.S. military be prepared to fight and win across the spectrum of conflict, from general war—high-intensity nuclear or conventional war—where national survival is at stake, to mid-intensity limited conventional wars, to low-intensity "peace operations."

And, throughout, it must maintain *escalation dominance*. "War is an act of force," said Clausewitz, "and there is no logical limit to the application of that force. Each side, therefore, compels its opponent to follow suit; a reciprocal action is started, which must lead, in theory, to extremes" (p. 77).

If the United States is not to be blackmailed into submission, it must have the military capability to escalate any conflict to the point where the adversary cannot respond in kind. When that cannot be achieved, against another nuclear-armed power, for example, the United States must have sufficient combat power to match enemy escalation to the point where a mutual standoff ensues.

Combat power has two interlocking dimensions, physical strength and political will. If escalation dominance is to be effective, the adversary must be convinced that the United States not only has the physical means to escalate the conflict, but also the political will to do so. That was the case in terminating the Korean War in 1953, and again in deterring the Iraqi use of weapons of mass destruction in the Persian Gulf War in 1990–91.

"There is now extensive documentary evidence," said Cornell University's Rosemary Foot in *The Wrong War* (1985), "to show that the use of atomic weapons became an integral part of the [Eisenhower administration's] planning designed to force a military solution in Korea." Foot went on to state that "the Chinese and North Koreans were intimidated by the threatened use of atomic weapons," leading to their "capitulation" in June 1953, and their signing of the Armistice Agreement the following month.

And in the Persian Gulf War, President George Bush's warning that the United States would escalate that conflict to the nuclear level if the Iraqis used chemical, biological, or nuclear weapons against the allied coalition proved to be an effective deterrent.

Eisenhower was able to muster the political will to threaten escalation to nuclear war because in 1953 the moral revulsion against the use of nuclear weapons was not as strong as it is today. Nuclear weapons were still seen, by the government and the military at least, as usable tools of war. Another major reason was that the United States had clear escalation dominance over North Korea and China, which at that time did not have the nuclear capability to respond in kind.

And Bush was even able to override the public aversion to the use of nuclear weapons because Saddam Hussein had threatened the first use of such weapons of mass destruction. If the enemy breaches the nuclear/biological/chemical threshhold, as Iraq threatened to do in the Gulf, the United States will respond in kind.

In July 1993, President Clinton threatened to respond with "all means necessary" (the generally understood euphemism for nuclear weapons) against North Korea, if that country breached the nuclear threshhold. In 1994, when North Korea issued a veiled nuclear threat to turn the South Korean capital of Seoul into a "sea of flames," the United States promised certain retaliation.

"Certainly the United States is not going to initiate a war," Defense Secretary William Perry said on NBC's "Meet the Press" on April 3, 1994. "And I believe that North Korea, looking at the catastrophe that would occur to their country if they initiated a war, is not going to either."

But U.S. first use of nuclear weapons remains another matter, as Senator Barry Goldwater found when he suggested their use in Vietnam during his unsuccessful 1964 bid for the presidency. Mindful of that lesson, when President Nixon escalated the Vietnam War in December 1972 to force North Vietnam to return to the negotiating table and end the war, he did it with purely conventional means. As discussed in Chapter 1, escalation to the nuclear level in the Vietnam War was ruled out not only by the President and the military; more importantly, it was ruled out by the American people.

"In actual practice," Clausewitz wrote, "war does not advance relentlessly toward the absolute as theory would demand. . . . Policy [defined as the interaction of peoples and their governments] converts the overwhelmingly destructive element of war into a mere instrument. . . . If war is part of policy, policy will determine its character" (p. 606).

As early as 1954, the use of nuclear weapons in Indochina to break the siege of Dien Bien Phu was ruled out by the United States, and when a nuclear planning group was organized by the Military Assistance Command Vietnam in 1967 to explore the possible use of nuclear weapons to break the North Vietnamese Army siege of Khe Sanh, it was ordered disbanded by the Pentagon. Both the U.S. government and the American people viewed nuclear means as disproportionate to the political ends to be achieved in Vietnam.

Instead of escalating the physical means of combat power, Nixon escalated its moral dimension. "We have the power to destroy [North Vietnamese] war-making capacity," President Nixon said in 1972. "The only question is whether we have the *will* to use that power. What distinguishes me from [President] Johnson is that I have that *will* in spades."

On December 18, 1972, Nixon launched an all-out air assault on Hanoi. For the first time, B-52 bombers were used in large numbers. Eleven days later, the North Vietnamese agreed to return to the negotiating table, and the next month they signed the Paris Peace Accords which ended direct U.S. participation in the war.

As an inducement for South Vietnam to agree to those accords, President Nixon promised that if North Vietnam failed to live up to its terms, he would reintervene and again escalate the conflict to a point where North Vietnam could not respond. But in the end it was North Vietnam that exercised escalation dominance.

When they flagrantly violated the Paris Accords in December 1974 with their corps-level cross-border assault on Phuoc Long province, the North Vietnamese raised the level of violence to a point at which the United States, paralyzed by Watergate, was by then unable to respond. President Gerald Ford cravenly limited his actions to feeble diplomatic remonstrances. This time it was North Vietnam, not the United States, that had the will in spades.

One final note on escalation dominance. When the strategy of "Massive Retaliation" was announced in 1954, Secretary of State John Foster Dulles justified this almost total reliance on nuclear weapons as providing for "a maximum deterrence at a bearable cost." "The Soviet Communists are planning for what they call 'an entire historical era,'" Dulles said, "and we should do the same thing. They seek, through many types of maneuvers, gradually to divide and weaken the free nations by overextending them in efforts which, as Lenin put it, are 'beyond their strength, so that they come to practical bankruptcy.'"

In fact, the precise opposite happened. It was the Soviet Union that became overextended to the point of practical bankruptcy. A major factor in that overextension was President Ronald Reagan's escalation, not of U.S. offensive nuclear capabilities, but of U.S. *defensive* nuclear capabilities.

"Looking to the future," Reagan said in January 1988, "the

Strategic Defense Initiative . . . would enhance deterrence by injecting greater uncertainties into Soviet estimates of their ability to achieve their military objectives should they attempt a first strike." Soviet attempts to counter these "Star Wars" initiatives, it has been said, overloaded their already faltering economy and were a major factor in their dissolution.

Short of retaliation in kind, escalation dominance in the foreseeable post–Cold War era remains limited to conventional means. While the United States would not rule out a preemptive strike on North Korea, Defense Secretary Perry told "Meet the Press," "I can't envision the circumstances in which the [first] use of nuclear weapons would be reasonable or prudent military action."

General Nuclear War

After the 1962 Cuban missile crisis during the Kennedy administration when the world came close to nuclear war, the first use of nuclear weapons was never again a serious option. Instead, the Cold War doctrine of "Mutually Assured Destruction" (MAD) was adopted, whereby both the United States and the USSR maintained sufficient nuclear weapons to ensure they could ride out a first strike by the other side and still have enough remaining strength to respond in kind. Although its morality was often called into question, the fact is MAD worked and nuclear war was avoided.

With the signing of the Strategic Arms Reduction Treaty (START I) between the United States and the USSR in July 1991; the May 1992 agreement that the four nuclear-armed republics of the former Soviet Union (Russia, Ukraine, Belarus, and Kazakhstan) would assume the obligations of the former USSR under the treaty; and the signing of a follow-on treaty (START II) by President George Bush and Russian President Boris Yeltsin on January 3, 1993, the nuclear era effectively came to an end.

By the year 2003, both countries are to have reduced their strategic warheads to between 3,000 and 3,500, notes the

1993–94 edition of *The Military Balance.* In addition to reducing the total number of warheads, START II limits submarine-launched ballistic missiles (SLBM) to 1,750 for each side, and bans intercontinental ballistic missiles (ICBM) with multiple independently targeted re-entry vehicles (MIRV).

The United States plans to limit the third leg of its nuclear triad to ninety-five B-52H and twenty B-2 bombers carrying nuclear-tipped ALCM (air launched cruise missiles) or advanced cruise missiles (ACM), and the nuclear-armed republics of the former Soviet Union will make similar reductions in their manned bomber fleets.

But the threat of nuclear war has not completely gone away. As JCS Chairman General Colin Powell warned in April 1991, "The Soviet Union will remain the one country in the world with the means to destroy the United States in 30 minutes in a single devastating attack." Even with the dissolution of the Soviet Union, that fact remains unchanged.

As of June 1, 1993, noted *The Military Balance,* the four nuclear-armed republics of the former Soviet Union—Russia, Ukraine, Belarus, and Kazakhstan—still held some 10,456 strategic nuclear warheads. Delivery systems included 1,204 ICBMs, 788 SLBMs, and 170 long-range bombers.

On May 31, 1994, the United States announced that it had completed the retargeting of U.S. strategic missiles away from points inside the former Soviet Union. The result of a January 1994 agreement between President Clinton and President Boris Yeltsin as a "symbolic gesture" of improved U.S.-Russian ties, Russia has supposedly followed suit. But, as a Pentagon spokeswoman admitted, that "can't be actively verified." In any case, "re-targeting [by either side] can take place fairly quickly."

As we shall see in the concluding chapter, defense against nuclear war must remain the bedrock of any U.S. military policy, for nuclear weapons pose the only credible threat to the American homeland. That said, the fact remains that the nuclear era per se is at an end, and with it the debilitating effects that nuclear weapons had on American warfighting doctrines.

With the dropping of the atomic bombs on Hiroshima and Nagasaki in 1945, a whole new "atomic age" had seemingly begun. "Thus far the chief purpose of our military establishment has been to win wars," wrote nuclear strategist Bernard Brodie in 1945. "From now on, its chief purpose must be to avert them. It can have no other useful purpose."

Deterrence was to become the name of the game. Conventional war was a thing of the past, said the nuclear enthusiasts, and all past military philosophies, all past military theories, and, most significantly, all past military experience were dismissed as irrelevant.

The Army's position, as stated in the 1949 edition of its operations manual, FM 100-5, was that even with nuclear weapons, "the fundamental principles of combat remain unchanged." Such a viewpoint would seem to have been validated by that most conventional of conflicts, the 1950–53 Korean War. But instead, that war was dismissed as an aberration. Air Force Secretary Thomas Finletter declared the Korean War a unique, never-to-be-repeated diversion.

The "true course" of future war was revealed by the Eisenhower administration's strategy of "Massive Retaliation," in which almost total reliance for national security was placed on nuclear weaponry. U.S. conventional military forces were cut to the bone, with the Army particularly hard hit. As the historian Russell Weigley noted, this nuclear strategy "left the Army uncertain of its place in the policy and strategy, uncertain that civilians recognized a need even for the Army's existence and uncertain therefore of the service's whole future."

The impact was even harder on the military's Reserve Components. There was no time for Reserve mobilization in a nuclear war that would be over within a matter of minutes. And the connector with the American people was cut as well. The constitutional duty of the citizenry to "provide for the common defense" did not seem to apply when war was waged by nuclear "wizards of Armaggedon," whose highly sophisticated weapons and convoluted strategies they could scarcely comprehend.

In the beginning, nuclear weapons were seen as usable instruments of war. In the 1954 edition of FM 100-5, the Army argued that nuclear weapons represented "additional firepower of large magnitude." That was the way Eisenhower evidently saw them when he threatened their use in Korea and Lebanon.

But it was soon discovered that Massive Retaliation was fatally flawed. As Army Chief of Staff General Maxwell D. Taylor pointed out after his retirement, it "could offer our leaders only two choices, the initiation of general nuclear war or compromise and retreat." When the Kennedy administration came to power in 1961, the strategy changed to "Flexible Response." Conventional forces were increased, but reliance was still placed on nuclear weapons at both the strategic and tactical levels.

Distracting the United States with its sponsorship of "Wars of National Liberation," the Soviets reached and then exceeded nuclear parity with the Americans. A "Mexican standoff" ensued where one side's nuclear arsenal canceled out the other. Except for defense of the homeland, nuclear weapons evolved from weapons of war to instruments of diplomacy, useful primarily to deter their use by other nuclear-armed powers.

Be that as it may, for the first time in forty-five years the nuclear Sword of Damocles no longer hangs over America's head. As long as its nuclear deterrent is maintained, general nuclear war is the least likely threat facing the United States today.

General Conventional War

General conventional war is equally unlikely, but you would not know it, for such wars, as exemplified by World War II, are the model for most Americans against which other wars are compared. General conventional wars are marked by the total destruction of the enemy's armed forces, the occupation of his homeland, his unconditional surrender, and the trial and execution of his leaders.

When the Korean War did not fit those standards, many Americans saw it as a defeat, even though the war's objective of ejecting North Korea and its Chinese allies from the South was achieved, and South Korea remains a free and independent nation over four decades later. Likewise, the U.S. victory in the Persian Gulf War has been called into question because it too did not fit the model. Yet, again, all of the stated objectives of the war, including the ejection of the Iraqis from Kuwait and the restoration of the Kuwaiti government, had been realized.

While for the victors, general conventional wars are the most soul-satisfying, they are also the most rare. As Dave Palmer notes, "Most wars . . . have been limited. One can dig back in history to say that the final Punic War—when Rome defeated Carthage, slaughtered the population, razed the city, plowed under the ruins, and sowed the furrows with salt— was not in any way limited. . . . But it is hard to find other examples; in some manner or other a limiting factor was always present."

Limited War

One of the reasons the American people look to the general conventional war paradigm as the model for war is that they agree with General of the Army Douglas MacArthur that "In war there can be no substitute for victory."

But "victory" does not necessarily mean total victory. "In war many roads lead to success," Clausewitz emphasized, "and they do not all involve the opponent's outright defeat. They range from the destruction of the enemy's forces, the conquest of his territory, to a temporary occupation or invasion to projects with an immediate political purpose, and finally [as was the case in the Cold War] to passively awaiting the enemy's attack" (p. 94).

This point was well made during the 1951 "Great Debate" in the U.S. Senate on the Korean War. Senator Brian McMahon of Connecticut questioned General of the Army Omar

Bradley, then Chairman of the Joint Chiefs of Staff, on what constitutes victory in war:

> General, in the course of our history I believe there have been a number of instances in which we accomplished our objectives without what might be called a final and complete defeat of the enemy such as we visited on Germany [in World War II]. Certainly in the War of 1812 we fought the British on the sea and on our own mainland to maintain the security of our commerce and the safety of our nationals.
>
> We didn't insist on a military victory over England as essential, did we? . . . Now, in the Spanish-American War when we accomplished the liberation of Cuba, we didn't proceed to Madrid to capture Madrid, did we?
>
> The point I want to make, to find out if you are in agreement with me, is that when you say that the object of war is victory, you must have a definition of what constitutes victory, don't you?
>
> I think you must, General Bradley replied, and you vary from being willing to accept a rather small thing that you start off to correct up to an objective which we set in World War II of unconditional surrender. There are many variations in between the two.

Senator William Knowland of California took issue with those statements:

> The fact of the matter is, is it not, General, that we did not satisfy the controversy with the Spaniards being left in control of half of Cuba; we did not settle the [1947–49] Greek War with the Greek Communists being left in control of a substantial part of Greece; and we did not finish the War of 1812 with the British being left in control of New Orleans. While it is true that we did not carry the war into their home countries, nevertheless, we did clean up the particular situation in which we were involved.

Bradley stuck to his guns. "We restored it in some cases to the status quo when we started the [Korean] war, and won our point. That boils down to what our point is," he emphasized.

His comment was incorporated into the Army's 1954 doctrinal manual. Limited war was defined as "wars of limited objective," returning to the pre–World War II definition that did not require total submission of the enemy, but only the realization of the objectives the war set out to achieve and a return to peace.

But this concentration on political ends as the limiting factor in war did not last. The nuclear-era 1962 manual dropped the concept of "wars of limited objective" and introduced instead the concept of "limited means." "The essential objective of United States military forces will be to terminate the conflict rapidly and decisively in a manner best calculated to prevent its spread to general [i.e., nuclear] war," it said.

Without realizing it, this definition surrendered the U.S. advantage of escalation dominance. During the subsequent war in Vietnam, as then Secretary of State Dean Rusk admitted in his autobiography, it was the Chinese who had escalation dominance, for it was their threat of escalation to the nuclear level that restricted U.S. prosecution of the war.

As a result of the debacle in Vietnam, there was a reexamination of the definition of limited war. The 1986 edition of the Army's strategic doctrinal manual, Field Manual 100-1, *The Army*, defined limited war as "armed conflict between two or more nations, at an intensity below that of general war, where means and/or ends are constrained." Although the fallacy of seeing war as limited by its means did not completely disappear, there was a major emphasis on war's political ends.

As the Army's strategic doctrinal manual went on to say, "Since war is primarily a politically directed act for political ends, the conduct of a war, in terms of strategy and constraints, is defined primarily by its political objectives. . . . The scope and intensity of warfare are therefore defined and limited by political purposes and military goals. The interactions of military operations, political judgements, and national will further define the objectives of a conflict and determine its duration and the conditions for its termination."

And when the Cold War drew to an end, the fallacious idea that the purpose of limited war was to avoid nuclear war, which had led to the U.S. loss of escalation dominance, was also discarded. As the Army's strategic doctrinal manual puts it, "The restrained use of nuclear or chemical weapons, or enemy use of biological weapons, is possible in limited wars." And the United States did indeed threaten escalation to the nuclear level during the 1990–91 limited war in the Persian Gulf.

Low-Intensity Conflict

Just as the Cold War had spawned the notion of *low-intensity conflict,* also known as *counterinsurgency, wars of national liberation,* and *people's war,* the end of the Cold War spelled its demise. But in its heyday from 1960 to 1973, low-intensity conflict distorted and dominated U.S. military thinking.

Defined in the 1986 edition of FM 100-5, low-intensity conflict is "a limited politico-military struggle to achieve political, social, economic, or psychological objectives. It is often protracted and ranges from diplomatic, economic, and psychological pressures through terrorism and insurgency."

In its beginning in 1960, low-intensity conflict, like high-intensity nuclear war at the other end of the conflict spectrum, was seen as a new kind of war that rendered conventional war obsolete. Although not evident at the time, high-intensity conflict and low-intensity conflict were in fact reciprocal. For the Soviet Union and China, low-intensity "wars of national liberation" and "people's wars" were ways to avoid U.S. nuclear superiority by using guerrilla surrogates to challenge American power in the zero-sum Cold War.

Failing to see the subterfuge, President Kennedy bought the challenge. When Army Chief of Staff General George H. Decker, a World War II infantryman, told Kennedy that "any good soldier can handle guerrillas," he was seen as hopelessly old-fashioned. Decker was soon replaced by the more compliant General Earle Wheeler, a consummate staff officer who could mouth the politically correct platitudes of this "new kind of war."

The doctrine of "counterinsurgency" dominated strategic thinking, especially after Kennedy made it clear that future promotions of high-ranking officers would depend on their demonstration of experience in the counterguerrilla or sub-limited war field.

As former CIA analyst Douglas Blaufarb pointed out, "There was a brief period in the late 1960s when military intellectuals were advancing the notion that the U.S. Army was the arm of the government best equipped to carry out in the field the entire range of activities associated with nation building." Eschewing warfighting, the 1968 edition of the Army's operational manual stated that "The fundamental purpose of U.S. military forces is to preserve, restore or create an environment of order or stability within which the instrumentalities of government can function under a code of laws."

Civilian academicians also jumped on board. "Even before Vietnam justifiably absorbed the attention of America, guerrilla-revolution had become a fashionable challenge to be met in elegant and complex ways but ways which need the talents, the scope, and capacities and the experience of various available careerists," noted Harvard's J. Bower Bell. "For the American intellectual theoreticians of order, the nature of the appropriate response . . . fit the prejudices and aspirations of the time . . . the guerrilla could be met by using the advanced tools of social science for the betterment of mankind."

More fuel was added to the fire in 1965 with the publication of "Long Live the Victory of People's War," by the Chinese defense minister at the time, Lin Piao (Lin Biao in the later Chinese transliteration), which became the doctrinal basis for "people's war." Using the Chinese civil war strategy of "encirclement of the cities from the countryside" as an example, he argued that a "people's war" waged by the "world countryside"—identified as "the oppressed nations and peoples of Asia, Africa and Latin America"—would rise up and destroy the "world cities" of the United States, West Europe, and industrialized societies generally.

During the 1960s, the Communist battle cry was "One, Two, Three, Many Vietnams!" and counterinsurgency/low-intensity conflict was seen by many Western strategists as the wave of the future. But that future never materialized.

Instead, in the final years of the Cold War the Communist concepts of "wars of national liberation" and "people's wars" were turned against their creators. As Georgetown University's Mark P. Lagon points out, President Ronald Reagan pledged assistance to "freedom fighters" in Third World nations seeking to overthrow Marxist governments who were clients of the Soviet Union. Taking a page from the Communist revolutionary manuals, the United States backed successful insurgencies in Afghanistan, in Angola, in Cambodia, and in Nicaragua.

The demise of the Cold War, Lagon argues, was brought about in part by this "reversal of the dominoes," which made the economically fragile Soviet Union's pursuit of global empire more expensive. This reversal proved to be containment's final form.

The post-Vietnam reassessment of U.S. military policy rejected the civilian-spawned notions of nuclear war and low-intensity conflict that had dominated strategic planning since World War II. In their place came a return to an emphasis on traditional conventional war. Beginning at the Naval War College in 1972, a renaissance in military thinking would sweep the armed forces and revitalize the long-suppressed study of conventional war.

But low-intensity conflict has not entirely faded from the scene. As will be examined in detail in Part III, one of its components, "nation building," is once more in vogue, and "peace operations" in the Third World has replaced counterinsursgency as the currently fashionable academic dogma. Yet, although the "various available careerists" are still with us, touting "operations other than war" as an alternative to armed conflict, this time those stratagems are being viewed with an increasingly jaundiced eye.

Conclusion

In the post–Cold War world, the spectrum of conflict has shrunk considerably. Low-intensity conflicts now fall under the rubric of "operations other than war." And with the end of the nuclear era, general nuclear war has become a remote possibility.

The term "strategic," once appropriated by the nuclear strategists to define only nuclear weapons, no longer fits that description. By definition the use of means to achieve ends, "strategic" applies today to the conventional forces of the United States. They, not nuclear forces, are now the prime military means for securing U.S. political ends.

But even these conventional forces have limited application. Given the "correlation of forces" in the world today, where the United States remains the world's sole surviving superpower, the possibility of a general conventional war on the order of World War II is also remote.

With one important exception, the most likely paradigm for future conflicts is that most forgotten of wars, the 1950–53 war in Korea. It was fought with conventional weapons. Its objectives were limited. It was both a joint (i.e., all-service) and a combined (i.e., multinational) operation; and it ended with a negotiated settlement. The exception, as discussed in the following chapter, is that it was fought on the strategic defensive rather than on the strategic offensive as was the case prior to (and after) the Cold War.

Forty years later, that revised Korean War paradigm proved to be the model for the war in the Persian Gulf. Today, Korea and the Persian Gulf, appropriately enough, have been selected as the two major regional areas of conflict for which the U.S. military is to be prepared to fight.

Chapter 5

Warfighting Doctrines

Any set of men who have read and studied the art of war independently and without collaboration are almost certain to have evolved varying conceptions of war and radically different individual doctrines.

But the reader will readily appreciate the utter confusion and the fatal dispersion of effort that would occur should an army or fleet be commanded by a body of men who have no common meeting ground of doctrine. . . .

—LIEUTENANT COMMANDER
DUDLEY W. KNOX, USN,
Naval Institute Proceedings
(MARCH–APRIL 1915)

The Strategic Defensive

"This hypothetical condition [referred to above] must assume a grave aspect," said Dudley Knox eighty years ago, "when it is recognized to be the condition of our own navy at the present time." Yet this lack of common ground was the condition not only of the U.S. Navy but of all the military during much of the Cold War.

As discussed in the previous chapter, Cold War warfighting doctrine was distorted first by nuclear weapons and then by guerrilla war. The civilian "wizards of Armageddon" (to use the journalist Fred Kaplan's felicitous phrase) then formulating nuclear doctrine, and the academic social scientists pushing nation building and counterinsurgency, agreed on one thing: all past military theory, all past military doctrine, and, most importantly, all past military battlefield experience was irrelevant to these so-called new nuclear and guerrilla wars.

One of the most influential of the civilians was the late Bernard Brodie. First as a faculty member at Yale University and the National War College, then as a full-time member of the RAND Corporation, and then as a professor at the University of California at Los Angeles, Brodie legitimized the study of military strategy by civilians lacking a military background.

As the Cold War began, the military either opted out or were forced out of military policy formulation. Only the civilian analysts had the revealed truth, and Brodie and others stimulated the introduction of analytic methods at places like RAND. Most nuclear policies were formulated at civilian "think tanks" by what former Air Force Chief of Staff General Thomas D. White called the "tree-full-of-owls type of so-called professional 'defense intellectuals.'"

And as Dave Palmer noted in his analysis of the Vietnam War, the ill-conceived "slow squeeze" strategy of gradual escalation that came to such grief in the Vietnam War was the brainchild of Assistant Defense Secretary John T. McNaughton, a Harvard University Law School professor on loan to the Pentagon.

One could not imagine World War II's Army Chief of Staff General George Marshall, Army Air Force Chief General "Hap" Arnold, or Admiral Ernest King, the Chief of Naval Operations, allowing civilians to usurp their role in strategy and policy formulation, or in operational military matters. And neither would the Commander in Chief, President Franklin D. Roosevelt.

In a letter to Secretary of War Henry Stimson in February 1942, President Roosevelt said that he wanted to "make it very clear that the Commander-in-Chief exercises his command function in relation to strategy, tactics and operations directly through the [Army] Chief of Staff."

The World War II military chiefs would have resigned in protest at such challenge to their military authority. But the Cold War military leaders, and the officer corps in general, registered little protest to this tacit vote of no confidence in their military council and advice. "Military professionals," said Alain C. Enthoven and K. Wayne Smith, two of Defense Secretary Robert McNamara's infamous "whiz kids," in 1971, "are among the most infrequent contributors to the basic literature on military policy and defense strategy."

An even more serious distortion of Cold War warfighting doctrines was triggered by the change in U.S. national policy during the Korean War. Up to that time, warfighting doctrine had rested on a military policy of the strategic offensive, in which the military seized the initiative and went on the attack to destroy the enemy's armed forces and break his will to resist.

While it was sometimes necessary to go on the defensive to buy time and build one's strength, as in the early days of World War II and Korea, this was seen as only a temporary condition. The offensive was resumed as soon as possible.

The U.S. military entered the Korean War with a national offensive policy of "rollback and liberation," the same policy with which it had fought World War II. Although during the opening months of the war, the U.S. was pushed back into the Naktong Perimeter and forced temporarily on the defensive, U.S. forces resumed the offensive with the Inchon invasion and the subsequent breakout from the Naktong Perimeter. By early November 1950, the North Korean Army had been destroyed and its government forced back into enclaves along the Yalu River separating North Korea from the Chinese province of Manchuria.

But with the Chinese entry into the war later that month,

U.S. national policy underwent a profound change. Faced with a nuclear-armed Soviet Union and the possibility of a land war with China, the United States abandoned its offensive policy of rollback and liberation in favor of a defensive policy of containment.

Modeled on diplomat George Kennan's famous 1946 "long telegram" from the Soviet Union, which argued that the best way to deal with communism was not to confront it directly but to contain its expansion and allow the contradictions inherent in Marxism-Leninism to destroy it from within, the national policy of containment would be a long-term success.

But in the short term it had a debilitating effect on U.S. military policies and strategies, primarily because no one in the military, including that master military strategist General Douglas MacArthur, understood its implications.

"When you say, merely, 'we are going to continue to fight aggression,' that is not what the enemy is fighting for," MacArthur told the Senate during the 1951 "Great Debate" on the war. "The enemy is fighting for a definite purpose—to destroy our forces in Korea."

What no one at the time could understand was that the defensive policy of containment required the military to adopt the operational strategic defensive on the battlefield as well. This posture was enacted not as a temporary expedient, as had earlier been the case, but as the warfighting strategy for the remainder of the war.

While defeat can be forestalled by defensive operations, battlefield victory is no longer possible, for the essence of defensive operations is waiting for the enemy to attack. After the massive twenty-seven-division Chinese attack in April 1951 was routed, the U.S. Eighth Army commander, General James A. Van Fleet, was forbidden by Washington from taking the offensive and completing the destruction of the Chinese Army.

Instead, he was ordered to remain in position. A bloody outpost war then ensued, as both sides entrenched themselves in fixed positions along the front lines and waited for diplomatic negotiations to bring the fighting to an end. Two years later, on July 27, 1953, the Korean Armistice Agreement was signed, bringing the war to an end.

As discussed at some length in my analysis of the Vietnam War elsewhere, the best possible battlefield result with the strategic defensive is *stalemate*. That's exactly what happened in the Korean War. And the same thing happened in the Vietnam War. Distracted by the false doctrines of nuclear war and guerrilla war, neither the military professionals nor the civilian "whiz kids" could understand the fundamental limitations imposed by the defensive national policy of containment.

Again, as in Korea, the best possible battlefield result in Vietnam was stalemate, and that was exactly what happened after the enemy's abortive 1968 Tet Offensive. As former Marine combat historian and now George Washington University professor Ronald H. Spector has pointed out, it took a year of hard fighting before that fact finally sank in. Again, as in Korea, the war ended through diplomatic negotiations and the signing of the Paris "Peace" Accords in January 1973.

In reaction to the Vietnam debacle, a "back to basics" movement swept the U.S. armed forces. Though the defensive policy of containment remained in effect at the strategic level, the military started to edge back toward the tactical and operational offensive. It began in 1972 at the Naval War College at Newport, Rhode Island.

The college's president at the time, Admiral Stansfield Turner, said bluntly that "our increased reliance on civilians and on 'think tanks' to do our thinking for us" reflected a failure of war colleges in general. "We must be able to produce military men who are a match for the best of the civilian strategists or we will abdicate control of our profession."

The military began to take charge of its own house. For example, the concept and details of the sea service's post-Vietnam "Maritime Strategy" (discussed below) were worked out at the Naval War College. Abandoning the defensive mind-set that had plagued the sea services during the Cold War, the Navy and Marine Corps went back on the operational offensive.

Among other things, the 1986 Maritime Strategy stressed the importance of conventional rather than nuclear war. It called for what it termed the "horizontal escalation" of a NATO–Warsaw Pact war, with Navy carrier battle groups and amphibious task forces not just supporting the central front in Europe, as had previously been the case, but also moving "horizontally" to apply pressure on the Soviet Union's Middle East and Pacific flanks.

The sea services would take the operational offensive to seize and maintain control of the high seas so that the sealines of communication would be secured, paving the way for creation of a sea bridge to Europe, where the mobilization capabilities of the United States could be brought to bear.

Meanwhile, in 1973, the Army established the Training and Doctrine Command (TRADOC) at Fort Monroe, Virginia, to revitalize Army warfighting doctrine. Reflecting the sad state of the Army at that time, still recovering from the Vietnam War, the 1976 version of the Army's warfighting doctrinal manual was very much a stopgap measure, concentrating on the defense of West Europe. But its concentration on a return to classic warfighting fundamentals began the revolution within the Army

As the Army leaders reexamined the dynamics of the battlefield, they realized that the previous division of warfighting into "strategy" and "tactics" was inadequate. Where "strategy" dealt with the use of the military to achieve the nation's political objectives, and "tactics" with the fighting on the battlefield, another intermediate level of warfare had been totally ignored.

This "operational" dimension had to do with the use of tactical battles to achieve theater-of-war-level objectives, which in turn would assist in attaining the war's strategic goals. For example, old doctrine had defined three types of attack—the frontal attack; the penetration attack; and the envelopment, where the enemy is attacked on his flanks or rear.

But instead of seeing each of these tactical forms of attack in isolation, as had previously been the case, the operational level of war now saw their use in coordination with each other. A commander may well launch a frontal attack with one of his units to pin the enemy down, while another unit envelops the enemy flanks.

Labeled "AirLand Battle" doctrine, to highlight the change from previous doctrine as well as to emphasize the multidimensions of warfare, this new doctrine focused on the operational level of war and on operational offensive operations. It defined the battlefield not only in terms of the line of contact, now called "close operations," but also in terms of "rear" operations and "deep operations" into the enemy homeland.

First promulgated in 1982, then refined in 1986, the notion that nuclear weapons had rendered all past history, theory, and experience irrelevant was itself pronounced irrelevant. As the historian John L. Romjue put it, "AirLand Battle was a return to the tried and true principles of experience in war."

For its part, since 1975 the Air Force's Tactical Air Command had been working with the Army's TRADOC to enhance joint employment of Army and Air Force tactical forces. In 1982, "Project Warrior" was begun to "improve the warfighting spirit and perspective of Air Force people [and] encourage an improved understanding of the theory and practice of war." In January 1983, under the aegis of the Air University at Maxwell Air Force Base, Alabama, the Center for Aerospace Doctrine, Research and Education (CADRE) was formed.

During the Cold War the Air Force had been what one critic called "SACumsized," with the Strategic Air Command and its nuclear strike mission dominating the entire Air Force. But, like the other services, after Vietnam the Air Force too regained control from, in its case, the civilian nuclear strategists. Conventional war was once again emphasized, and the 1984 *Basic Aerospace Doctrine of the United States Air Force* stressed that belief. The Air Force's first mission, stated the manual, was "to neutralize or destroy an enemy's war-sustaining capabilities or will to fight [through] attacks . . . directed against an enemy's key military, political, and economic power base."

Back on the Offensive

These post-Vietnam warfighting doctrines, designed primarily to seize the battlefield initiative and take the tactical and operational offensive against Soviet and Warsaw Pact forces, were the ones that governed the conduct of the 1990–91 Gulf War.

Making these warfighting doctrines even more effective was the change at the strategic level. With the collapse of communism, the national defensive policy of containment came to an end. For the first time since World War II, the Soviet Union was our ally, not our adversary, and the forty-year constraint imposed by fear that massive application of military force would provoke a nuclear confrontation no longer applied.

Thus the national policy reverted to what it had been during World War II, "rollback and liberation," with the specific stated objectives of ejecting the Iraqi forces from Kuwait and restoring the Kuwaiti government to power.

Military policy followed suit, reverting to a strategic offensive in which the war was carried to the enemy homeland and the full fury of American military might was brought to bear, to destroy Iraqi warmaking capabilities and break their will to resist. The United States was able to do this because for the first time since World War II it could mass its forces against the enemy at hand, something it was unable to do during the Cold War.

Simply stated, "mass"—one of the principles of war—dictates that one should *mass*, i.e., bring the bulk of one's forces to bear, on the primary objective and use an *economy of force* against secondary objectives. In both the Korean and Vietnam wars, the United States massed its forces against the Soviet Union—the only power capable of destroying the United States in minutes—and used an economy of force to fight the shooting wars in Asia.

As Henry Kissinger has said, "Our perception of the global challenge at the same time tempted us to distant enterprises and prevented us from meeting them conclusively." But in the

Gulf, there was no longer the need to devote the majority of U.S. assets and attentions to guarding against the Soviet threat.

With the Soviet Union now on its side, the United States could commit not only its XVIII Airborne Corps "Third World" contingency forces, but also the U.S.-based heavy divisions previously earmarked for NATO reinforcement. Most importantly, it could withdraw its VII Corps from Europe, where it had been stationed for decades to guard against a Soviet–Warsaw Pact attack, and move it to the Gulf, where its 1st and 3d Armored Divisions and 2d Armored Cavalry Regiment could provide the muscle for the main attack.

Back on the strategic offensive at the strategic level, as in World War II the United States temporarily adopted a defensive posture to gain strength for the coming offensive. As it had envisioned in its "Maritime Strategy" doctrine, the Navy built a sea bridge to the Persian Gulf to bring U.S. mobilization capability to bear.

"It was the quickest and largest military sealift buildup since World War II," General H. Norman Schwarzkopf told the 1991 Naval Academy graduating class, "an 8,000 mile, 250-ship haze-gray bridge, one ship every 50 miles from the shores of the United States to the shores of Saudi Arabia. And they offloaded some nine million tons of equipment and petroleum products. . . ."

Anticipating "horizontal escalation" in the Middle East in the event of a NATO war, the Navy was already on station when the 1990 Gulf crisis began. In the largest naval deployment since World War II, the Navy sent some 120 warships to the Gulf region, including six carrier battle groups which flew 23 percent of the war's combat missions. Its surface warships conducted Maritime Interception Operations to enforce the UN sanctions against Iraq, and its submarines launched TOMAHAWK cruise missile attacks against the Iraqi homeland.

For their part, the Marine Corps validated the "Amphibious Warfare" portion of the Maritime Strategy by manning the Amphibious Task Force in the Persian Gulf, tying down several Iraqi divisions in coastal defense. And the two divisions of the I Marine Expeditionary Force (I MEF) also validated their post-Vietnam warfighting doctrine. Some would argue that their supporting attack along the Gulf coast in fact became the main attack when I MEF rapidly penetrated the Iraqi defenses and advanced into Kuwait itself.

In the largest ground campaign since World War II, the Army's AirLand Battle doctrine proved itself as well, especially its concepts of maneuver and deep operations. VII Corps's massive turning movement outflanked the enemy's defenses to destroy the Republican Guard armored divisions of the Iraqi strategic reserve. And XVIII Airborne Corps's 101st Airborne Division's 175-mile-deep aerial assault seized crossings over the Euphrates River, while its 24th Infantry Division, in just 100 hours, attacked 370 kilometers deep into the enemy's flanks and rear—the farthest and fastest mechanized attack in history.

Not as widely noted as its combat operations, Air Force airlift played a crucial role in sustainment of the war. Thanks to the aerial-refueling techniques pioneered during the Vietnam War, Military Airlift Command was able to fly more than 15,800 missions and deliver more than half a million passengers and nearly half a million tons of supplies to the war zone.

Although the Air Force did not win the war all by itself, as some of its more zealous airpower advocates may have wished, Air Force doctrine was also validated in the Gulf. The air campaign accomplished just what that doctrine called for: "to neutralize or destroy an enemy's war-sustaining capabilities [by attacks] directed against an enemy's key military, political, and economic power base."

The forty-three-day air campaign was one of the most brilliantly executed in history. Orchestrated by Lieutenant General Charles Horner, the Joint Forces Air Component Commander (JFACC), it included some 2,700 aircraft from 14 different national or service components. "Gulf War lesson number one is the value of air power," said President George Bush. "The Gulf War taught us we must retain combat superiority in the skies."

It was the Korean War model fought on the strategic offensive. But this time the battlefield was not stalemated by a defensive posture, and the Gulf War was won by force of arms. The war ended when the enemy asked for and was granted a battlefield cease-fire.

Giving the lie to German Field Marshal Helmuth von Moltke the Elder's observation during the Franco-Prussian War that "no plan survives contact with the enemy," the military's post-Vietnam warfighting doctrines were confirmed in combat against real enemies on the Persian Gulf battlefield. As a result, one might suppose that the military would be content to rest on their laurels. But that was not the case. Their first postwar priority was to refine their doctrines for war.

Doctrines for the Twenty-first Century

"Operation Desert Shield/Desert Storm was certainly the classic example of a multi-service operation," stated the U.S commander in the Gulf, General Schwarzkopf, "a truly joint operation."

Three months later the Joint Chiefs of Staff published a doctrinal manual, *Joint Warfare of the U.S. Armed Forces*, known as "Joint Pub 1." Although practically all past wars have been multiservice affairs, Joint Pub 1 was the first time a joint warfare doctrine had been formalized. "Joint warfare is essential to victory," the manual declares. "Accordingly this publication is written to help ensure members of the US Armed Forces fight successfully together."

In defining the military's purpose, the manual stated that "Defense of the national security rests first on the concept of deterrence. . . . If deterrence fails, then our single objective is *winning the nation's wars*. When we fight, we fight to win." While warfighting is its primary focus, Joint Pub 1 also noted that "we have along history of *military support for national goals short of war* ranging from general military service to the nation . . . to a wide range of actions abroad in support for foreign policy."

The heart of joint operations is the campaign. Campaigns

"represent the art of linking battles and engagements in an operational design to accomplish strategic objectives . . . and serve as the unifying focus for our conduct of warfare."

Joint Pub 1 lists several "foundations of the joint operational art." They include securing *air and maritime superiority and space control* to ensure freedom of action and to secure a mobility differential over the enemy. Another essential is the capability for amphibious, airborne, and air assault *forcible entry* in order to achieve strategic and operational leverage. Reflecting the fact that in strategic terms the United States is a world island, *transportation* is a third absolute.

Transportation enables the joint campaign to begin and to continue. "Without secure air, sea, space and land lines of communication," says Joint Pub 1, "we cannot reliably move forces and material, reinforce forward-deployed forces, or sustain the campaign."

Reflecting the post–Cold War reversion of the military to the strategic offensive, another foundation is "the *direct attack of the enemy's strategic centers of gravity* by air, missile, special operations and other deep-ranging capabilities. . . . In certain types of campaigns (for instance, those devoted to assisting in the internal defense of a foreign ally against an insurgency) *special operations* may assume a leading role."

The joint campaign should *exploit the information differential.* Space power is crucial to establishing superiority in command, control, communications, intelligence, navigation, and information processing. "Weather, mapping, charting, geodesy, oceanography, and terrain analysis are all areas where the joint force should achieve significant advantages."

But the centerpiece of joint operational art is *leverage among the forces.* "Engagements with the enemy may be thought of as *symmetric* if our forces and the enemy forces are similar (land versus land, etc.) or *asymmetric* if our forces and the enemy forces are dissimilar (air versus sea, sea versus land, etc.). . . . In years past, the sea was a barrier to soldiers and a highway to the sailor; the different mediums of air, land, sea and space were alien to one another. To the joint force team, *all forms of combat power present avenues for exploitation.*"

That having been said, *sustained action on land* is still key. "Many elements of the joint operations discussed above may be directed at enabling land power to be projected and directed against the foe. The ability to establish presence on the ground . . . can be fundamental to achieving the joint campaign's objectives and bringing it to a successful conclusion."

While advancing joint warfare doctrine, Joint Pub 1 acknowledges that "Service skills [i.e., the skills of the Army, Navy, Air Force, and Marine Corps] form the very core of our combat capability. Joint warfare does not lessen Service traditions, cohesion, or expertise. Successful joint operations are impossible without the capabilities developed and embodied in each Service." Each of the services would develop its own post–Gulf War warfighting doctrine to carry it into the twenty-first century.

From the Sea

Among the most radical of these post–Gulf War doctrines was the Navy and Marine Corps September 1992 White Paper, ". . . From the Sea," subtitled "Preparing the Naval Services for the 21st Century." This new doctrine, stated the White Paper, "represents a fundamental shift away from open-ocean warfighting on the sea toward joint operations conducted *from* the sea."

However, some open-ocean or "blue water" missions remain. "As long as the United States maintains a policy of nuclear deterrence, our highly survivable nuclear powered ballistic missile submarines will remain *critical* to national security," emphasizes the White Paper. And sealift, the movement of men and materiel by ship from the United States to a theater of war, as in the Gulf War, remains "an enduring mission for the Navy."

Showing the flag also remains a mission for naval forces, as it was when President Theodore Roosevelt sent the "Great White Fleet" on a round-the-world cruise in 1908. Filling the gap as the United States withdraws from its overseas bases, "the Navy and Marine Corps [will] operate forward to project a positive American image, build foundations for viable coalitions, enhance diplomatic contacts, reassure friends, and demonstrate U.S. power and resolve."

But the primary thrust of the Navy's "new direction" is Naval Expeditionary Forces, a shift in focus from a traditional "blue water" Navy operating primarily on the high seas to a "brown water" Navy operating in the waters of the "littoral" or coastlines of the earth. The Navy and Marine Corps Team, the new doctrine emphasizes, will concentrate on littoral warfare and maneuver from the sea, the tactical equivalent of maneuver warfare on land.

". . . From the Sea" includes three principal tenets. First is *battlespace dominance,* bringing decisive force to bear on and below the sea, on land, in the air, and in space as well. As the "heart of naval warfare," battlespace dominance ensures access from the sea to permit the effective entry of equipment and resupply, and "effective transition from open ocean to littoral areas, and from sea to land and back, to accomplish the full range of potential missions."

A second tenet is *power projection.* It involves the use of Marine expeditionary forces, carrier-based aircraft, land-based expeditionary aircraft, TOMAHAWK missiles from surface forces and attack submarines, and naval gunfire support to apply offensive military force against the enemy.

A third and final tenet is *force sustainment.* "American influence depends on its ability to sustain military operations *around the globe,*" states the new doctrine. It requires open sealanes of communication so that passage of shipping is not impeded by an adversary. "Forward logistics, prepositioning, and strategic sealift, coupled with strategic airlift, are the keys to force sustainment."

To refine this new doctrine, in the wake of the Persian Gulf War the Navy created a Naval Doctrine Command at Norfolk, Virginia, thus bringing the Naval Services on par with the Army and Air Force, which in the aftermath of Vietnam established TRADOC and CADRE to develop their warfighting doctrine.

Just as TRADOC had developed and published the Army's basic AirLand Battle manual and CADRE had done the same for aerospace doctrine, in March 1994 the Naval Doctrine Command published Naval Doctrine Publication (NDP) 1, *Naval Warfare*. It was a milestone event, for unlike the other services, the Navy had not formally stated its operational doctrine in many years.

Naval Warfare incorporates the guidance contained in ". . . From the Sea," and stresses the shift from "a global struggle envisioned under Cold War maritime strategy . . . to preparation for regional challenges." "Our warfighting philosophy," it concludes, "incorporates the principles of war while making the best use of the inherent characteristics and advantages of our naval forces."

The Navy Doctrine Command has its work cut out for it. In a sense, ". . . From the Sea" is "the epitaph to the command of the sea ethic that has dominated naval thought since the late 16th century," says Dr. Jan Breemer, an assistant professor at the Naval Postgraduate School. Command of the sea is synonymous with naval strategy itself, he says. But the new emphasis on battlespace dominance stresses primacy of land warfare in fleet operations. "Superficially this may not sound terribly revolutionary," he writes, "but it represents a 180 degrees reversal from the classic relationship between sea control and naval power projection."

Land control has traditionally been a mission for the Army, thus a major unresolved question in this new naval strategy is how much land control should be the aim of warfare from the sea. Does "littoral" mean coastal, or does it mean, as one Navy map portrays it, lying anywhere within the 650-nautical-mile-range of naval strike capabilities? "The only areas of the world thus excluded," writes Breemer, "are the very central portions of Canada, South America, Africa, and Siberia."

But it would appear the Navy has no such ambitions. Acting as an "enabling force," states *Naval Warfare*, "the naval component may conduct operations initially to seize a hostile port facility or airfield as a precursor to the arrival of airlift, sealift and prepositioned assets. After achieving maritime and air superiority, naval forces can continue to operate as an integrated part of a larger joint operation or disengage to respond to another need for their presence."

"We are in the midst of two simultaneous revolutions," Navy Secretary John Dalton told the Naval War College on June 14, 1994. "First is a major technological revolution that is fundamentally changing the ways in which we conduct warfare. And second, a strategic revolution that is changing our national military strategy as well as our naval strategy. We must embrace the challenges that accompany those revolutions."

While ". . . From the Sea" is "our foundation . . . a starting point for what lies beyond," Dalton announced that he had directed the Chief of Naval Operations and the Commandant of the Marine Corps "to begin work on the framework for . . . a new maritime strategy . . . to provide the strategic bridge between our doctrine for warfighting and the objectives of our peacetime operations. It will examine the relationships between forward presence and crisis prevention and detail the transition of naval forces across the entire spectrum of conflict. . . ."

Global Reach, Global Power

The Air Force's strategic planning framework, *Global Reach—Global Power,* was actually published in June 1990, on the eve of the Persian Gulf War, but, like the Navy's ". . . From the Sea," it was intended to lead the Air Force into the twenty-first century.

As with the Navy's post–Cold War doctrine, the Air Force stresses its role in nuclear deterrence with its manned bombers and intercontinental ballistic missiles, as well as its critical role in strategic and theater airlift and in aerial refueling. It also stresses its role in space, "the high ground of the future." But the emphasis of its new doctrine is warfighting.

With one refueling, long-range bombers operating from

Guam, Diego Garcia, and U.S. bases can deliver a large conventional bombload anywhere on the entire globe. And "modern fighter forces can respond anywhere in the world on short notice."

To enhance its combat capabilities, the Air Force underwent a major reorganization after the Gulf War. As noted earlier, during the Cold War the Strategic Air Command (SAC) and its nuclear mission dominated the Air Force. But with the collapse of the Soviet Union, its time had past. "We have moved beyond the phase when strategic bombing, standing alone, is in any way adequate to describe our purposes," said Air Force Chief of Staff General Merrill A. McPeak in June 1992.

Adding to that need for reorganization was the fact that internal roles and missions had become entangled. In both Vietnam and the Gulf, tactical fighter-bombers conducted most strategic air operations over the enemy homeland, while strategic B-52 bombers operated primarily in support of tactical ground operations. Meanwhile, the SAC tanker fleet actually flew most of its missions in support of intercontinental airlift transports.

After the Gulf War, the Air Force did away with its old fiefdoms and reorganized itself into "movers" and "shooters." The transport aircraft of the Military Airlift Command, plus some of the SAC aerial-refueling tankers, were assigned to the new Air Mobility Command at Scott Air Force Base in Illinois under the operational control of the Defense Department's U.S. Transportation Command.

The "shooters"—combat aircraft of the former Tactical Air Command—plus the former SAC bombers and tankers not part of the Defense Department's U.S. Strategic Command's nuclear deterrent force, were formed into composite wings and assigned to Air Combat Command at Langley Air Force Base in Virginia, which is now under the operational control of U.S. Atlantic Command.

"The establishment of Air Combat Command is both a sign of our maturity and a signal that the new gospel is airpower integration," said General McPeak. That new gospel was contained in the March 1992 edition of Air Force Manual 1-1, entitled *Basic Aerospace Doctrine of the United States Air Force*. Elevation above the earth's surface is singled out as the key to the differences between aerospace and surface-bound forces. Aerospace forces were divided into four categories: *aerospace control* (counterair and counterspace operations); *force application* (strategic attack, interdiction, and close air support); *force enhancement* (airlift, air refueling, electronic combat, surveillance, and reconnaissance); and *force support* (base operability and logistics).

Elaborating on this new doctrine in his June 1992 speech, General McPeak spelled out the Air Force mission: "to defend the United States through control and exploitation of air and space."

Control is easy to understand, he said. Because in the Korean, Vietnam, and Gulf wars the U.S. Air Force immediately established and maintained total air control over the battlefield, "It's been nearly 40 years now since a U.S. soldier was killed by enemy aircraft. . . . No one now serving in our ground forces has even come under attack by enemy aircraft.

"To 'exploit' air and space," McPeak continued, "means to understand this arena and to possess efficient and effective means to operate there. We cannot know where the next trouble spot will be, but we do know that every interesting location on Earth is visited several times a day by our large constellation of satellites." And B-2 bombers "can be overhead, anywhere in the globe, in less than one day."

As the United States withdraws from forward overseas bases such as Clark Air Force Base and the Subic Bay naval facilities in the Philippines, the global reach provided by air and space systems becomes increasingly critical. "This seems to me to be of particular importance," McPeak went on to say, "as we move away from the system of forward bases and toward more emphasis on U.S.-based forces configured for expeditionary action."

But while acknowledging the Air Force's role in support of ground operations, General McPeak was still not ready to abandon the conceit that the Air Force could go it alone.

"Make no mistake," he stressed, "our approach to the mission genuinely separates us from our colleagues in the other services.

"For them, air operations are seen as an extension of surface activity, needed to make possible safer, more effective maneuver on land or at sea. We, on the other hand, seek to control and exploit air and space not to facilitate operations somewhere else, but to achieve national objectives in and through this dimension. Thus, the way we perceive the mission is different from the other services . . . we are, in fact, unique."

In October 1994, on the eve of his retirement from active duty, McPeak made another bid for Air Force primacy. While he would give up the close air support of ground operations, which since World War I many airpower proponents have felt was beneath their dignity, McPeak staked out a claim for almost total control of the deep-battle portion of the Army's AirLand Battle doctrine. He would eliminate Army long-range artillery and anti-missile defenses, and restrict the role of its attack helicopters.

"It's ironic that at a time in which the Pentagon's emphasis has been on joint military operations," complained Major General Thomas L. Wilkerson, the Marine Corps's senior planner, "the Air Force's answer is to try to put up walls between itself and the others." It is doubtful whether such walls will stand.

AirLand Battle

Unlike the Air Force, the Army has no illusion that it can operate autonomously. "The first sentence of the first paragraph of the first chapter" of the June 1993 edition of its post–Gulf War doctrine, Army Chief of Staff General Gordon Sullivan points out, "says America's Army is a member of the joint team."

Unless we go to war with Canada or Mexico again, a most unlikely eventuality, the Army knows it is absolutely dependent on Navy sealift and Air Force airlift to get it to the point of action. "Our strategic 'center of gravity,'" said one officer, "will be getting there." The Army is likewise dependent on Air Force, Navy, and Marine air support for battlefield survival and success. "The Army will not operate alone," the new doctrinal manual emphasizes repeatedly.

Written under the direction of the commander of the Army's Training and Doctrine Command, General Frederick Franks, who led VII Corps in the Gulf War, the latest version of FM 100-5, *Operations,* in one sense revalidates the AirLand Battle doctrine that led to victory in the Gulf. But it is more than that.

While original AirLand Battle doctrine emphasized rear, close combat, and deep operations, the new manual stresses depth and simultaneous attack. "Depth is the extension of operations in time, space, resources and purpose," it states, putting the Army in direct conflict with General McPeak's October 1994 claims.

One important addition was a chapter on "Operations Other Than War," which will be discussed in more detail in Part III. There was a fear that in the post–Cold War environment the Army would slip back into the social science fallacies of the counterinsurgency era. But that was not the case. "The Army organizes, trains, and equips to fight and win the nation's wars," says the new manual. "That remains its primary mission."

Instead of the Air Force's claims for exclusivity, the Army stresses greater cooperation with the other services. As then TRADOC Commander General Franks noted in a February 1993 interview with *Jane's Defence Weekly,* the new doctrine "reflects the shift to stronger joint operation [and] extends AirLand Battle into a wider interservice integration. . . . The doctrine allows for an Army more disposed to force projection than to forward defense."

The Army is also attempting to institutionalize its ability to prepare for the future, evolving what General Sullivan, the current Army Chief of Staff, calls "a new force for a new century—Force XXI." Battle Labs were formed in 1992 to "rapidly develop requirements for a Force Projection Army through experimentation that encourages innovation and multi-disciplined participation," and in 1993 the Louisiana Maneuver concept was announced to "energize and focus the force of change."

In August 1994, the Army's Training and Doctrine Command published Pamphlet 525-5, "not doctrine, rather a document of ideas," to provide a concept for early twenty-first-century operations. As General Franks put it, "It describes in general terms how the Army will function in the future as the primary land force executing joint multinational operations in War and Operations Other than War to achieve established objectives in operations where domination of terrain or control of population is central to victory."

"We do not know exactly what lies ahead," said General Sullivan, "but we are moving forward."

Conclusion

Doctrine is a dynamic process, and all of the armed services continue to refine and develop how they will fight and win on the battlefields of the future. As the Air Force's General Mc-Peak, quoted above, made clear, the Air Force is somewhat at odds with this process, still believing it can operate autonomously. But that view will not prevail. The Joint Chiefs, who have the whip hand, are emphatic that "Joint [i.e. multi-service] warfare is essential to victory," and their joint warfare doctrinal manual was written specifically "to help ensure members of the US Armed Forces fight successfully together."

Chapter 6

Reorganization for Combat

The Clinton Administration defense program . . . is based on tomorrow's requirements. It is a product of a comprehensive, broadly collaborative review based upon the real dangers that face America in the new era. It has produced a lean, mobile, high-tech force, ready to protect Americans in this new time.

—SECRETARY OF DEFENSE LES ASPIN, SEPTEMBER 1, 1993

The Nuclear Deterrent

During the Clinton administration's detailed "bottom-up review" of U.S. defense programs, discussed in detail later in this chapter, conventional force levels were closely scrutinized. Not so with so-called strategic (i.e., nuclear) forces. "The reason we didn't spend a lot of time on that," said JCS Chairman General Colin Powell in September 1993, just prior to his retirement,

was that as a result of actions taken over the last several years [i.e., the Strategic Arms Reduction Treaty agreements] strategic forces are going down to their bottom-up review level without any help needed at this time.

In the four years I have been Chairman, we have put in place arms control agreements and we have done unilateral things within the Armed Forces reflecting the post–Cold War environment, that has resulted in us reducing . . . our nuclear weapons level by about 70 percent. . . .

Without a whole lot of prompting from anybody [the military] decided let's get rid of artillery-fired [nuclear] projectiles in the Army [and it] bit the bullet on taking tactical nuclear weapons off our ships at sea. The Navy, the Marine Corps and the Army now totally rely on the Air Force for any potential future nuclear weapons they need on the battlefield. . . . I'm very pleased that the JCS [has] been in the forefront of getting rid of capability that is no longer needed in the post–Cold War environment.

But, Powell went on to add, "at the end of the day . . . you have to look at the reality of the nuclear weapons and make sure that we always have the capability on our side to deter their use. And that's what we have tried to do in structuring our own strategic forces and bringing them down in size, to make sure that no military planner anywhere on the face of the earth who might have access to nuclear weapons would ever contemplate a successful strike against the United States."

There has already been a major reduction in nuclear weaponry. Beginning in 1945, the United States produced some 70,000 nuclear warheads. In 1967, the peak U.S. stockpile was 32,500 warheads, which was reduced to 16,500 by 1994, with 10,500 active warheads and 6,000 awaiting disassembly. The Soviets, beginning in 1949, produced some 55,000 nuclear warheads. In 1986, their peak stockpile was 45,000 warheads, which was reduced to 32,000 by 1994, with 15,000 active and 17,000 awaiting disassembly.

And they are slated to be reduced even further. U.S. nuclear force levels were set by the START II agreements signed by President George Bush and Russian President Boris Yeltsin on January 3, 1993. By the year 2003, the total number of nuclear warheads that can be deployed may not exceed 3,500. While the nuclear triad of ground-launched, sea-launched, and air-launched missiles will continue, their numbers will be drastically reduced from the 9,970 U.S. nuclear warheads deployed when START II was signed. All land-based intercontinental ballistic missiles have to be downloaded from three warheads to one. Submarine-launched ballistic missiles have to be reduced to no more than 1,750. And the bomber force will be limited to ninety-five B-52H and twenty B-2 bombers.

In September 1994, President Clinton approved Presidential Decision Directive 34, a year-long classified Pentagon study meant to spell out U.S. nuclear policy through the year 2002. "That decision," reported *The Washington Post,* "rules out for the present any new U.S. push for further reductions in nuclear arsenals than previously planned or any new strategic role for these weapons." Specifically rejected was a proposal that the United States move to a "no-first-use" policy, thereby retaining the U.S. option of a "last resort" nuclear retaliation after a non-nuclear attack on U.S. forces.

As has been true from the beginning, the initial authority to use nuclear weapons remains reserved to the President alone. He exercises that authority through the Secretary of Defense to the Commander in Chief, U.S. Strategic Command (STRATCOM), at Offnut Air Force Base in Nebraska.

As with all unified commands, STRATCOM reports directly to the Secretary of Defense. Formed in July 1992, it replaced the Air Force's Strategic Air Command (SAC) and the U.S. Joint Strategic Targeting Planning Staff (JSTPS), which was established in 1960 to coordinate Air Force and Navy nuclear targeting. Now STRATCOM, commanded alternately by an Air Force general and a Navy admiral, is responsible for the planning, targeting, and wartime employment of all U.S. nuclear forces.

Combatant Commands

While the reorganization of the nuclear command and control system was prompted by the major post–Cold War reductions in nuclear weaponry, there had also been major changes in the military's conventional command and control structure.

One aspect remained unchanged, however—civilian control of the military. Although the uniformed Chiefs of Staff of the Army and the Air Force, the Chief of Naval Operations, and the Commandant of the Marine Corps are charged with organizing, training, and equipping America's military, they are forbidden by law from actual command. And that goes for the JCS Chairman as well.

The President of the United States, in his role as Commander in chief, legally commands the armed forces of the United States. In fact, however, he has delegated that authority to the Secretary of Defense, who is the de facto commander of the American military. The Secretary exercises his command function through the commanders in chiefs (CINCs) of the nine unified commands that actually command military forces in the field.

Though some of these commands have been in existence for many years—both the European Command (EUCOM) and the Pacific Command (PACOM) were formed in 1947—their authority was limited until the Goldwater-Nichols Department of Defense Reorganization Act of 1986, named after its sponsors, Senator Barry Goldwater (R-AZ) and Representative Bill Nichols (D-AL).

The Goldwater-Nichols legislation was an outgrowth of the debacle of the Vietnam War in which command and control was so distorted and convoluted that it severely hampered the prosecution of the war. Unlike World War II, where General Dwight Eisenhower was the commander of the European Theater of Operations and coordinated all air, sea, and land operations, General William C. Westmoreland was the field commander only.

He had no control over air strikes against the Ho Chi Minh Trail, the enemy's main line of supply and communication, or over strikes against North Vietnam. And he had no authority over naval operations outside South Vietnam's territorial waters. These were the province of the CINC PACOM in Honolulu, 6,000 miles away.

The Goldwater-Nichols Act greatly strengthened the authority of the commanders of the combatant commands, as was evidenced during the Persian Gulf War. Unlike West-moreland in Vietnam, General H. Norman Schwarzkopf, the CINC of the U.S. Central Command (CENTCOM), was very much the equivalent of Eisenhower, having total command of all theater air, sea, and land operations.

The five geographical unified commands are EUCOM, PA-COM, and CENTCOM; the U.S. Southern Command (SOUCOM), which is responsible for U.S. military operations in Latin America; and the newest geographical command, the U.S. Atlantic Command (USACOM), which was restructured in October 1993.

The largest of all the unified commands, USACOM controls all U.S. military forces in the continental United States. In addition to its responsibilities for military operations in the Atlantic and the Caribbean, it is tasked with providing reinforcements to the overseas commanders. The first test of that mission turned out to be providing such "adaptive force packages" to its own Haitian invasion force.

Admiral Paul David Miller, USACOM commander at the time, had said earlier that "We need to break with the momentum of the past, and actively explore new ways to provide our theater commanders with the capabilities they really need. . . . From my personal vantage point an aircraft carrier is 4.1 acres of mobile real estate. . . . And we need to be able to have whatever capability the U.S. needs to operate from that carrier."

True to his word, for the September 1994 Haitian invasion force, Admiral Miller embarked the Army's 10th Mountain Division on the aircraft carrier U.S.S. *Eisenhower,* and special operations forces, including helicopters and Army Rangers, on the carrier U.S.S. *America.* This break with tradition is evidence of the degree to which the U.S. military is adapting for the twenty-first century.

Another adaptation is the post-Vietnam creation of four single-mission unified commands. These include STRAT-COM, discussed above, and the new U.S. Space Command (SPACE) responsible for U.S. activities in space as well as the nation's aerospace defense.

Also new is the U.S. Transportation Command (TRANSCOM), responsible for directing the airlift efforts of the Air Forces Air Mobility Command and the sealift efforts of the Navy's Military Sealift Command. Finally, there is the U.S. Special Operations Command (SOCOM) at MacDill Air Force Base in Florida, responsible for worldwide military special operations.

One Gulf War lesson, noted the Congressional Research Service's John Collins, was that "It is not enough for each U.S. Armed Service to be well prepared for unilateral operations. The Army, Navy, Air Force and Marine Corps also must be ready to work smoothly with each other and, when required, with allies as well." That was the very reason for the creation of the multiservice unified commands in the first place and was the focus of the 1986 Goldwater-Nichols reforms.

But the validation of the reorganization of the military command and control structure was only one of the lessons of the Gulf War. Other lessons that shaped the internal organization of the U.S. military include the role of women in the military and the role of the Reserve Components, including the Army, Navy, Air Force, Marine, and Coast Guard Reserves, and the Army and Air National Guard.

Women in the Military

During the Gulf War, the United States crossed the Rubicon on the issue of women in the military, and there is no turning back. A matter of considerable debate and discussion before the Gulf crisis, their battlefield performance during the war confirmed beyond question their fitness to serve.

Although women had served in past wars, especially in nursing and administrative positions, they had not been truly integrated into the force. But all that changed in the Gulf War.

Women played a vital role in that war. According to the official statistics, by late February 1991 more than 37,000 military women were in the Persian Gulf, making up approximately 6.8 percent of U.S. forces. Approximately 26,000 Army, 3,700

Navy, 2,200 Marine, and 5,300 Air Force women were deployed.

For the first time in American military history, the majority of the women were not nurses. They served in a variety of assignments, including truck drivers, military policewomen, helicopter pilots, radio operators, electronic warfare repair technicians, chaplains, and as crew members aboard hospital, supply, oiler, and ammunition ships. Women commanded combat support and combat service support brigade-, battalion-, company-, and platoon-sized units in the Kuwait Theater of Operations.

Women endured the same hardships under the same harsh conditions as their male counterparts, and the official Department of Defense report on the war concluded that "Women performed admirably and without substantial friction or special consideration." But it was not without cost.

For the first time in American military history, the casualties included enlisted women as well as officers. The six women killed in action were Army helicopter pilot Major Marie Rossie; helicopter crewman Sergeant Cheryl O'Brien; medic Specialist Cindy Beaudoin; and supply technicians Specialist Beverly Clark, Specialist Christine Mays, and Private Adrienne Mitchell. Another seven women died in accidents and from other non-hostile causes. Twenty-one women were wounded in action, and two women—Army flight surgeon Major Rhonda Cornum and truck driver Specialist Melissa Rathbun-Nealy—were captured. Fourteen women Marines were awarded the Combat Action Ribbon for having returned fire against bypassed Iraqi troops.

As a result of their performance in the Gulf War, overall opportunities for military women increased substantially. On April 28, 1993, Secretary of Defense Les Aspin repealed the exclusion of women from combat aircraft and ships. On January 13, 1994, he repealed the "risk rule" that had barred women from serving in non-combat units where the risk was as great as that in combat units. "We've achieved some historic gains," he said:

First, in the Air Force, women are now flying combat aircraft and more than 99 percent of Air Force jobs are open to women. Second, the Navy has expanded the number of flying squadrons where women can serve from 42 to 200, and women are taking off in tactical aircraft from Navy aircraft carriers. Third, in the Army, women are piloting helicopters in combat aviation units. More than 9,000 aviation positions are now available to women. And finally, the Navy has opened 18 additional ships to women so that there are 9,000 . . . sea billets available. And in November [1993] Congress adopted and President Clinton signed the legislation repealing the law barring women from serving on combat ships.

Our policy says that women will not serve in units that engage in direct ground combat. And today we are uniformly defining "direct ground combat" for the first time. The definition has three parts, all of which must be present to prevent service by women:

Women may not serve in units that one, first of all, engage an enemy on the ground with individual or crew-served weapons; that two, are exposed to hostile fire; and that three, have a high probability of direct physical contact with the personnel of a hostile force. . . . That is a definition of a ground combat unit. And that is a definition of a unit in which the women will not be allowed to serve.

Women now comprise some 11.6 percent of the active military force, up from 1.9 percent in 1972 when the all-volunteer military began. And these numbers will rise. Projections are that the number of women enlisting in the Army will increase to 20.5 percent in fiscal year 1994. Because of the lifting of the ban on women serving on combat ships, Navy female recruits will increase to 15 percent. The Air Force, which already has a high percentage of women, will increase female accessions to 22.6 percent. And even the Marine Corps will almost double the number of its female recruits, from 2.5 percent to 4 percent.

Within NATO, the United States has by far the most women in uniform, both in actual numbers and (except for Canada) as a percentage of the force. According to a 1991

Western European Union report, France had 20,000 women in uniform (3.6% of the force), the United Kingdom 17,747 (5.9%), Canada 9,056 (10.6%), Greece 4,671 (2.8%), Belgium 3,092 (3.6%), the Netherlands 2,795 (2.9%); the rest of the WEU force (except Italy and Iceland, which had none) had less than 1,000. By comparison, in 1990 the United States had 223,154 women under arms, or 11 percent of the force.

While the gross numbers have declined as a result of the post–Cold War drawdowns, the percentages will continue to climb.

The Reserves

Another lesson learned—or, more properly, relearned—in the Gulf War was the critical importance of the Reserve Components. "Operations Desert Shield and Desert Storm required the largest mobilization and deployment of Reserve Component forces since the Korean Conflict," says the official Department of Defense (DOD) report on the war. Over 230,000 reservists from the Army and Air National Guard, and the Army, Navy, Air Force, Marine Corps, and Coast Guard Reserves were ordered to active duty in support of the Gulf crisis. More than 105,000 of these men and women served in the KTO (Kuwait Theater of Operations).

The comparison with the Korean War is apt, for that war would have been lost without the Reserves. And the same is true of the war in the Persian Gulf. Active-duty military units simply would have been overwhelmed. For example, much of the U.S. airlift capability was provided by Air National Guard and Air Reserve units, and a large proportion of the Army's logistics units came from the Reserve Components.

Their mobilization was a validation of the "Total Force" concept that grew out of the Vietnam War experience. Although there had been a token partial mobilization during the Vietnam War, for the first time in American military history the Reserve Components did not play a major part in that war. That failure to mobilize either the Reserves or the American people was a major factor in America's failure to achieve its strategic objectives.

To prevent a recurrence of that debacle, Army Chief of Staff General Creighton Abrams set out to restructure the Army so that it could not be committed to sustained combat without action by the President and the Congress to mobilize the Reserves, which perforce would require mobilization of the country as well.

His 1973 Total Force concept called for a closer affiliation of the Reserves with the active force, including the rounding out of active Army divisions with National Guard brigades. Although General Abrams died in office in 1974, his initiatives were carried forward by his successor, General Frederick C. Weyand, and others, particularly Generals Walter Kerwin and John Vessey.

As a result, 70 percent of the Army's combat support and combat service support units necessary to sustain the Army in the field was in the Reserve Components, including 77 percent of its combat engineers, 77 percent of its hospital units, 71 percent of its supply and service units, 57 percent of its Signal Corps units, and 97 percent of its civil affairs units.

The Army was not alone in its dependence on the Reserves. One hundred percent of the Navy's combat search and rescue squadrons and logistic airlift squadrons were in the Reserves, as were 93 percent of its cargo-handling battalions, 85 percent of its minesweepers, 68 percent of its SEABEE mobile construction battalions, and 50 percent of its fleet hospitals.

One hundred percent of the Marine Corps's civil affairs units were in the Reserves, as were 62 percent of its bulk fuel companies, 50 percent of its force reconnaissance units, 40 percent of its tank battalions, 40 percent of its beach and port operations companies, and 33 percent of its heavy artillery.

Fifty-nine percent of the Air Force's tactical airlift was in the Air Guard and Air Reserve, as was 55 percent of its tactical air support. Ninety-two percent of its aeromedical evacuation personnel also were in the Reserve Components, 50 percent of its strategic airlift, 71 percent of its aerial port capability, 69 percent of its engineering personnel, 66 percent of its combat communications, 59 percent of its combat logistics support squadrons, and 23 percent of its aerial refueling.

The roundout brigade concept did not work as planned, as we shall see in the following chapter, but some Army Reserve Component combat forces did serve in the Gulf, including two Army National Guard field artillery (FA) brigades. The 142d FA Brigade from Arkansas and Oklahoma supported the British 1st Armoured Division, and the 196th FA Brigade from Tennessee, West Virginia, and Kentucky supported XVIII Airborne Corps. Also deployed was the Army Reserve's 416th Engineer Command, which served as the theater Army Engineer Command.

The Marine Corps sent a substantial portion of its reserve 4th Marine Division, 4th Marine Aircraft Wing, and 4th Service Support Group to the Gulf, including four infantry battalions, elements of two tank battalions, several artillery batteries, and composite attack and transport helicopter squadrons.

Air Force National Guard and Reserve deployments included three tactical fighter squadrons, one special operations group, two special operations squadrons, and a tactical reconnaissance squadron. Navy Reserves included two minesweepers, the U.S.S. *Adroit* (MSO 509) and *Impervious* (MSO 449), two combat search and rescue squadrons, one SEABEE battalion, four logistics squadrons, and several mobile inshore undersea warfare detachments. For the first time in its history, the Coast Guard mobilized three reserve Port Security Harbor Defense units and deployed them to the Gulf.

At the peak of the mobilization, a total of 231,000 reservists had been called to active duty. More than 105,000 reservists were serving in the KTO at the time of the cease-fire on February 28, 1991, including 37,692 from the Army National Guard, 35,158 Army reservists, 6,625 Navy reservists, 13,066 Marine reservists, 10,800 Air National Guard reservists, and 281 Coast Guard reservists.

The Gulf War was concrete evidence of the importance of the Reserve Components. Not only were the physical contributions of the Reserves validated; even more so were its psychological dimensions.

By activating 798 Army, Navy, Air Force, Marine Corps, and Coast Guard Reserve Component units from over two thousand towns and cities in every state across the country, public support for the war was almost guaranteed. As General Edwin H. Burba, Jr., then commander of U.S. Forces Command, told an audience of reservists, "When you come to war, you bring America with you."

The Legacy of Unpreparedness

"We continue to follow a regular cycle in the doing and undoing of measures for the National Defense," said Major (later General of the Army) George C. Marshall in a remarkably prescient address in June 1923. Using examples from the War of 1812, the Mexican War, the Civil War, the Spanish-American War, and World War I, Marshall noted that

> from the earliest days of this country, [the military] was materially increased in strength and drastically reduced with somewhat monotonous regularity.
>
> We talk of Valley Forge in Revolutionary days, and do not realize that American soldiers experienced something like Valley Forge over in France in the fall of 1917. I have seen soldiers of the First Division without shoes and with their feet wrapped in gunny sacks marching ten or fifteen kilometers through the ice and snow. . . . I have seen so many horses of the First Division drop dead on the field from starvation, that we had to terminate the movements in which they emerged.

This situation, Marshall went on, "reflects the general condition of unpreparedness with which we entered the war, and it was only the strength of our Allies who held the enemy at bay." His words would come back to haunt him sixteen years later when he took over as Army Chief of Staff and found a military again woefully unprepared. As in 1917, the price was paid in blood at Pearl Harbor, at Bataan and Corregidor, and at Faid and Kasserine Passes in North Africa to buy time while America mobilized.

And Marshall must have recalled those words again when he took over as Secretary of Defense during the Korean War. The first American ground unit committed to action in July 1950, the 1st Battalion, 21st Infantry (called Task Force Smith after its commander, Lieutenant Colonel Charles B. Smith), was cut to pieces because it was outgunned by the advancing North Korean Army.

And so was its parent 24th Infantry Division, which fought a fighting retreat back into the Pusan Perimeter. A truly hollow force, it had two rifle battalions instead of three in its infantry regiments, two firing batteries instead of three in its field artillery battalions, and a company of light M-24 tanks whose 75mm guns could not stop the North Korean T-34s, instead of the heavy tank battalion that was authorized.

Again, the price was paid in blood. And yet again, as in earlier wars, America's mobilization capability was eventually brought to bear and the battlefield imbalance corrected.

In his 1923 speech, with words that still ring true over seventy years later, Marshall speculated on why such fluctuations occurred. After each war, he said, "the public mind ran away from the tragedies of the War and the reasons therefor, and became obsessed with the magnitude of the public debt and the problem of its reduction. Forgetting almost immediately the bitter lesson of unpreparedness, they demanded and secured the reduction of the Army, which their representatives had so recently increased for very evident reasons."

The same pattern was repeated after the Cold War. The military buildup during the Reagan administration that helped bring that conflict to an end was rapidly dismantled. In a move unprecedented in history, President George Bush in August 1990 announced a major reduction in the size of the U.S. military on the very same day he committed the United States to the Persian Gulf War.

Even as the war was raging, U.S. military combat units were being phased out and deactivated. The two combat brigades of the 2d Armored Division, for example, were committed piecemeal because their parent division was being deactivated. One rounded out the 1st Infantry Division, whose 3d Brigade was in the process of deactivation, and the 1st Armored Division had to be augmented by a brigade from the 3d Infantry Division.

In the wake of the Gulf War, once again "obsessed with the magnitude of the public debt," the military was substantially reduced. "Our future military will be smaller," said President Bush in August 1991. "By mid-decade our force can be some 25 percent smaller than the force we maintained in the last days of the Cold War . . . these planned reductions will cut our force to a minimally acceptable level—to a Base Force below which further reductions would not be prudent."

The Base Force

The Bush administration's fiscal year 1993 "base force" reductions called for organizing the military into four packages: a truncated nuclear-triad-force package for deterrent and retaliatory purposes (later overtaken by the January 1993 START II agreements), and three force packages for forward presence and crisis. These included an Atlantic force package, a Pacific force package, and a Contingency force package.

The *Atlantic* force would include a two-division Army corps and three Air Force fighter wings on the ground in Europe, plus a Navy carrier battle group, an amphibious ready group, and a Marine Expeditionary Unit on station in the Mediterranean and Indian oceans. U.S.-based reinforcements would include three active and six Reserve Army divisions, two active and ten Reserve Air Force fighter wings, four Navy carrier battle groups, and a Marine Expeditionary Force.

The *Pacific* force would include an Army division and an Air Force fighter wing forward deployed in Korea, an Air Force fighter wing, a Marine Expeditionary Force, and a Navy carrier battle group and amphibious ready group forward deployed in Japan. U.S.-based reinforcements would include an Army corps, one active Air Force fighter wing and one Reserve fighter squadron, and five Navy carrier battle groups.

Contingency forces would include a five-division Army corps, seven Air Force fighter wings, and one Marine Expeditionary Force.

As President Bush said, force levels would fall by almost 25 percent, from their 1980s peak of 3,358,000 to 2,554,000—a reduction of some 804,000 personnel. Active Army divisions would be reduced from eighteen to twelve, and Reserve divisions from ten to six. Active Navy battle force ships would fall from 568 to 432, including cutting aircraft carriers from 15 to 12 and reducing reserve warships from 31 to 16. The Air Force would lose twelve active and three Reserve fighter wings. Although they would lose 51,000 personnel, only the Marine Corps' force structure would remain unchanged at three divisions and three air wings.

The Bottom-Up Review

With the Army reduced to some 536,000 active-duty personnel, down 57,000 from its "hollow army" strength on the eve of the Korean War, it would appear that cuts had reached what President Bush had called the "minimally acceptable level."

But that proved not to be the case. The "base force" concept lasted less than two years, replaced by the Clinton administration's "bottom-up" review announced on September 1, 1993, in a joint press conference by Secretary Aspin and JCS Chairman General Colin Powell.

This "start-from-scratch" review of U.S. security requirements was subtitled "Forces for a New Era." It was, said Aspin, "a very extensive collaborative process," involving a number of working groups that looked at force structure options, modernization choices, initiatives, and foundations.

Every one of these working groups had personnel from the Office of the Secretary of Defense, the Joint Chief of Staff, the service staffs, and from the Commanders in Chief of the combative commands in the field. "And this [was] just the collaboration within the building," said Aspin. "The White House staff, the president himself was involved in the process.

"The first step in this bottom-up review was . . . to go to the fundamental question, 'What do you need a defense for?' And we began with the question of 'What are the dangers that face the United States now in the post–Cold War, post-Soviet world?'"

The review came up with four such threats. First was "the new nuclear threat, a handful of nuclear weapons in the hands of some terrorist organization or terrorist state, perhaps delivered by unconventional means." Second was the conclusion "that we needed a defense establishment to deal with regional dangers. There is still in the world today a handful of bad guys who, while they cannot threaten the continental U.S. in any meaningful way, they can threaten American interests or American allies or American friends."

Third was "dangers to democracy." Aspin cited "a tenuous movement toward democracy today . . . in the former Soviet empire and in the developing world," but warned that a reversal of this trend "would pose a different national security situation for the United States." The fourth danger, Aspin said, was that of "a weak economy. In the short run the national security of the United States is protected by a strong military force; in the long run, the national security of the United States is protected by a strong economy."

It was a restatement of John Foster Dulles's 1954 warning not to become "permanently committed to military expenditures so vast that they lead to 'practical bankruptcy.'" Thankfully, Aspin did not follow Dulles's simple-minded solution and place total reliance on nuclear weapons for U.S. defenses.

While the bottom-up review retained the nuclear forces provided for in START II—eighteen ballistic missile submarines, ninety-four B-52 and twenty B-2 bombers, and five hundred Minuteman III single-warhead ICBMs—primary reliance was on conventional forces.

Forward deployment of such forces remained critical.

"Peacetime overseas presence is the single most visible demonstration of our commitment to defend U.S. and allied interests . . . around the world," the review stated. It "deters adventurism and coersion by potentially hostile states, reassures friends, enhances regional security [and improves] ability to respond effectively to crisis or aggression when they occur."

In Europe, the President and Secretary Aspin had reaffirmed that 100,000 troops would be the number, said JCS Chairman General Colin Powell, and in East Asia, about 98,000 troops, "keeping our two brigades in Korea, an Air Force wing in Japan. . . . We have roughly 20,000 troops prepositioned [in Southwest Asia] now."

But the most controversial objective established by the bottom-up review was that the United States must be capable of fighting and winning two major regional conflicts nearly simultaneously with a high probability of success, while minimizing American casualties. As General Powell explained:

> It seems to us, that it is essential that the United States armed forces in the name of the American people be prepared to fight and win a major regional war in . . . Southwest Asia. Why? Because we have alliances there, we have vital interests there, the oil of the Western world is located there. . . .
>
> Similarly, we think we should be able to do the same thing in Northeast Asia. . . . North Korea has not changed its stripes [and] our interest is so great in this part of the world that we should have the ability to do this as well. We believe it is sound, and wise and prudent for us to be able to do these two near simultaneously.
>
> But, history teaches that the forces you buy based on these reasonable assessments might well be used for a conflict you never dreamed of. The forces we are buying now . . . are for a force that will be with us for years to come. . . . So we always have to be thinking about the future, the unknown, the uncertain, and I think that is what Secretary Aspin has clearly done in . . . the bottom-up review.

Another controversial aspect, discussed in more detail in Part III, is to prepare U.S. forces to participate effectively in multilateral peace enforcement and unilateral intervention operations that could include peacekeeping, humanitarian assistance, counterdrug and counterterrorism activities.

Here even General Powell expressed his concern. "We're warriors," he emphasized.

> Now at the same time, because we are able to fight and win the nation's wars, because we are warriors, we are also uniquely able to do some of these other new missions that are coming along—peacekeeping, humanitarian relief, disaster relief—you name it, we can do it.
>
> And we can modify our doctrine, we can modify our strategy, we can modify our structure, our equipment, our training, our leadership techniques, everything else to do these other missions, but we never want to do it in such a way that we lose sight of the focus of why you have armed forces—to fight and win the nation's wars.

With all these changes contained in the bottom-up review came another reduction in U.S. military strength, beyond the Bush administration's post–Cold War base force level. There was a further 196,000 reduction in U.S. military personnel, bringing the Army to its lowest level since before World War II. Active divisions were cut from twelve to ten and Reserve divisions from six to five. Navy warships were cut from 438 to 336 and aircraft carriers from 12 to 11.

Active Air Force fighter wings were reduced from fifteen to thirteen, and Reserve fighter wings from eleven to seven. Again, as in the Bush reductions, the Marine Corps remained unchanged at three Marine Expeditionary Forces, each with a Marine division, a Marine Aircraft Wing, and a combat service support element.

Readiness

As these reductions began to take effect, there were increasing questions as to whether the decade-long cuts in defense spending had gone too far and whether the United

States was once again repeating its legacy of unpreparedness.

Although earlier he had denied it, after the November 1994 congressional elections Defense Secretary Perry admitted that three of the Army's twelve divisions were far below peak readiness, and that two of the Army's main quick-reaction units would be unable to fulfill some of their missions if they were ordered into combat immediately.

In fact, the lead armor battalion for the 24th Infantry Division (Mechanized) had been sent to Kuwait in October 1994 suffering from major training deficiencies. Due to funding shortfalls, some platoon leaders had never taken their platoons into the field for training exercises, tank crews had not completed their crew-drill evaluations, and platoons had not been evaluated in a live-fire exercise.

In a throwback to the heights of unpreparedness on the eve of World War II, when U.S. troops had to train with wooden rifles, tankers in the 2d Armored Division's 1st Battalion, 67th Armor, had to park their tanks and conduct their platoon training dismounted, with soldiers walking the ranges and pretending to be tanks.

The readiness of the other services had been lowered as well. "The anecdotal evidence of a serious readiness problem is overwhelming," warned Representative Floyd Spence (R-SC), the new chairman of the House National Security Committee (formerly the Armed Services Committee).

Air Force units in Europe were so overextended in supporting peacekeeping operations that training for their primary mission had been seriously degraded. "This means that should a contingency action arise in the near term," said Spence, "we would not be able to deploy a single F-15E [fighter-bomber] crew out of Europe that has not suffered recent training deficiencies."

Similarly, naval operations in Cuba and Haiti had seriously overextended the Navy surface combatants involved. The available sixty-one ships, Spence said, were forced to do the job of the seventy-three ships actually required for those operations. "Due to depleted Operations and Maintenance funding," Spence continued, "28 Marine Corps and Navy tactical aviation squadrons had to ground 50% of their aircraft for the entire month of September 1994. Eight East Coast Marine Corps aviation squadrons were completely grounded for the month of September 1994."

Senator Strom Thurmond (R-SC), the new head of the Senate Armed Services Committee, also expressed his concerns, saying, "Many of us have observed that evidence of a new hollow force has steadily emerged over the last year."

"No one really knows how to measure readiness," he told Defense Secretary Perry in October 1994, "but experienced people are generally able to recognize it when they see it. Mr. Secretary, you have a readiness problem."

To its credit, the Clinton administration acknowledged that defense cuts had gone too far, and recommended a $25 billion increase in defense spending over the next six years. But this was not good enough for the new Republican Congress, whose "Contract with America" had called for strengthening America's defenses. In January 1995, the House National Security Committee called for boosting defense spending by some $126 billion over the next five years, and the Senate Armed Services Committee called for a $100 billion increase over the same period.

Conclusion

Whatever the outcome of these budget proposals, it is clear that after ten straight years of cuts in the Pentagon budget, the post–Cold War drawdown of the U.S. Armed Forces has finally bottomed out. While substantial increases in force structure are unlikely, there will be no further reductions either.

And there is likely to be little change in the U.S. military's organization for combat either. In 1993, the Congress created an eleven-member independent Roles and Missions Commission, chaired by Harvard University's John White, to make recommendations for the future structure of the armed forces.

Among the most controversial of the twenty-five issues the

commission is to address are the question of "four air forces" (i.e., the fact that each of the four services has its own aviation component) and the "appropriate overall size and mix of capabilities between the Army and the Marine Corps for forcible entry and sustained land combat." The debate no doubt will be acrimonious, but the chances for a major reorganization of service roles and missions remain slight, for the present structure, combat-tested in the Gulf War, has served the nation well.

Chapter 7

Combat Operations

The aggressor is always peace-loving (as Bonaparte always claimed to be); he would prefer to take over our country unopposed. To prevent his doing so one must be willing to make war and be prepared for it. . . . Thus decrees the art of war.

—CARL VON CLAUSEWITZ, *On War*, P. 370

Major Regional Conflicts

What James Madison called "the means and dangers of attack" have always formed the basis for U.S. military policy. During the Cold War, it was the nuclear and conventional forces of the Soviet Union. Today, when it comes to warfighting, it is what Defense Secretary Les Aspin called regional dangers. "Now," he said, "our focus is on the need to project power into regions important to our interests and to defeat potentially hostile regional powers, such as North Korea and Iraq.

"Although these powers are unlikely to threaten the United States directly, these countries and others like them have shown they are willing and able to field forces sufficient to threaten important U.S. interests, friends and allies."

At the turn of the century, the British satirist Hilaire Belloc neatly summed up British regional military policy in a simple couplet: "Whatever happens we have got/The Maxim Gun and they have not." But today everyone has the modern equivalent of the "Maxim Gun," an early version of the machine gun.

Iraq and North Korea, the potential regional aggressors, so the Defense Department *Bottom-Up Review* stated, are each capable of fielding forces in the range of 400,000–750,000 troops; 2,000–4,000 tanks; 3,000–5,000 armored fighting vehicles; 2,000–3,000 artillery pieces; plus 100–1,000 SCUD-class ballistic missiles, some possibly with nuclear, chemical or biological warheads; 500–1,000 combat aircraft; 100–200 naval vessels, primarily patrol craft armed with surface-to-surface missiles; and some submarines. (North Korea currently has twenty-five submarines and Iraq is reportedly acquiring a submarine capability.)

Two planning scenarios were selected to assess the warfighting forces needed for the future: an attack by "a re-militarized Iraq against Kuwait and Saudi Arabia and by North Korea against South Korea." As the review noted, "neither of these scenarios should be regarded as a prediction of future conflicts, but each provides a useful representation of the challenges presented by a well-armed regional power initiating an aggression thousands of miles from the United States. As such, the scenarios serve as yardsticks against which to assess, in gross terms, the capabilities of U.S. forces."

Assumptions included an aggressor's short-notice, armor-heavy combined arms offensive against the outnumbered forces of a neighboring state. Only minimal American forces were assumed to be on the ground when hostilities commenced, requiring U.S.-based reinforcements to quickly deploy to the region, supplement the forces of the ally under attack, halt the invasion, and defeat the aggressor.

"Our first priority in preparing for regional conflicts," says *The Bottom-Up Review,* "is to prevent them from occurring. This is the purpose of our overseas presence forces and operations, joint exercises and other military capabilities—to deter potential regional aggressors from even contemplating an attack."

Four Phases of Combat Operations

But if deterrence failed, it was envisioned that combat operations would unfold in four main phases. Phase 1 would be *to halt the invasion* as quickly as possible in order to minimize the territory and the critical facilities the invader could capture. Rapid reaction is crucial, says *The Bottom-Up Review*, for "the more territory the enemy captures, the greater the price to take it back." The primary responsibility for halting the enemy advance rests with the nation under attack, assisted by those forward-deployed U.S. forces, if any, in the theater of war. But as the United States draws down its overseas presence, the bulk of American reinforcements would have to come from U.S. bases.

"This places a high premium on rapidly deployable, yet highly lethal forces to blunt an attack," *The Bottom-Up Review* states, and goes on to lay out six major tasks to be performed in Phase 1, where, while remaining on the strategic offensive, U.S. forces would temporarily assume the tactical (i.e., battlefield) and operational (theater-of-war) defensive in order to buy time in preparation for future battlefield and theater counterattacks.

First would be to help allied forces establish a viable defense. Second would be to use a combination of U.S. land- and sea-based strike aircraft, heavy bombers, long-range tactical missiles, ground-maneuver forces with anti-armor capabilities, and special operations forces to delay, disrupt, and destroy the enemy ground forces and damage the roads on which they were moving in order to halt the attack.

Third would be to protect friendly forces and rear-area assets such as ports, supply depots, and staging areas from attack by enemy aircraft or cruise missiles, using U.S. land- and sea-based aircraft, ground- and sea-based surface-to-air missiles, and special operations forces.

The fourth task would be to establish air superiority and suppress enemy air defenses as a prelude to the fifth task, the destruction of enemy high-value targets such as weapons of mass destruction and central command, control and communications facilities. The sixth task would be to establish maritime superiority in order to ensure access to ports and sealines of communication, and as a precondition for amphibious operations.

Phase 2 would continue the operational defensive in order *to build up U.S. combat power in the theater while reducing the enemy's power.* Many of the same forces employed in Phase 1 would be used in Phase 2, to continue to grind down the enemy while additional U.S. reinforcements arrived in theater.

"As more land and sea-based air forces arrive," says the study, "emphasis would shift from halting the invasion to isolating enemy ground forces and destroying them, destroying enemy air and naval forces, destroying stocks of supplies, and broadening the attack on military-related targets in the enemy rear area." Meanwhile, heavy ground forces would begin arriving in the theater to strengthen the defensive line and prepare for the counteroffensive.

In Phase 3, U.S. forces would move from the operational strategic defensive to the operational offensive in order *to decisively defeat the enemy.* U.S. and allied forces would mount a large-scale air-land counteroffensive to attack the enemy centers of gravity, retake territory he had occupied, destroy his warmaking capabilities, and defeat his armed forces on the field of battle so as to break his will to resist.

"Combat power in this phase would include highly mobile armored, mechanized and air assault forces, supported by the full complement of airpower, special operations forces, and land and sea-based fire support. Amphibious forces would provide additional operational flexibility to the theater commander."

The final phase, Phase 4, would *provide for postwar stability.* Although a majority of U.S. forces would begin returning to their home bases, some forces might remain to help repatriate prisoners, occupy or administer some of the enemy territory, or ensure compliance with the provisions of war termination or cease-fire agreements.

"These forces," said *The Bottom-Up Review,* "might include a carrier battle group, one or two wings of fighters, a division or less of ground forces, and special operations units."

Supporting Capabilities

While only combat forces were discussed above, combat support and combat service support capabilities would play an essential role throughout all phases of combat operations. First is the matter of getting U.S. force to the scene of the action. The airlift capabilities of U.S. Transportation Command's (TRANSCOM) Air Mobility Command would be critical in the early days of a conflict, moving troops and supplies into the battle area.

In Operation Desert Storm/Desert Shield, the United States delivered to the Gulf region, on average, more than 2,400 tons of material per day by airlift, notes *The Bottom-Up Review*. It anticipates that at least the same level of lift capability will be needed to support high-intensity military operations in the opening phases of any future major regional conflict, and to help sustain operations thereafter.

Aerial refueling is an integral part of airlift operations, as well as in the overseas deployment of fighter aircraft and in the operation of surveillance aircraft. "Large numbers of aerial-refueling aircraft would be needed to support many components of a U.S. theater campaign."

Sealift by TRANSCOM's Military Sealift Command would also be critical, for, as in the Gulf War, most combat equipment—including tanks, armored fighting vehicles and heavy artillery, ammunition, fuel, and supplies—would come by sea. To cut down on sealift requirements and to accelerate movement of critical warfighting equipment and supplies to the battle area, increasing reliance would be placed on the prepositioning of supplies aboard ships in forward areas.

Extensive use was made of such prepositioned supplies during the Gulf War. The thirteen cargo ships of the three Navy Maritime Prepositioning Squadrons (MPS) enabled the rapid deployment of the Marine Expeditionary Force. MPS-2, for example, sailed from its base at Diego Garcia in the Indian Ocean on August 7, 1990, and met up with the Marine Expeditionary Brigade airlifted to the Gulf from the United States on August 15, 1990.

Likewise, the Army and Air Force had supplies aboard eleven Afloat Prepositioning Ships (APS) at the beginning of the Gulf War. They included tankers with water and fuel, lighter-aboard ships (LASH) (two with Air Force ammunition), break-bulk cargo ships, and one float-on-float-off (FloFlo) ship with harbor craft and barges.

In 1994, in addition to four prepositioned ships previously loaded with supplies and port-opening equipment, the Army began prepositioning afloat another four ships with the equipment of a heavy combat brigade, consisting of two armored and two mechanized battalions. Equipment includes 123 MlAl Abrams main battle tanks, 154 Bradley infantry fighting vehicles, 24 155mm self-propelled howitzers, nine Multiple Launch Rocket Systems, 344 other tracked vehicles, and a number of wheeled vehicles. Yet another three roll-on/roll-off ships will be loaded with sustainment supplies.

Another critical support area has to do with winning the information war, especially in the areas of battlefield surveillance and command, control, and communications. "Accurate information on the location and disposition of enemy forces is a prerequisite for effective military operations," stresses *The Bottom-Up Review*. Advanced systems that proved so effective in the Gulf War, such as the Joint Surveillance and Target Attack Radar System (JSTARS), the Airborne Warning and Control System (AWACS), and MIL-STAR satellite communications systems, would be deployed early.

Advanced munitions are also critical. The Gulf War demonstrated the effectiveness of precision-guided munitions such as laser-guided bombs, and *The Bottom-Up Review* noted that "new 'smart' and 'brilliant' munitions under development hold promise of dramatically improving capabilities of U.S. air, ground, and maritime forces to destroy enemy armored vehicles, halt invading ground forces [and] destroy fixed targets at longer ranges."

Force Enhancements

In order to compensate for lower force numbers, *The Bottom-Up Review* noted a number of force enhancements "especially geared toward buttressing our ability to conduct a successful initial defense in any major regional conflict."

They included improving strategic mobility, as noted above, through more prepositioning as well as through enhancing airlift and sealift. "We will either continue the program to purchase and deploy the C-17 airlifter or purchase other airlifters to replace our aging C-141 transport aircraft." The surge sealift fleet capacity will be increased by purchasing additional roll-on/roll-off ships, and the readiness and responsiveness of the sealift Ready Reserve Force will be improved.

The Navy will improve its strike potential by upgrading its F-14 Tomcat carrier aircraft with precision ground-attack capabilities and by acquiring stocks of new "brilliant" anti-armor weapons. During a crisis, additional squadrons of F/A-18 Hornet fighters would be dispatched to forward-deployed aircraft carriers. The Army is developing new "smart" submunitions that can be delivered by either missiles or tube artillery. Air Force B-1 and B-2 long-range heavy bombers will be modified to deliver "smart" conventional munitions against advancing enemy forces. All-weather munitions are also being developed to "dramatically increase our capability to attack and destroy critical targets in the crucial opening days of a short-warning conflict."

Reserve Reinforcements

In order to respond to the requirement to fight two nearly simultaneous major regional conflicts, several initiatives were taken to improve the readiness and flexibility of Army National Guard combat units and other Reserve Component forces.

As noted earlier, the criticality of Reserve mobilization was one of the major lessons of the Persian Gulf War. Over 230,000 reservists were called to active duty and some 105,000 served in the Kuwait Theater of Operations, including 37,692 from the Army National Guard, 35,158 from the Army Reserve, 6,625 Navy reservists, 13,066 Marine reservists, 281 Coast Guard reservists, and 10,000 from the Air National Guard and Air Force Reserve.

When it came to buttressing American public support for the war and providing logistical support for the active-duty combat elements, their contribution was invaluable. While Air Force and Marine Corps combat elements were successfully deployed, the Army's Reserve combat elements were limited to two National Guard artillery brigades.

The "roundout" concept, whereby Army National Guard combat brigades were supposed to form the third brigades of active Army units, did not work as planned. The 24th Infantry Division had to leave its roundout brigade, the Georgia National Guard's 43d Infantry Brigade, behind when it deployed to the Gulf in August 1990, replacing it at the last minute with the active Army 197th Infantry Brigade from Fort Benning, Georgia.

The 43d Infantry Brigade was not even called to active duty until November 1990, and was not certified as combat-ready until February 28, 1991, the day the war ended. The same was true of Mississippi's 155th Armor Brigade, which was supposed to round out the Army's 1st Cavalry Division. Instead, the 1st Cavalry Division deployed with the "Tiger Brigade" of the 2d Armored Division.

While some analysts claim this was proof that, given the enormous complexities of the modern battlefield, it is impossible to train a maneuver (i.e., infantry or armor) brigade on a part-time basis, others blame the delay on their late call-up, equipment shortages, and last-minute changes in readiness standards.

In any event, said *The Bottom-Up Review,* "In the future, Army National Guard combat units will be better trained, more capable, and more ready." To that end, on December 10, 1993, Secretary Aspin announced agreements on plans to restructure the Army Reserve Components. Gone was the "roundout" concept, replaced by a "roundup" plan where all ten of the Army's active divisions would have three active-duty brigades and would be "rounded up" in the event of war, with an additional National Guard combat brigade.

On August 30, 1994, the Army announced the selection of twelve Army National Guard infantry brigades, two armor brigades, and an armored cavalry regiment as "enhanced readiness" units. These will be fully manned, trained and equipped, and modernized at the same level as the active unit with which they are affiliated.

These brigades are to be maintained at a high level of readiness, ready to be deployed overseas to reinforce active-duty combat units within ninety days of mobilization. In addition, in November 1994 the Secretary of the Army also designated eight National Guard divisions as a strategic reserve combat force. Fully structured but manned and equipped at less than 100 percent, these divisions will be maintained at readiness levels that will allow them to mobilize in the event of extended crisis or protracted operations.

During his election campaign, President Clinton had called for a major role for the Reserves. While active Army strength is scheduled to decrease from 751,000 in fiscal year 1990 to 495,000 in FY 1999, a decrease of 34 percent, Army National Guard and Army Reserve strength will decrease from 736,000 in FY 1990, to 670,000 in FY 1994, to 575,000 in FY 1999, a decrease of 22 percent, with the Army Reserve taking the brunt of the cuts.

Meanwhile, combat organizations within the Army Reserve will be shifted to the Army National Guard. The Army Reserve would focus on "providing the combat service support mission during wartime," while the Guard would be focused on "a wartime combat mission and a peacetime domestic emergency mission."

The Major Regional Conflict Force

What would the combat force for a major regional conflict in either the Persian Gulf or Korea look like? Based on "detailed analysis of future major regional conflicts, coupled with military judgements of the outcomes," said *The Bottom-Up Review*, a single military regional conflict would require four to five Army divisions, four to five Marine Expeditionary Brigades, ten Air Force fighter wings, one hundred Air Force heavy bombers, four to five Navy aircraft carrier battle groups, and a number of special operations forces.

"If the initial defense fails to halt the invasion quickly, or if circumstances in other parts of the world permit," decision makers might decide "to commit more forces than those listed. . . . But our analysis also led to the conclusion that enhancements to our military forces . . . would both reduce our overall ground force requirements and increase the responsiveness and effectiveness of our power-projection forces."

A simultaneous second regional conflict would require essentially the same forces described above, but "certain specialized high-leverage units or unique assets [B-2 bombers, JSTARS and AWACS command and control aircraft, etc.] might be 'dual tasked.'" It would also require sufficient strategic air- and sealift—aircraft and ships already in use in supporting and sustaining the ongoing first conflict—to deploy the forces to where they were needed and to sustain them on the battlefield.

Conclusion

The Bottom-Up Review of September 1993 spelled out the reasons for a declared two-war strategy: "First was to avoid leaving an opening for another aggressor to attack its neighbor while the U.S. was totally occupied elsewhere. Second, having the capability to fight two wars near simultaneously provided a hedge against the possibility that a future adversary or coalition of adversaries might provide the U.S. with a larger-than-expected threat."

But does the United States really have "the capability to fight two wars near simultaneously"? The last time we fought in Korea in 1950–53, six active Army divisions and one Marine division were initially committed to combat there. That stretched our ability to cover other strategic threats so thinly that eight National Guard divisions were mobilized and two served in combat in Korea.

And the last time we fought in the Middle East during the 1990–91 Persian Gulf War, two Marine divisions and seven active Army divisions, plus combat brigades of two additional divisions, were sent into combat there. Today, that commitment alone would exhaust all of the Army's ten-division active force, including the divisions now deployed in Western Europe and Korea, leaving nothing whatsoever in the active force to fight the other contingency, much less fight it "near simultaneously."

By claiming to be able to do what in fact it is unable to do, the United States is not only bluffing—a most dangerous thing to do—but even worse, is kidding itself into a false sense of security.

PART III

OPERATIONS OTHER THAN WAR

Governments and commanders have always tried to find ways of avoiding a decisive battle and of reaching their goals by other means. . . . This line of thought has brought us almost to the point of regarding . . . battle as a kind of evil brought about by mistake. . . .

The fact that slaughter is a horrifying spectacle must make us take wars more seriously, but not provide an excuse for gradually blunting our swords in the name of humanity. Sooner or later someone will come along with a sharp sword and hack off our arms.

—CARL VON CLAUSEWITZ,
On War, PP. 259–260

Chapter 8

Peace Operations

Properly constituted, peace operations can be one useful tool to advance American national interests and pursue our national security objectives. The U.S cannot be the world's policeman. Nor can we ignore the increase in armed ethnic conflicts, civil wars and the collapse of governmental authority in some states—crises that individually and cumulatively may affect U.S. interests.

—President Bill Clinton, Presidential Decision Directive 25, May 3, 1994

Peace Enforcement and Intervention

Warfighting operations are the primary basis for the size and shape of the U.S. military. But *The Bottom-Up Review* created a second criterion as well: "peace enforcement and intervention." It was assumed that the threat from such operations would include a mix of regular and irregular forces, armed with light weapons and some moderately sophisticated anti-tank and anti-ship missiles, surface-to-air missiles, land and sea mines, T-54 and T-72 tanks, armored personnel carriers, and towed artillery and mortars. Enemy forces might also include a limited number of older aircraft such as the MiG-21 or MiG-23, patrol craft, and even a few submarines.

In most cases, *The Bottom-Up Review* stated, the United

States would operate as part of a multinational effort under the auspices of the United Nations or another international body such as NATO. *Peace enforcement* operations would include several key objectives. One might be forced entry to secure airfields, ports, and other facilities. Others might include enforcing a blockade or quarantine, controlling the cross-border movement of troops and supplies, establishing and defending zones to protect civilians from internal threats, and preparing to turn over responsibility for an area to reconstituted local authorities.

The planning force for such a major intervention or peace enforcement operation would include an Army air assault or airborne division, an Army light infantry division, a Marine Expeditionary Brigade, one or two Navy carrier battle groups, one or two composite Air Force wings, special operations forces, civil affairs units, airlift and sealift forces, and combat support and service support units for a total of some 50,000 troops.

Noting that these capabilities can be provided largely by the same forces needed for major regional conflicts, so long as they had the appropriate training, *The Bottom-Up Review* warns that "this means that the United States would have to forego the option of conducting sizable peace enforcement or intervention operations at the same time it was fighting two major regional conflicts."

As defined by *Peace Operations*, the Army's December 1994 doctrinal manual on operations other than war, *peace enforcement* (PE) "is the application of military force or the threat of its use, normally pursuant to international authorization . . . to maintain or restore peace. . . . PE may include combat action. . . . Forces conducting PE may, for example, be involved in the forcible separation of belligerent parties or engaged in combat with one or all parties to the conflict. The U.S. participation in operations in Somalia in 1992–1993 is an example of PE."

Although cloaked in new terms, "peace enforcement" sounds suspiciously like the "counterinsurgency" doctrine of the 1960s and the "low-intensity conflict" notions of the

1980s. And it suffers from the same critical deficiencies—the lack of clearly defined and attainable objectives, and a precise understanding of what constitutes success.

Recognizing that main stumbling block, *Peace Operations* emphasizes that "a clearly defined mission statement is the key to the successful planning and execution of a peace operation. Commanders must continually work with higher authorities to ensure that the mission is well-defined. In peace operations, the conditions for success are often difficult to define." To help remedy that situation, *Peace Operations*, in an important addition to previous doctrinal manuals, defines what that "end state" should be:

> The end state describes the required conditions that, when achieved, attain the strategic and political objectives or pass the main effort to other national or international agencies to achieve the final strategic end state. The end state describes what the authorizing entity desires the situation to be when operations conclude. . . . The peace operation should not be viewed as an end in itself, but part of a larger [diplomatic, economic, informational or humanitarian] process that must take place concurrently.

That was never the case in "peace enforcement" operations in Vietnam, where during the course of the war some twenty-two conflicting official justifications were issued. The most damning statistic of the war was Brigadier General Douglas Kinnard's finding that "almost 70 percent of the generals who managed the war were uncertain of its objectives." This, he went on to say, "mirrors a deep-seated strategic failure: the inability of policy-makers to frame tangible, obtainable goals."

It was a failure repeated once again in Somalia in 1993, which led in turn to congressional pressure to terminate the mission there. And the failure to frame tangible, obtainable goals plagued Clinton administration attempts at "peace enforcement" in Bosnia and, initially, in Haiti in 1994.

As Defense Secretary Caspar Weinberger said a decade earlier, a critical precondition for U.S. military intervention abroad is "reasonable assurance" of public and congressional support. Both have been missing in recent "peace enforce-ment" attempts and may ultimately be a bar to future such operations.

Another critical deficiency in "peace enforcement" was singled out by Chinese Defense Minister Lin Piao in his 1965 treatise, "Long Live the Victory of People's War." Self-reliance, he said, is an absolute precondition for victory. A combatant that relies exclusively on foreign assistance cannot win; and even if it did achieve temporary victory, it could not sustain itself in power.

While the United States can provide arms and equipment to a beleaguered ally, and even military advice and assistance, it cannot provide the will and self-reliance necessary for ulti-mate success. The United States cannot do for an ally what it is unwilling to do for itself. The real danger is that the U.S re-sponse will be so overwhelming, and its attitude so impatient and condescending, that it smothers what will and self-reliance does exist.

Vietnam was a case in point. After the fall of Saigon in 1975, a high-ranking South Vietnamese staff officer was asked, "What mistakes do you think the Americans made in prepar-ing South Vietnamese to fight the war?"

"Two things," the officer replied. "First, when American troops came to Vietnam, they try to do everything. And they make the Vietnamese lose the initiative. . . . So the Viet-namese don't rely on themselves. They rely on the Ameri-cans."

One of the most telling passages in *A Bright Shining Lie,* veteran war correspondent Neil Sheehan's epic work on the Vietnam War, is his account of how the South Vietnamese military and civilian leadership were cowed by their North Vietnamese counterparts. The North Vietnamese had fought for independence from France with the Viet Minh in the First Indochina War, while many South Vietnamese leaders had served in the ranks of the French colonial army.

And now in the Second Indochina War North Vietnam was going it alone again, with only material support from China and the Soviet Union, while South Vietnam was relying almost exclusively on foreign troops and assistance. As with U.S. domestic welfare programs, America had set out to help its South Vietnamese ally stand on its own two feet and act independently; but instead the United States had created a welfare dependent, who collapsed as soon as the aid and support were withdrawn.

A key objective of "peace enforcement," states *The Bottom-Up Review* is "preparing to turn over responsibility for security to peacekeeping units and/or a reconstituted administrative authority." But such disengagement is something the United States finds extremely difficult to do. A case in point was the seemingly highly successful Combined Action Program (CAP) organized by the U.S. Marine Corps in Vietnam.

The concept involved assigning a Marine rifle squad with a Navy medical corpsman to a South Vietnamese "Popular Force" home guard militia unit at the village level. At its height in 1968, there were four Combined Action Groups with some 102 Combined Action Companies, each with several Combined Action platoons. Because of their ties to the U.S. logistic base, they were able to bring to bear resources the Vietnamese government could not begin to match. The CAP teams were quite successful at "winning the hearts and minds" of the local villagers.

But these U.S. tactical successes were at the expense of its strategic purpose. While the CAP concept rested on the premise that eventually village security would be turned over to local South Vietnamese authorities, that never happened. The South Vietnamese government lacked the resources and, in some cases, the will to assume such responsibilities.

Thus, the very effectiveness of the CAP teams highlighted the weaknesses and deficiencies of South Vietnamese officialdom, and weakened the ties between the villages and their government. Yet the U.S. purpose for being in Vietnam in the first place was to strengthen that very government.

Drawing on that experience, as well as the later debacle in Somalia, the new *Peace Operations* manual emphasizes that "Failure to fully understand the mission and operational environment can . . . result in actions that are inconsistent with the overall political objectives."

As in the principles of war, the first principle of peace operations, says the manual, is the principle of the objective: "A clearly defined and attainable objective—with a precise understanding of what constitutes success—is critical when the US is involved in peace operations."

Failure to appreciate the importance of that principle plagued initial Clinton administration attempts to garner public support for peace enforcement operations in Haiti. "Nearly 80 years ago," noted the July 10, 1994, *Washington Post*, "Woodrow Wilson dispatched Marines to Haiti for many of the same reasons that appear to be motivating Clinton. That intervention led to a 19-year occupation that ended in a failure to foster democracy." As in 1915, "armed intervention would probably meet little resistance," but also as in the past, there is no strategic concept for achieving democracy there.

Taking those criticisms to heart, President Clinton began to build public consensus, culminating with the dispatch of former President Jimmy Carter, Senate Armed Services Committee Chairman Sam Nunn, and former JCS Chairman Colin Powell to Haiti to try—successfully, as it turned out—to reach a peaceful settlement.

"Our objective over the past three years has been to make sure the military dictators leave power and that the democratically-elected government is returned," said President Clinton in his September 18, 1994, address to the American people. "This agreement guarantees both those objectives."

But he was quick to establish the "end state" for the commitment of U.S. troops. "I want to emphasize," the President said, "that in a matter of months, the United States troops will hand over to the United Nations the responsibility for completing this mission and for maintaining basic security." From a high of 20,000 in September 1994, U.S. troop strength declined to 6,000 by January 1995, and declined still further when the mission was turned over to the United Nations in May 1995. Of the 6,000-man UN force to take over in Haiti, about half are from the United States.

In his November 1994 statement on "the thinking behind our decisions about where and how to use force in the post–Cold War world," Defense Secretary William Perry outlined the rationale for the Haitian intervention. "In Haiti we were prepared to use force because we have interests in protecting democracy in this hemisphere, preventing the flow of refugees and putting a halt to a cruel, systematic reign of terror over the Haitian people.

"When we had exhausted all other alternatives the United States and its allies threatened to use force to remove the junta from power. In Haiti this proved to be sufficient."

But Perry was careful to point out that in other cases, "our use of force will be selective and limited, reflecting the relative importance of the outcome to our interests." This, he went on to say, was specifically not the case in Bosnia, where "the level of blood and treasure" required to achieve peace "is not commensurate with our national interests."

Humanitarian Assistance

At the opposite end of the "peace operations" spectrum is humanitarian relief. While peace enforcement involves mainly the combat use of military forces, *humanitarian assistance* primarily involves their non-combat use. But even humanitarian assistance may have a warfighting dimension.

A high-ranking military speaker at a 1993 Naval Institute conference in San Diego, California, praised the "peacekeeping" skills of the U.S. Marine Corps for their success during their initial intervention in Somalia in December 1992 to provide humanitarian assistance to the starving peoples there.

But it was not their "peacekeeping" skills that made the Marine Corps effective, otherwise they would have been hunkered down behind the berm at the Mogadishu airport with the Pakistani "peacekeepers" already there. What made them effective was their warfighting skills.

Tribal warlords and armed anarchy had prevented the international non-governmental relief organizations (NGO) and private voluntary relief organizations (PVO) already present in Somalia from distributing food supplies to the starving. The United States made it clear that it was there to ensure that such deliveries would resume, and it was ready and able to use military force against anyone who interfered. It further stated that it would not wait until attacked to use such force, but would take preemptive military action if it felt threatened in any way.

And it did just that, using deadly force to impose its will impartially on all factions that were blocking the movement of relief supplies. These efforts were quite successful, and movement of relief supplies by the NGOs and PVOs soon resumed throughout the country. It was only when the mission shifted (as we shall see in the following chapter) from humanitarian assistance to "nation building" that the U.S. effort collapsed in confusion.

As defined by the Army's 1994 *Peace Operations* manual, humanitarian assistance (HA) "includes programs conducted to relieve or reduce the results of complex emergencies involving natural or man-made disasters, or other endemic conditions such as human pain, disease, hunger or privation that might present a serious threat to life or that can result in great damage to or loss of property." Although not included in the manual's formal definition of peace operations, "HA programs will probably be conducted simultaneously in almost every peace operation."

As Andrew S. Natsios, the former assistant administrator of the Agency for International Development (AID) in the Bush administration, noted, "The man-made Somalia crisis and others like it in Bosnia, Sudan, Liberia and Cambodia, differ from the traditional relief responses to natural disasters. . . .

"These complex humanitarian emergencies involve . . . civil strife, mass starvation, the collapse of civil society . . . refugees and displaced persons and complex political negotiations over the transportation of food and relief commodities through areas of conflict." And they are increasing in number.

Natsios attributes the increase to three causes: "the failure of democratic experiments (Sudan, Peru, Yugoslavia, Haiti, Tajikistan and Angola); long-standing ethnic and tribal conflicts (Northern Iraq, Liberia, Sudan, Armenia and Azerbaijan, Yugoslavia, and Somalia); and systematic collapse of autocratic regimes under pressure for free-market reforms and democratization (Zaire and Albania).

"The novel aspect of these crises," he says, "is that intervention often requires a military component and hence involves difficult choices about the use of forces." These include the dispatch of ground combat forces with the authority to engage combatants interfering in relief efforts, such as in Somalia and Kurdistan, and the use of air and naval forces engaged in enforcing "no-fly" zones or sea blockades, such as in Iraq.

For instance, a major U.S. post–Cold War humanitarian assistance operation was Operation Provide Comfort, the April 1991 U.S. relief campaign which established a "safe zone" in northern Iraq for some 1.5 million Kurds and moved more than 7,000 tons of relief supplies into the area.

A more traditional type of humanitarian assistance is the use of the military to deliver relief supplies to affected areas. These operations have a long history, including the 1948 Berlin airlift in which U.S. pilots flew 277,000 missions to deliver 2 million tons of coal, food, and other necessities to Berlin in the face of a Soviet ground blockade. Air Force Secretary Donald Rice noted in 1991 that the Air Force had performed over 360 such humanitarian operations since World War II.

A recent example of such traditional humanitarian assistance was Operation Sea Angel, the 1991 relief operation in the wake of the cyclone and floods that had taken as many as 100,000 lives in Bangladesh. At the request of the Bangladesh government, some 8,000 U.S. sailors and Marines from the eight-ship amphibious task force centered on the U.S.S. *Tarawa* tendered water-purification and reconstruction services, and provided 1.7 million people with 6,000 tons of food and medicine.

Traditional military humanitarian assistance operations

like Operation Sea Angel are an effective instrument of foreign policy. They are generally non-controversial and enjoy a high degree of public support. Not only are they the right thing to do from a moral standpoint, but from a practical standpoint they help spread U.S. influence in the world.

Unlike *humanitarian intervention* operations involving combat forces, they also enhance rather than degrade wartime skills. Most of the military units engaged in traditional humanitarian assistance are from support units. They include airlifters, medical teams, water-purification specialists, and other combat support and combat service support personnel who practice their wartime skills while providing humanitarian assistance. Parachuting relief supplies to the Kurds, for example, sharpens the skills necessary to airdrop supplies to U.S. forces on the battlefield.

"We're the nation's 911 force," said Major General Thomas L. Wilkerson, the Marine Corps planner, in July 1994, and JCS Chairman General John M. Shalikashvili noted that "We have the capability like almost no one else to help with tragedies of the magnitude we're witnessing now in Rwanda."

But these humanitarian efforts can conflict with the military's primary warfighting mission. This almost became the case with the Rwandan crisis, which coincided with rising tensions in Korea, one of the major regional crisis areas specified in *The Bottom-Up Review*. As *New York Times* correspondent Eric Schmitt noted at the time, the U.S. Army "has sent five ships full of trucks, medical supplies and tents from Saipan, Thailand and Diego Garcia—supplies earmarked to supply American troops in Korea if a war erupts there—to the crisis in central Africa." Fortunately, tensions in Korea eased and the mission conflict was averted.

"My fear," said General Shalikashvili in September 1994, as U.S. forces began to withdraw from Rwanda, "is we're becoming mesmerized by operations other than war and we'll take our mind off what we're all about, [which is] to fight and win our nation's wars." Ironically, while the Pentagon was concerned that the military had done too much, relief officials were complaining that it had not done enough.

"The gap between the Clinton administration's public promise and the military's performance has distressed some U.S. aid officials and senior officers at the Geneva-based U.N. High Commissioner on Refugees," reported the *Washington Post*'s R. Jeffrey Smith on September 5, 1994. According to U.S. officials, "the friction between relief officials and U.S. military commanders . . . partly reflects a larger disagreement about the Pentagon's present and future role in humanitarian disasters."

In November 1994, Defense Secretary William Perry made clear the U.S. policy on humanitarian assistance. Generally, he said, "the military is not the right tool to meet humanitarian concerns. The U.S. government has established ongoing programs to assist international and nongovernmental agencies in providing humanitarian relief." But, he went on to add,

> under certain conditions the use of our armed forces is appropriate:
> First, if we face a natural or manmade catastrophe that dwarfs the ability of the normal relief agencies to respond. Second, if the need for relief is urgent and only the military has the ability to jump start the effort. Third, if the response requires resources unique to the military. And fourth, if there is minimal risk to the lives of American troops.

Rwanda met all the conditions "for the use of Defense Department capabilities." But, Perry concluded, "ordinarily the Defense Department will not be involved in humanitarian operations because of the need to focus on its war-fighting missions. We field an army, not a Salvation Army."

Sanctions

Sanctions are another "peace operation" enjoying much popularity in the post–Cold War world. In its first four decades the United Nations imposed sanctions only twice, against Rhodesia in 1966 and South Africa in 1977. In the last four years alone, however, sanctions have been imposed four times—in Iraq, the former Yugoslavia, Libya, and Haiti—and arms embargoes have been imposed against Somalia, Liberia, and the Khmer Rouge area of Cambodia.

As James Ngobi, secretary of the UN Sanctions Committee, noted at an April 1993 conference at Notre Dame University, there is now a "flurry of activity" on the sanctions issue within the United Nations "to use sanctions as a tool for regulating international behavior." That is unusual, for while sanctions have some symbolic value, their overall success rate has been low.

A 1991 study at the U.S. Military Academy found that "Most blockades and embargoes have failed to force an opponent to yield." According to another study from the Institute for International Economics, the overall effectiveness rate of the 115 cases of sanctions used since World War II has been 34 percent.

The sanctions imposed against Iraq in the wake of their 1990 invasion of Kuwait are a case in point. Imposed by UN Security Council Resolution 661 on August 6, 1990, all trading and dealing with Iraq, except for medicine and food, and all transshipment of Iraqi or Kuwaiti oil was forbidden.

"These sanctions, now enshrined in international law, have the potential to deny Iraq the fruits of aggression," said President Bush on August 8, 1990, "while sharply limiting its ability to either export or import anything of value, especially oil." Many at the time, including Senator Sam Nunn, chairman of the Senate Armed Services Committee, and by some accounts, General Colin Powell, Chairman of the Joint Chiefs of Staff, felt that these sanctions could be an effective alternative to war.

Ninety percent of Iraqi oil went by pipeline across Turkey to the Mediterranean and across Saudi Arabia to the Red Sea, and shortly after the Iraqi invasion of Kuwait both of these pipelines were closed. On August 25, 1990, UNSC Resolution 665 ordered enforcement of sanctions by inspection and verification of cargo and destinations of ships in area and Maritime Interception Operations (MIO) began. Thirteen nations, in addition to the six Gulf Cooperation Council states, provided 165 ships to intercept shipping in the Persian Gulf, Gulf of Oman, Gulf of Aden, the Red Sea, and the eastern Mediterranean.

Although Iraq lost 90 percent of its imports, 100 percent of its exports, and had its gross national product cut in half, the imposition of sanctions did not cause it to renounce its aggression and withdraw from Kuwait. Instead, military action was necessary to force its withdrawal.

After the Gulf War, the sanctions were continued in order to ensure Iraqi compliance with the terms of the cease-fire agreement. Even though some argued that by 1994 Iraq was in compliance, sanctions remained in effect. "The Clinton Administration," editorialized The New York Times on August 1, 1994, "insists on retaining sanctions as long as Mr. Hussein remains in power . . . putting domestic political posturing ahead of the problem of containing Iraq's military power." Two months later, that argument was rendered moot by Iraq's abortive military power play. The sanctions are not liable to be lifted soon.

But the main problem with sanctions is that they don't work. As U.S. News & World Report noted in May 1993, "While ordinary Iraqis have suffered fearfully under the international sanctions, smugglers and clandestine sales of Iraqi oil have kept [Saddam] Hussein and his murderous coterie of hangers-on in relative comfort. . . . Had George Bush listened to the go-slow proponents of sanctions and no use of force, the Iraqi Army might still be billeted in Kuwait City."

And Lieutenant General Raoul Cedras might still be ensconced in the Presidential Palace in Port-au-Prince as well, for the U.S. sanctions against Haiti, while causing terrible suffering among the Haitian people, failed to force him from power. Again, military action, or more precisely the threat of military action, was ultimately necessary to enforce U.S. policy.

Why, then, the reliance on such measures? It is because the United States has adopted a policy of "exclusion" as a replacement for "containment" as the basis of its post–Cold War national policy, argues Air Force Colonel Jeffery R. Barnett.

"Whenever any country, alliance, organization or corporation challenges U.S. international interests," he wrote in an article early in 1994, "Washington's immediate reaction is predictable: exclude the challenger from sources of trade, capital and aid. The usual vehicle is sanctions. In 1993, sanctions were central to U.S. security response in Haiti, Iraq, Iran, North Korea, Guatemala, Libya, the former Yugoslavia, and Nigeria.

"Exclusion plays to America's strengths," says Barnett. "It has the added benefit of mitigating major American weaknesses. These weaknesses involve casualty intolerance [and] impatience." Armed intervention raises "the specter of casualties [and] inhibits the national leadership from committing armed forces." Exclusion, on the other hand, "offers the possibility of coersion without attack; casualties should be minimal."

Impatience is another American weakness. "No sooner are troops committed than deadlines for their withdrawal are demanded. Potential adversaries are aware of this American characteristic, which lessens the coersive value of military threats. . . . Conversely, Americans have little problem imposing Exclusion over the long term [i.e., Cuba since 1959]. . . . Exclusion seems to be unaffected by American impatience."

But an exclusion policy is not risk-free, as the 1994 North Korean crisis made clear. "As the noose tightens on a state's economy, the victim may pursue a highly risky course of action . . . that it otherwise would not have hazarded," noted the 1991 Military Academy study on embargoes. "Today, with the proliferation of chemical, biological, and nuclear weapons, any such escalation could be extremely problematic, if not outright dangerous."

Engagement and Enlargement

A centerpiece of the Clinton administration's foreign policy was to be "engagement" and "enlargement." In a speech to the United Nations General Assembly on September 27, 1993,

President Clinton called isolationism a "poison" and pledged continued U.S. engagement. Administration spokespeople gave two primary reasons for this policy. First was the interconnectedness of the global economy. Second was the need to avoid reversals in the current international situation, such as a reversion to dictatorship in the former Soviet Union, which would threaten U.S. security.

Assessing the policy of engagement, the Congressional Research Service's Mark Lowenthal noted a sense of drift in and diminution of U.S. public support for foreign policy in the aftermath of the Cold War. "The predominant basis for U.S. engagement abroad throughout this century," he notes, "has been perceived major threats to the international status quo."

But, Lowenthal asks, to what extent do current "threats" such as nuclear proliferation, terrorism, ethnic and subnational violence, hunger and disease, and environmental concerns "constitute genuine 'threats' as opposed to obvious problems that must be dealt with?" And none, he points out, "pose a comparable threat—either in degree or in vividness— to that of the nuclear-armed Soviet Union.

"Thus, these 'threats' become dubious rallying points for U.S. public opinion. Indeed some people may argue that these are not threats, feeling instead that these issues are being used largely to substitute for the late 'evil empire.'"

Be that as it may, the term "engagement" has been incorporated into U.S. military policy. There is "forward engagement" with the NATO allies. There is "constructive engagement" with the former Soviet Union. And there is "cooperative engagement" in the U.S. Pacific Command.

But "engagement" is not an end in itself. "The successor to a doctrine of containment must be a strategy of enlargement," said national security adviser Anthony Lake in a September 21, 1993, speech, "enlargement of the world's free community of market democracies." Democracies, he argues, "tend not to wage war on each other or sponsor terrorism."

Enlargement, as Lake defines it, has four components. First is to strengthen the core community of free market democracies. That involves domestic renewal both at home and abroad. Second is to foster democracies and free market economies in "states of special significance and opportunity" such as Russia and the Ukraine, the new democracies in Central and Eastern Europe, the Asian-Pacific, and the Western Hemisphere, which have "large economies, critical locations, nuclear weapons, or the potential to generate refugees."

Third is to counter the aggression of and attempt to liberalize states hostile to democracy and free markets. Iran, Iraq, and North Korea were cited as examples of such states. As discussed in Chapter 7, if these states threaten Americans or American interests, the United States "must be prepared to strike back decisively and unilaterally."

Fourth is to pursue a "humanitarian agenda" via aid, to see democracies and market economies expand to "regions of greatest humanitarian concern." But there is a difference between humanitarian assistance and humanitarian intervention. "Relatively few intra-national and ethnic conflicts [will] justify our military intervention," Lake says, and goes on to emphasize that the United States will have to "pick and choose" among other humanitarian needs.

Selected "to serve as a contrast to its predecessor, 'containment,'" the main problem with the enlargement concept, Lowenthal maintains, "is the dearth of details as to what the United States is willing to do in terms of programs and policies to see that these four steps come to fruition."

Conclusion

Operations other than war, not warfighting, were to be the prime focus of Clinton administration military policy. Following what Charles Krauthammer had called a left-isolationistic agenda, with humanitarian interests and multilateralism setting the tone, this new policy would be a radical departure from the past.

Two years later, this agenda had been almost totally repudiated. Peace enforcement and intervention under United Nations auspices had come a cropper in Somalia, and the prospects for such action in Bosnia had become increasingly repugnant. Humanitarian assistance in Rwanda revealed that such operations could adversely affect U.S. military warfighting readiness. And sanctions proved to be an ineffective foreign policy tool, certainly no substitute for the use of military force.

Although, as of this writing, the U.S. military intervention in Haiti has been successful, the Clinton administration made clear that this operation was *sui generis* and not likely to serve as a model for the future. As Defense Secretary Perry's November 1994 remarks attest, there has been a shift in administration policy from left-isolationism and humanitarian concerns to right-isolationism, so that, as Perry said, "our interests should dictate where we get involved and the extent of our military involvement."

Chapter 9

Peacekeeping

First, and foremost, our national interests
will dictate the pace and extent of our engagements. In all cases, the costs and risks of
U.S. military involvement must be judged to
be commensurate with the stakes
involved . . . our military engagement must
be targeted selectively on those areas that
most affect our national interests.

—PRESIDENT BILL CLINTON, *A National Security Strategy for Enlargement and Engagement, July 1994*

Mission Creep

"Mission creep," a relatively new buzzword, actually describes a phenomenon as old as war itself. "The original political objects can alter greatly in the course of the war and
may finally change entirely," observed Clausewitz in his 1832
treatise, "since they are influenced by events and their probable consequences." President Clinton's remarks in the epigraph above reveal just how much "events and their probable
consequences" have caused a mission creep in his national security strategy.

What had begun as a focus on multilateralism and humanitarian concerns has evolved into a focus on unilateral concerns and the national interest. This was probably inevitable,

for "mission creep" seems to be the very hallmark of peace-keeping operations.

That has been true of the very term itself. When the Charter for the United Nations was drawn up in 1945, there was no specific mention of "peacekeeping." And that is still true to-day. "Peacekeeping" is an outgrowth of Chapter Six of the Charter, which gives the United Nations the power to mediate international disputes between states and recommend terms of a settlement.

But they also impinge on Chapter Seven as well, which gives the United Nations the authority to use the armed forces of member states to "maintain or restore international peace and security." Former UN Secretary-General Dag Hammarskjold labeled early peacekeeping efforts as "Chapter Six and a Half" operations, in recognition of their tenuous legitimacy.

"It is commonly accepted," said Canadian Brigadier General Ian C. Douglas during our April 14, 1994, panel appearance at the U.S. Air Force Academy, that peacekeeping operations as they now are known were the brainchild of Canada's Lester B. Pearson, as an idea to help the Middle East situation in 1956. The result was United Nations Emergency Force One at the Suez Canal.

These early efforts, as analyst John F. Hillen III puts it, were "sufficiently unambiguous to merit approval by the super-powers and their clients." A principle of such Cold War peacekeeping efforts was that such operations should not have an obvious superpower presence, but should use the volunteer forces of so-called middle nations.

That was a reflection of the Duke of Wellington's admonition in the early nineteenth century that "Great nations do not fight small wars." He did not mean, as some have misconstrued his warning to mean, that great nations did not fight wars that were small in size. Wellington meant that once a great nation gets involved in a war, regardless of its size, it is no longer a small war, for the prestige of the great nation is on the line. And because it is on the line, it is almost impossible for that nation to disengage or to seek a settlement less than battlefield victory.

That was one of the problems of the U.S. involvement in Vietnam. And it remains a problem today. When in his February 19, 1994, radio address to the nation on ending the conflict in Bosnia, President Clinton said that "we have an interest in showing that NATO [read the United States], the world's greatest military alliance, remains a credible force for peace in the post–Cold War world," he came perilously close to again, as in Vietnam, involving a "great nation" in a "small war" from which it would find itself impossible to disengage.

Another principle was that UN troops were deployed with the consent of all parties involved and only after a political settlement had been reached between the warring factions. But as Sir Brian Urquart, the former UN Under-Secretary for Special Political Affairs, pointed out during our joint September 21, 1993, testimony to the Congress, these Cold War peacekeeping operations primarily involved disputes between sovereign states.

These early operations included the dispatch of UN troops to supervise the 1948 Arab-Israeli truce, the monitoring of the India–Pakistan–Kashmir dispute that began in 1949, and the Cyprus dispute between Greece and Turkey that began in 1964. All achieved some limited success, he said, for there are centuries of experience and a vast body of knowledge on how to settle disputes between nation states.

But since the end of the Cold War, there has been a "mission creep" in such operations. Now there is a trend to involve UN peacekeepers in disputes not so much *between* nation states as *within* nation states. At the time of President Clinton's inauguration in January 1993, the United Nations had thirteen peacekeeping operations under way. Six of these operations—in the Middle East, Iraq/Kuwait, western Sahara, the former Yugoslavia, Cambodia, and Somalia—involved U.S. military forces. Except for the former Yugoslavia and Somalia, however, most involved individual service members serving on UN teams rather than military units.

It is noteworthy that the more recent missions were within areas previously deemed "essentially within the domestic jurisdiction" of member states. Unlike disputes between nations, these disputes within nations are much more resistant to outside solutions. In fact, there is some doubt as to whether such missions are doable at all, especially through the use of military force.

Reflecting the traditional military aversion to involvement in nonmilitary tasks, JCS Chairman General John M. Shalikashvili said in April 1994, after a trip to Zagreb, Sarajevo, and Skopje in the Balkans, "I do not believe you can bring peace to the area through the barrel of a gun. That peace over there can come only through a negotiated settlement."

General Shalikashvili's words were echoed that same month by General Douglas at the Air Force Academy Symposium. A veteran of UN peacekeeping operations in Cyprus, in Central America, and most recently in Liberia, Douglas emphasized that a peacekeeping force "does not have the right to impose its mandate by force of arms and indeed negotiations and consensus are the main means by which it achieves its objective."

The Importance of Being Neutral

Unlike *peace enforcement*, in peacekeeping operations it is the non-use rather than the use of military force that is important. Strict neutrality is a must. While a peacekeeping force must have the authority to defend itself, said General Douglas, "the first OFFENSIVE round which is fired by the peacekeeping forces causes the peace process to end, and the problem then reverts back to a much earlier, and violent stage, with the UN now on one side and then the other.

"Somalia . . . might well fall into that category," Douglas went on, "where the use of offensive UN force disrupted the peace process/cycle, and caused not only a slowing down of the process, but indeed saw the UN force becoming part of the problem." The United States should have known that full well, for almost a decade earlier the same thing happened in Beirut, Lebanon.

Disaster in Beirut

In the wake of the June 1982 Israeli invasion of Lebanon, the United States, Italy, and France formed a Multinational Force (MNF) to interpose itself between the warring factions and oversee the safe evacuation of Palestine Liberation Organization troops. To that end, the 1,800-man 32d Marine Amphibious Unit (MAU), part of the U.S. Sixth Fleet's Mediterranean Amphibious Ready Group (MARG), was landed, ostensibly for a thirty-day stay.

The 800-man French paratroops and Foreign Legionnaires took up position around the French Embassy, and the 400-man Italian contingent deployed along the "green line" between East and West Beirut. The U.S. contingent would secure the port area.

"No offensive weapons, not even mortars, were to be taken ashore," noted Eric Hammel in his analysis of the disaster, "because, it was feared, the fragile agreement underlying the evacuation might dissolve if the PLO and Syrians felt there was real danger of a major confrontation."

On September 1, 1982, the last of the PLO troops were evacuated, and on September 10, the Marines returned to their ships and set sail. Having served its purpose, the MLF was disbanded, only to be reconstituted almost immediately following the massacre of some eight hundred Palestinian civilians at the Sabra and Shatila refugee camps by Christian militiamen eight days later. But in so doing, there was a fatal mission creep. Instead of being neutral observers, this time the U.S. forces became an interested party. The Reagan administration committed itself to the reestablishment and strengthening of the legitimate Lebanese government in the wake of the destructive Lebanese civil war.

On September 20, 1982, the 32d MAU was ordered back

into Beirut, this time to "establish a presence." It was a phrase, Hammel noted, "no Marine commander had even before seen on an operation order." For the next seven months, as MAUs rotated through the area, "The presence mission . . . appeared to be reaping benefits far beyond the commitment in manpower and material."

But that euphoric perception changed radically on April 18, 1983, when a pickup truck loaded with an estimated 2,000 pounds of explosives was detonated at the U.S. Embassy in Beirut. Incidents involving U.S. Marines began to escalate.

Then, on May 17, 1983, in what was to prove a fatal mistake, President Reagan made the Marine mission creep official. "The MLF went there to help the new government of Lebanon maintain order until it can organize its military and its police to assume control of its borders and its own internal security," he said. As Hammel notes, "President Reagan thus positively identified U.S. servicemen with the besieged [President Amin] Gemayel government." The consequences were not long in coming.

On October 23, 1983, disaster struck. In what was called the largest non-nuclear explosion ever detonated on the face of the earth, a 12,000-pound bomb wrapped in canisters of flammable gases exploded at the Marine barracks, killing 241 U.S. servicemen and wounding another 128. Just over three months later, on February 8, 1994, President Reagan announced that the Marines would be withdrawn to their ships.

"Events and their probable consequences" had forced his hand. The loss of life coupled with the lack of a clearly articulated rationale for the Marine presence there had resulted in a loss of public confidence and growing congressional disapproval. It was a pattern that would be repeated.

Déjà Vu in Mogadishu

Those words could have been written almost a decade later about the U.S. withdrawal from Somalia in March 1994. Tragically, warning of the similarity had been blatantly ignored. In

November 1992, Smith Hempstone, then the U.S. Ambassador to Kenya, was asked for his assessment of the wisdom of U.S. intervention in Somalia. "If you liked Beirut," he replied, "you'll love Mogadishu." But, as he wrote later, "That was not the advice the [State] Department expected or wanted."

As with the U.S. peacekeeping operation in Lebanon, the operation in Somalia began with an entirely different mission from that into which it eventually evolved. President George Bush's December 4, 1992, address to the nation is quoted below at length to show in his own words how the original U.S. involvement in Somalia was justified to the American people.

His emphasis on the limited nature of the commitment was clearly stated, as was his specific promise to the Somalians that the United States would not dictate political outcomes:

> Every American has seen the shocking images from Somalia. Already, over a quarter million people, as many people as live in Buffalo, New York, have died in the Somali famine. In the months ahead, five times that number, 1.5 million people could starve to death. . . .
>
> There is no government in Somalia. Law and order have broken down. Anarchy prevails. One image tells the story. Imagine 7,000 tons of food are literally bursting out of a warehouse at the dock in Mogadishu while Somalis starve less than a kilometer away because relief workers cannot run the gauntlet of armed gangs roving the city.
>
> Confronted with these realities. relief groups called for outside troops to provide security so they could feed people. It's now clear that military support is necessary to ensure the safe delivery of the food Somalis need to survive. . . .
>
> After consulting with my advisors, with world leaders and the congressional leadership, I have today told [United Nations] Secretary General Boutros-Ghali that America will answer the call. I have given the order to [Defense] Secretary Cheney to move a substantial American force into Somalia. As I speak, a Marine amphibious ready group, which we maintain at sea, is offshore Mogadishu. These troops will be joined by elements of the First Marine Expeditionary Force based out of Camp Pendleton, California and by the Army's 10th Mountain Division out of Fort

Drum, New York [to] assist in Operation Restore Hope. . . .

In taking this action I want to emphasize that I understand the United States alone cannot right the world's wrongs, but we also know that some crises in the world cannot be resolved without some American involvement. . . . Only the United States has the global reach to place a large security force on the ground in such a distant place, quickly and efficiently, and thus save thousands of innocents from death. . . .

And here is what we and our coalition partners will do. First, we will create a secure environment in the hardest-hit parts of Somalia, so that food can move from ships over land to the people in the countryside now devastated by starvation.

And second, once we have created that secure environment, we will withdraw our troops, handing the security mission back to a regular UN peacekeeping force. Our mission has a limited objective—to open the supply routes, to get food moving, and to prepare the way for a UN peacekeeping force to keep it moving. This operation is not open-ended. We will not stay one day longer than is absolutely necessary. . . . We have no intent to remain in Somalia with fighting forces, but we are determined to . . . secure an environment that will allow food to get to the starving people of Somalia. To the people of Somalia I promise this: we do not plan to dictate political outcomes. We respect your sovereignty and independence.

As in Lebanon almost a decade earlier, the initial U.S. involvement in Somalia was quite successful. Security for relief workers was established and food began to flow to the countryside. Mohammed Sahnoun, the UN envoy to Somalia, before the U.S. intervention was quoted as saying that Operation Restore Hope "established a security framework for emergency relief and demonstrated that a well-organized endeavor by the United States for humanitarian purposes can have a positive impact."

But when President Clinton took office in January 1993, he had a much more ambitious role in mind for U.S. military forces in Somalia. Committed to "assertive multinationalism," Clinton's Secretary of State, Warren Christopher, told the Congress in March 1993 during his confirmation hearings that "international peacekeeping—especially by the UN—can and must play a crucial role." And Somalia was to be the test case for this new policy.

Bush's promise not to dictate political outcomes was brushed aside, and Madeleine Albright, the U.S. Ambassador to the United Nations, announced that "nation building" as part of a UN peacekeeping effort was to be the new role for U.S. forces in Somalia. As in Beirut earlier, it was to prove a disastrous mistake.

"The neutrality of the U.S. dominated UN force was compromised after confrontations between UN troops and gunmen believed to be supporters of Somali warlord Mohammed Farah Aidid," noted Robin Wright in the *Los Angeles Times*. UN envoy Jonathan Howe, a retired U.S. Navy admiral, ordered a manhunt for Aidid after twenty-four Pakistani peacekeepers were killed by Aidid's men.

In the ensuing search, eighteen U.S. servicemen were killed and seventy-eight wounded in a shoot-out in October 1993. As discussed earlier, televised pictures of dead American Rangers being dragged through the streets of Mogadishu enraged the American people and prompted a congressional ultimatum for the total withdrawal of U.S. troops from Somalia. All were pulled out before the March 31, 1994, deadline subsequently agreed to by the President.

What *The Washington Post* would later label the "nation building fiasco" in Somalia had far-reaching implications. "It will clearly influence and make the United States more reluctant about decisions to undertake missions of this kind elsewhere in the world," said former Defense Secretary Frank Carlucci at the time. "In terms of the humanitarian mission I'd say it achieved its initial purpose," he went on. "But when the mandate changed to nation-building—an impossible task, especially for a multilateral organization—I'd have to give it an 'F.'"

Hesitation in Bosnia

The immediate effect of the Somalia "peacekeeping" debacle was on Bosnia, where U.S. military intervention had earlier seemed almost inevitable. Even before his election, Clinton had pledged firm action, as *The New Republic* for August 17 and 24, 1992, put it, "to punish the Serb aggressors in Bosnia," including air strikes "against those attacking the [UN] relief effort."

"Bosnia Is 'Top Priority,'" was the front-page headline in the January 28, 1993, *Washington Times* shortly after Clinton took office. "President Clinton's National Security Council will meet for the first time today to consider new policies to deal with the conflict in the former Yugoslavia," it reported. "The meeting reflects the conviction of top Clinton administration foreign policy officials that resolving the crisis is crucial to hopes for a stable world order after the collapse of communism."

The reason for this "Top Priority" was the enormous public pressure that then existed for U.S. intervention to stop the "holocaust" in Bosnia. "Last August [1992], an ad appeared in the New York Times," noted Richard Cohen in *The Washington Post* on February 23, 1993. "'STOP THE DEATH CAMPS,' it was headlined. . . ."

It was signed by the American Jewish Committee, the American Jewish Congress and the Anti-Defamation League. The ad was typical—typical of other ads placed by Jewish organizations, typical of their press releases, typical of the arguments and the pleas they have made to both the Bush and Clinton administrations.

It was characteristic also of arguments made by a bevy of columnists and editorial writers who find U.S. policy toward the former Yugoslavia both flaccid and immoral. George Bush was compared to Neville Chamberlain, the British Prime Minister who appeased Hitler. Other writers have used the words "holocaust" and "genocide" to suggest that Europe had seen "ethnic cleansing" before.

There were lurid reports of Serbian "death camps" and "rape camps" and reports of mass starvation. But these assertions, both as to the matter of policy and to the numbers of women raped, are hardly indisputable . . . there's little doubt that the Serbs have behaved abominably. But so, too, on occasion, have the Muslims. . . .

Still, the consensus of Western observers, journalists and diplomats alike is that the Serbs are the bad guys in the war. . . . But the world is full of bad guys, and usually the mostly liberal American intelligentsia has rarely, if ever, united behind U.S. intervention.

Bosnia has been different. . . . Some of these same liberals [urging military intervention] opposed the Vietnam War, Operation Desert Storm and, really, every U.S. military intervention since the Korean War.

The reason for the difference was simple—to them, what was happening in Bosnia was a repeat of the Nazi Holocaust. Cohen, who had just returned from a trip to Bosnia and Croatia, rejected the comparison, saying it "exaggerates the crimes of the Serbs and diminishes those of the Nazis—and, of course, obscures suffering elsewhere: Afghanistan, Angola, Liberia, and Sri Lanka, just to name several on-going civil or ethnic wars. . . .

"If the United States and the West are going to intervene, the decision has to be based on a realistic appraisal of the situation," Cohen concluded, "not a pathetically tardy response to Nazism . . . if [history] does indeed repeat itself, there's more reason to think that in Bosnia it will come back not as the Holocaust but as Vietnam."

Sensing that danger, Clinton's first response to the public pressure to intervene was to use the cloak of multilateralism to deflect demands for action. The United Nations would deal with the Bosnian problem. To that end, Clinton appointed a high-level interagency group chaired by deputy national security adviser Samuel A. Berger to work out the details. The result, tentatively entitled "Presidential Decision Directive [PDD] 13," was reportedly approved for the President's signature on June 13, 1993.

Providing for the desired multilateralist cloak, this draft "welcomed the 'rapid expansion' of UN peace enforcement operations" and said the United States "would sometimes contribute armed forces 'under the operational control of a United Nations commander.'" But this initial version received so much criticism that it was never signed.

"Officials said the policy had been redrafted twice since its initial disclosure," reported *The Washington Post* on September 23, 1993, "and its basic thrust is moving away from committing U.S. forces routinely under UN control."

A post-Mogadishu March 1994 draft of PDD 13 marked a further retreat from Clinton's campaign pledge to create a UN "rapid deployment force" to deal with aggression and peace-keeping in Bosnia and elsewhere. Instead of playing to public sentiments as the earlier Bosnian proposals had done, the UN cloak was becoming counterproductive. "The Administration realizes they've got an albatross around their necks with this," a Senate aide told the *Washington Times*.

Putting aside the UN cloak, Clinton then turned to the NATO cloak to cover the lack of unilateral U.S. action. As he explained to the American people in a February 19, 1994, address, the United States had participated in the enforcement of sanctions against Serbia, initiated airdrops of food and medicine, and participated in the Sarajevo airlift to relieve starvation there.

"In August [1993] at our initiative, NATO declared its willingness to conduct air strikes to prevent the strangulation of Sarajevo, and other population centers," he said. Clinton then went on announce a NATO ultimatum requiring the withdrawal within ten days of all heavy weapons within twenty kilometers of Sarajevo unless such guns were placed under UN control.

"The United States as part of NATO—never unilaterally, as part of NATO—is making air power available to further the peace process," stated JCS Chairman General Shalikashvili at an April 5, 1994, Pentagon news conference after an official trip to Eastern Europe, Bosnia, Macedonia, and Croatia.

But, his denials notwithstanding, unilateralism was beginning to burst through the multilateral cloak. As far as commitment of U.S. ground troops was concerned, General

Shalikashvili stated that "America's position on that issue has been clear from the very beginning. . . . We should be prepared, in consultation with Congress, to provide forces to help implement an overall peace agreement, but we should not now, in a piecemeal fashion, become involved in an area where peace still eludes them, and where we don't have an assurance that a comprehensive peace can be attained in the end."

By November 1994, the United States had dropped the multilateral pretexts altogether and returned to the traditional unilateral interest basis for U.S. foreign and military policy. As noted earlier, Secretary of Defense William Perry made that policy shift explicit in his speech that month on "Rules of Engagement." In Bosnia, he said, "it would take hundreds of thousands of troops and probably significant casualties to impose the outcome we want—peace. That's a level of blood and treasure that is not commensurate with our national interests.

"Our actions need to be proportional to these interests," Perry emphasized. "We're not about to enter the war as a combatant." The policy shift had been coming for some time. As will be seen, it was hidden in the pages of President Clinton's May 1994 Presidential Decision Directive 25.

Peacekeeping Policy

The antithesis of the Clinton administration's left-isolationist emphasis on multilateralism and humanitarianism had been the "Weinberger Doctrine," laid out by the Reagan administration's Defense Secretary Caspar Weinberger in November 1984. Charles Krauthammer, who coined the phrases, labeled it "a remarkable right isolationist text . . . remarkable because of its insistence in the hallmarks of right isolationism: nationalism and unilateralism."

Equally remarkable, that Weinberger Doctrine, after the disasters and near disasters in Somalia and Bosnia, became the basis for the Clinton administration's PDD 25 peacekeeping policy. Although never publicly acknowledged, that fact is apparent when the two documents are compared. First, the Weinberger Doctrine:

> I believe the postwar period has taught us several lessons, and from them I have developed six major tests to be applied when we are weighing the use of U.S. combat forces abroad. . . .
>
> (1) *FIRST*, the United States should not commit forces to combat overseas unless the particular engagement or occasion is deemed *vital* to our national interest or that of our allies. . . .
>
> (2) *SECOND*, If we decide it *is* necessary to put *combat* troops into a given situation, we should do so wholeheartedly, and with the clear intention of winning. . . .
>
> (3) *THIRD*, If we do decide to commit forces to combat overseas. we should have precisely defined political and military objectives. . . .
>
> (4) *FOURTH*, The relationship between our objectives and the force we have committed—the size, composition and disposition— must be continually reassessed and adjusted if necessary. . . .
>
> (5) *FIFTH*, Before the U.S. commits combat forces abroad, there must be some reasonable assurance we will have the support of the American people and their elected representatives in the Congress. . . .
>
> (6) *FINALLY*, The commitment of U.S. forces to combat should be a last resort.

Compare those tests with the standards laid out in PDD 25: *The Clinton Administration's Policy on Reforming Multilateral Peace Operations*. After specifying the factors to be considered before the United States votes in favor of a proposed new UN peace operation, "the Administration will continue to apply even stricter standards when it assesses whether to recommend to the President that U.S. personnel participate in a given peace operation:

> —Participation advances U.S. interests and both the unique and general risks to American personnel have been weighed and are considered acceptable;
> —Personnel, funds and other resources are available;
> —U.S. participation is necessary for operation's success;
> —The role of U.S. forces is tied to clear objectives and an

endpoint for U.S. participation can be identified;
—Domestic and Congressional support exists or can be marshalled;
—Command and control arrangements are acceptable.

Additionally, even more rigorous factors were to be applied "when there is the possibility of significant U.S. participation in . . . operations that are likely to involve combat":

—There exists a determination to commit sufficient forces to achieve clearly defined objectives;
—There exists a plan to achieve those objectives decisively;
—There exists a commitment to reassess and adjust, as necessary, the size, composition, and disposition of our forces to achieve our objectives.

After all its rhetoric, the Clinton administration had abandoned its idealistic left-isolationist policies and adopted instead the pragmatic right-isolationist policies of the Reagan administration. As Clausewitz had written, this change was prompted by "events and their probable consequences."

The tests laid out in the Weinberger Doctrine and the standards specified in PDD 25 have one thing in common. They were both drawn up in the wake of military debacles, the 1983 Beirut disaster for one and the 1993 Mogadishu disaster for the other.

"They are intended to sound a note of caution," Secretary Weinberger concluded, in words President Clinton would almost certainly endorse, "caution that we must observe prior to committing forces to combat overseas. When we ask our military forces to risk their lives in such situations, a note of caution is not only prudent, it is morally required."

Conclusion

Since PDD 25 was announced in May 1994, the notes of caution on peacekeeping policy have continued to grow. Secretary Perry expressed them clearly in his November 1994 address on rules of engagement. And the new Republican Congress, sensing what one member called "a neo-isolationist mood," is moving to codify these cautions. In January 1995, Senate Majority Leader Robert Dole introduced the "Peace Powers Act," which would restrict the President's authority to commit U.S. forces under UN command and cut funds for UN peacekeeping.

Testifying against such proposals, U.S. Ambassador to the UN Madeleine Albright told a congressional committee that if such legislation was approved, "It would become literally impossible for the UN to manage or sustain peace operations, thereby leaving us with the stark choice between acting unilaterally or not at all when global emergencies arise."

The reply from Republicans, reported *The Washington Post*, "is essentially, yes, we know. 'It would end peacekeeping as we know it,' said a key Senate Republican aide."

Like the attempts by the Kennedy-Johnson administrations to use the military as a counterinsurgency force to deal with world instability in the 1960s, Clinton's plan to use U.S. forces for international peacekeeping in the 1990s may already have come and gone.

Chapter 10

Dangers to Democracy

Overseas humanitarian and nation-building assignments proliferated. Though these projects have always been performed by the military on an ad hoc basis, in 1986 Congress formalized that process. It declared overseas humanitarian and civic assistance projects to be "valid military missions" and specifically authorized them by law . . . humanitarian missions were touted as the military's "model for the future." That prediction came true.

—Colonel J. Dunlap, Jr., USAF,
"The Origins of the American
Military Coup of 2012"

A Hollow Military

The use of the military in non-traditional roles has great appeal. But such a diversion can have severe unintended consequences, both to the military establishment and to the society itself. First is its impact on the primary mission of the U.S. Armed Forces, to be prepared to fight and win on the battlefield. There is a major concern that operations other than war will dangerously undermine combat readiness.

Earlier, in Chapter 6, that eventuality was explored, with both the new chairman of the Senate Armed Services Committee, Strom Thurmond, and the chairman of the House National Security Committee, Floyd Spence, decrying the current state of readiness. While some might chalk up their remarks to Republican partisan politics, no one could make that claim about Representative Ike Skelton (D-MO), a respected military analyst and architect of the post-Vietnam military.

"Peace-keeping commitments may so degrade the armed forces' warfighting capability that it will be impossible to carry out the national military strategy," Skelton said in an October 1993 speech. "If the commitments-forces mismatch continues to develop as current trends suggest, the military will be unable to carry out the strategy.

"Both the Bush and Clinton administrations have embraced the socalled 'win/win' strategy which requires sizing the military for two major regional conflicts." But, Skelton went on to say, "We may have a win/win strategy, but we are in fact drawing the Army down to a win/zero capability. Peace-keeping missions may even undermine the first 'win.'"

The reason, he explained, is that military units are not deployed overseas indefinitely. After a certain period of time they must be rotated back to their home stations and replaced by another such unit. That unit in turn will also eventually be replaced. Each unit on the ground, therefore, requires the commitment of two addition units for backup and replacement.

In 1993, plans were to commit some 34,000 U.S. troops to peacekeeping operations around the world. Applying the three-to-one rule, Skelton pointed out that "the United States is contemplating engaging over 100,000 Army troops to peace-keeping, one-fifth of the entire post-drawdown Army, and the equivalent of between four and five divisions." As he concluded:

> This is alarming, in light of the Bottom-Up Review proposal of cutting the U.S. Army to only 10 divisions. Three of these divisions will be stationed overseas, in Europe and Asia. A major regional contingency would require the rapid deployment of at

least five divisions (in the Persian Gulf it was seven; in the Korean War it was seven). If the equivalent of five divisions are devoted to peacekeeping when a crisis erupts and will require re-training before they can be deployed for combat, there is no way that the U.S. Army will be in a position to respond rapidly to the crisis.

And as a matter of fact, that's exactly what happened a year later, when the U.S. 24th Infantry Division (Mechanized) was ordered to deploy from Fort Stewart, Georgia, to Kuwait to counter the Iraqi buildup on the border. As Congressman Spence reported in his December 1994 *Military Readiness* report, some tank platoon leaders in the lead battalion were sent into the combat area despite never having taken their platoon to the field; some tank crews had not completed crew drill; and some platoons had not been evaluated in a live-fire exercise. It was a recipe for disaster, a disaster averted only because the Iraqis chose not to fight.

The Corruption of an Army

In addition to the physical erosion of the military by peacekeeping operations, there is also a concern about the corruption of the military's reason for being as well. This concern is well founded, for an example can be found in our neighbor to the north.

Lieutenant Colonel John A. English of the Princess Patricia's Canadian Light Infantry, then on the faculty of the National Defense College of Canada, wrote in 1991 that such an internal corruption was exactly what happened to the Canadian military between the world wars.

Their senior officers were corrupted not by money or power. They were corrupted by their desire to be loved, to be politically correct, in the anti-military climate of the times. To that end, they involved themselves and their military almost entirely in good works in the civilian sector. Tragically, they did so at the expense of maintaining their professional military skills and their battlefield expertise.

They paid for this error with the blood of the soldiers they had been entrusted to command. In Normandy alone, the Canadians suffered 18,444 casualties, many through sheer military incompetence.

As Colonel English concludes: "Those who had been paid excessively high wages to keep the military art alive, adopted instead the bankrupt policy of searching for other roles. They shamefully forgot that the main purpose of a peacetime military establishment is to prepare for the day when armed forces might have to be used against a first-class enemy."

During that same period, the American military was also involved in such civil relief operations as the Civilian Conservation Corps, but they accomplished those tasks as an adjunct to, rather than a replacement for, their fundamental military duties. Given what has been called the long and proud tradition of American anti-militarism, they had no illusions about being loved. Their focus remained on the battlefield.

As T. R. Fehrenbach noted in his masterful analysis of the Korean War, *This Kind of War,* "Before 1939 the United States Army was small, but it was professional. Its tiny officers corps was parochial, but true. Its members devoted their time to the study of war.

"There was and is no danger of military domination of the nation," Fehrenbach continued.

> The Constitution gave Congress the power of life or death over the military, and they have always accepted the fact. The danger has always been the other way around—the liberal society, in its heart, wants not only domination of the military, but acquiescence of the military toward the liberal view of life.
>
> Domination and control society should have. . . . But acquiescence society may not have, if it wants an army worth a damn. By the very nature of its mission, the military must maintain a hard and illiberal view of life and the world.

For a time in the closing days of the Vietnam War, it appeared that the military would not so much lose as surrender its soul in order to be "relevant" to civilian society. The

Army's recruiting slogan became "The Army wants to join you," and the "Modern Volunteer Army" project began elimination of standards of discipline (called "irritants") that might offend the new recruits. Admiral Elmo Zumwalt, then Chief of Naval Operations, sponsored similar "liberalization" projects within the Navy, and the Air Force and Marine Corps followed suit.

But instead of reversing the disintegration of the military then under way, these moves exacerbated it. Common sense soon intervened, and the "back to basics" movement described earlier included, as one of its first steps, a reimposition of what Fehrenbach calls "the hard and illiberal view of life."

Eroding Societal Foundations

Not only are the underlying principles of the military in peril. So is the very foundation of American democracy, for there is a real danger that the current emphasis on operations other than war may end up hoisting America on its own petard.

In medieval siege warfare, the enemy's fortifications were undermined by saps or trenches extended beneath the city or castle walls. A bomb (petard) was then exploded to cause a breech through which an assault could be made. But if extreme care was not taken, one could be blown up (hoisted) by one's own bomb.

A powerful warning of such an eventuality was Air Force Lieutenant Colonel (now Colonel) Charles E. Dunlap's award-winning 1992 National War College student essay, "The Origins of the American Military Coup of 2012."

Written from the perspective of a senior military officer about to be executed for opposing the coup, this presumed takeover was "the outgrowth of trends visible as far back as 1992," including "the massive diversion of military forces to civilian uses."

Congress, which is the constitutional guardian of the rules

for the regulation and government of the military, may be furthering that trend. Among the examples Dunlap cites is the Military Cooperation with Civilian Law Enforcement Agencies Act of 1981, "which was specifically intended to force reluctant military commanders to actively collaborate in police work."

That law deliberately undermined the Posse Comitatus Act of 1878, which had removed the military from such sensitive civilian activities. In 1986, Congress "declared overseas humanitarian and civic assistance activities to be 'valid military missions' and specifically authorized them by law." In 1992, Secretary of State James A. Baker III pronounced that in airlifting relief supplies around the world, "We will wage a new peace."

"In truth," Dunlap wrote from the vantage point of 2012,

> militaries ought to "prepare for war," and leave the "peace waging" to those agencies of the government whose mission is just that. Nevertheless, such pronouncements—seconded by military leaders—became the fashionable philosophy. The result? People in the military no longer considered themselves warriors.
>
> Instead they perceived themselves as policemen, relief workers, educators, builders, health care providers, politicians—everything but warfighters . . . it is little wonder its [the military's] traditional apolitical professionalism eventually eroded.

Dunlap, who served as deputy Staff Judge Advocate of the U.S. Central Command and as such took part in the 1992–93 Somalia deployment, expanded on his original thesis with an article in the *Wake Forest Law Review* for Summer 1994.

Posing the question "How does the increasing military involvement in nontraditional missions undermine civilian control of the military?" Dunlap highlights "the increased politicization of today's armed services." This, he believes,

> is another vestige of the Vietnam War. . . . One theory partially attributed the defeat in Vietnam to the failure of the military leadership to assert themselves and their views more forcefully in the political realm. Profoundly affected by that experience, mili-

tary officers developed the skills and determination to effectively express themselves. . . . Thus, military leaders eroded the customary practice of privately expressing disagreement with civilian leaders, if at all. . . . To many in the military, the lessons of Vietnam hold that a discreet approach to confronting political authority is outmoded.

Retired former JCS Chairman Admiral William J. Crowe, Jr., who in a break with the military's apolitical tradition publicly backed Clinton in his campaign for the presidency and was subsequently appointed U.S. Ambassador to Great Britain, observes in his autobiography that "few officers today achieve high rank without a firm grasp of international relations, congressional politics, and public affairs. . . . The old military was gone."

Accordingly, notes Dunlap, "today's officers are intellectually prepared to challenge political leaders, particularly when they believe military interests are at risk."

Dunlap's observations were confirmed in conversations with my Vietnam War company and field-grade contemporaries who have now risen to flag rank. One three-star Army general, now retired, who commanded a division in the Gulf War, spoke of what he called the "never again" syndrome among Vietnam veterans. Never again, he said, would they sit on their hands like the senior generals of the Vietnam War, and remain silent while their soldiers were being slaughtered through lack of a coherent strategy.

Like JCS Chairman General Powell and Central Command's General Schwarzkopf and Schwarzkopf's deputy, Lieutenant General Calvin Waller, during the Gulf War they would speak up when they saw things going wrong.

Ironically, anti-military protest groups have unwittingly contributed to this weakening of civilian control. During the Vietnam War, they urged soldiers not to obey the orders of their civilian leaders to go to Vietnam, and publicly villified those who did. As noted in my earlier analysis of the Vietnam War, *On Strategy*, "By attacking the *executors* of Vietnam policy rather than the *makers* of that policy, the protestors were striking at the very heart of our democratic system—civilian control of the military."

Such politicization of the military continues today, Dunlap says in his *Wake Forest Law Review* article.

> For example, opponents of the military's homosexual exclusion policy have challenged military recruiters and education programs on many university campuses.
>
> The complainants apparently ignored the fact that the homosexual policy is ultimately a matter to be decided *not* by military commanders but by *civilian* leaders. The misguided activists send the military community a troubling message. In effect, they suggest that the defiance of the policies of civilian authorities by military commanders is appropriate ... military officers should condition their actions not on the lawful dictates of the civilian leadership but on their own assessment of the present—and future—political climate.
>
> Given the military's intensifying involvement in domestic affairs, the potential arises for military officers to defy or subvert the directives of the civilian leadership when they decide that the civilian leadership is out of step with fashionable thinking.

Shortly after those words were written, that potential became a reality.

In July 1994, Admiral Jeremy Boorda, the Chief of Naval Operations, in effect countermanded President Clinton's earlier nomination of Admiral Stanley R. Arthur to be the Commander in Chief, Pacific Command. On his own authority he forced Arthur to withdraw his name because he deemed that Arthur—the commander of the Seventh Fleet during the Gulf War and widely acknowledged as the best choice for the job—had been not sufficiently politically correct in dealing with a junior female officer's complaint, a fact that might undermine Boorda's liberal image when it came out during the Senate confirmation hearings.

As former Secretary of the Navy James Webb, a Marine combat veteran of the Vietnam War, noted on July 10, 1994, in *The New York Times*, "it is a grim omen for the future of the U.S. military when competent warriors are sent home by political admirals." It was a grim omen as well when neither President Clinton, Defense Secretary William Perry, nor Navy Secretary John Dalton protested this gross subversion of the principle of civilian control.

And, cowed by the climate of political correctness that they themselves had engendered, neither did the majority of the news media and the intellectual community who had previously been so sensitive to even a hint of military usurpation of power.

"Postmodern Militarism"

Because of these and other factors, Dunlap believes that we have entered an era of what he calls "postmodern militarism." Unlike conventional militarism, "postmodern militarism is *not* marked by overt military dominance or even a societal embrace of martial values." Instead, it "looks to the armed forces for answers to perplexing societal problems without apprehending the long-term implications of military-derived solutions."

And he is not alone in noting this erosion of civilian control over the military. Russell F. Weigley, the distinguished military historian, decried this trend in an article entitled "The American Military and the Principle of Civilian Control from McClellan to Powell," in the *Journal of Military History* (October 1993).

Even more critical was A. E. Bacevich, executive director of the Foreign Policy Institute at the Paul H. Nitze School of Advanced International Studies at Johns Hopkins University, Baltimore. Bacevich, a retired Army colonel who had served in combat in Vietnam, taught at West Point, and commanded the 11th Armored Cavalry Regiment in Germany, noted in the *National Review* for December 13, 1993, what he called the growing "military distemper."

"The post–Cold War military environment—institutional uncertainty (how deep will the cuts go?), burgeoning technological change (what is the face of modern warfare?), renewed interest in social experimentation (what role for women and gays?), combined with *expanding* expectations of what the military can and ought to do to make peace, succor the afflicted, and respond to disasters," he warns, is eroding the professional ethic that forms the basis for military subordination to civilian authority, and "fosters conditions where civil military harmony should not be taken for granted."

Bacevich recommends several actions needed to shore up this professional ethic. But, he notes,

> As long as Clinton remains in office, one danger will loom above all others as a threat to civil-military relations—the scenario in which the President on record as loathing the military dispatches Americans to die in some distant land where the stakes are obscure, the sacrifices substantial, and success elusive.
>
> Recriminations from the field could undermine the military professional ethic in a way that could leave the Clinton Presidency—and much more—in shambles. As the United States flirts with the notion of marrying its ideals (presumed to possess universal applicability) to its military preeminence (thought to be unassailable) President Clinton would do well to preserve the essential balance of civil-military relations . . . by protecting it from the forces that threaten the ethic of military professionalism.

Especially controversial was the criticism leveled by Richard H. Kohn, chairman of the Curriculum in Peace, War, and Defense at the University of North Carolina at Chapel Hill, who had served as the Chief of Air Force History from 1981 to 1991 and is a respected authority on U.S. civil-military affairs.

In the Spring 1994 issue of *The Public Interest,* Kohn launched a scathing attack on what he saw as the military's alienation from its civilian leadership and on former Chairman of the Joint Chiefs of Staff General Colin Powell personally.

Kohn even saw Dunlap's 1992 article as a sign of that alienation: "An Air Force legal officer wrote a thesis at the prestigious National War College hypothesizing the conditions that would lead to a coup—something officers *never* mention in public and barely even whisper in private—and won the top writing prize and publication in the Army's leading professional journal."

Tracing "the breakdown in the peacetime balance between civilian and military" to the Vietnam War, Kohn described how Defense Secretary Robert McNamara "ignored or dismissed military advice, disparaged military experience and expertise, and circumvented or sacked generals and admirals who opposed him. . . . The reaction against McNamara . . . reversed the trend toward greater civilian control. . . .

"McNamara provoked a tremendous backlash from the military," and as a result, "the professional military became politicized, abandoning its century-and-a-half tradition of non-partisanship." Into this situation, says Kohn, stepped a new set of military leaders. First was Admiral William J. Crowe, Jr., who served as JCS Chairman from 1985 to 1989.

Crowe is quite open, notes Kohn, about how he used his position to influence foreign policy, to rein in President Reagan's Strategic Defense Initiative, and in his "conscious cultivation of the press and the military's manipulation of Congress." After his retirement, Crowe took the unprecedented step of becoming publicly active in partisan politics during Clinton's election campaign.

But while Crowe operated mostly behind the scenes, his successor, Army General Colin Powell, who succeeded Crowe in 1989, was much bolder.

"If civilian control is defined first by the relative influence of the military as opposed to civilians in military affairs, and secondly the appropriateness of the areas in which the military exercises its influence," writes Kohn, "then it was under Colin Powell's tenure that civilian control eroded most since the rise of the military establishment in the 1940s and 1950s. . . . Colin Powell has been the most powerful military leader since George C. Marshall, the most popular since Dwight D. Eisenhower, and the most political since Douglas MacArthur."

In his first two years as Chairman, says Kohn, on his own initiative Powell pushed through the most significant changes in our military establishment since the 1940s. In so doing, Kohn acknowledges that he was filling a vacuum. The Bush administration's National Security Council, State and Defense Departments "were so devoid of a vision of the future international system that their only response to the growing pressures from Congress and the public for new foreign and national security policies was a slogan called 'the new world order.'"

Sadly, Kohn's analysis at times degenerates into a partisan *ad hominem* attack on Powell himself. In an overwrought section entitled "Mutiny in the Ranks," he goes on at length over Powell's opposition to lifting the ban on homosexuals, calling it, in a fit of hyperbole, "the very worst breach of civilian control."

He also repeats the canard that Powell encouraged the firing of Air Force Chief of Staff General Michael Dugan at the start of the Gulf War "because General Dugan had visited the war theater before the Chairman, taking reporters along with him, and because Dugan had been an all-too-effective advocate for air power."

Kohn's real quarrel, which he fitfully acknowledges, is not so much with General Powell the person as with the expanded role of the Chairman of the Joint Chiefs of Staff. There he is on more solid ground, for the 1986 Goldwater-Nichols Defense Department Reorganization Act had given the JCS Chairman enormous new powers, powers that Powell had not hesitated to use.

"Under his leadership," says Kohn, "the uniformed military gained an enormous public voice on the subject of when, where, and in what circumstances American military power should be used. His opposition to intervention in Bosnia now approaches legend; perhaps more than any single individual he restrained first the Bush, and then the Clinton administration from action."

Kohn does, however, quote approvingly former "whiz kid" Adam Yarmolinsky, who noted in 1974 that "The problem is not the overwheening military, but the inadequate civilians. . . . The danger . . . is not that the military may take over the country, but that the country is not able to preside over the military."

Conclusion

There has never been a military coup in the United States, but they have been endemic in Central and South America. When I lectured to a group of senior Latin American political leaders at Georgetown University in 1994 at a U.S. Information Agency–sponsored symposium on U.S. civil-military relations, one of their main questions was how such coups could be avoided.

The way to minimize that danger, I pointed out, was laid out by Harvard's Samuel P. Huntington almost forty years ago. "Subjective" military control, he said, achieves its ends by civilianizing the military, making them the mirror of the state, with the resulting danger that they may become the state.

"Objective" civilian control, on the other hand, is gained by maximizing military professionalism, which renders the military "politically sterile and neutral." Until the recent "operations-other-than-war" fad, that's what the United States had always done with its own military, and that's what it has been encouraging the Latin American military to do as well through its Inter-American Defense College in Washington, D.C., and its much-maligned School of the Americas at Fort Benning, Georgia.

Criticized as a "school for dictators," the School of the Americas is in fact the precise opposite. By promoting military professionalism, the School has helped wean the Latin American military from politics and has had a hand in the transformation of Latin American governments from almost total control by military juntas several decades ago to total control (with the exception of the Communist regime in Cuba) by democratically elected representatives today.

You wouldn't know it from Kohn's argument, but such focus on military professionalism was precisely what General Powell had emphasized. "We're warriors," he said in September 1993. "And because we're warriors . . . that's why you have armed forces within the United States structure."

The trend toward "operations other than war" as the primary role for the military in the post–Cold War world has now begun to fade, and the military has returned to its traditional warfighting focus. With that change, the trends such as they were toward a military coup in the United States have faded as well.

PART IV

A MILITARY POLICY FOR AMERICA'S FUTURE

It is clear that war should never be thought of as *something autonomous* but always as an *instrument of policy*. . . . Only this approach will allow us to approach the problem intelligently. . . .

—CARL VON CLAUSEWITZ,
On War, P. 88

Chapter 11

The Ten Commandments

Of all the elements contained in this strategy, none is more important than this: our Administration is committed to explaining our security interests and objectives to the nation; to seek the broadest possible public and congressional support for our security programs and investments; and to express our leadership in the world in a manner that reflects our best national values and protects the security of this great nation.

—PRESIDENT BILL CLINTON, *A National Security Strategy of Engagement and Enlargement*, JULY 1994

The Past Is Prologue

Reviewing the Army's post–Vietnam War study on future military strategy, which rejected counterinsurgency in favor of a return to conventional military operations, General Fred C. Weyand, then the Army Chief of Staff, quoted three lines from T. S. Eliot's *Four Quartets*, "And the end of all our exploring/Will be to arrive where we started/And know the place for the first time."

Those words have even greater relevance to America's

post–Cold War military policy now that that policy has come full circle during the first two years of the Clinton administration. From an initial concentration on humanitarian concerns and multilateral operations under UN auspices, it has arrived where it started with a traditional emphasis on U.S. national interests and the exercise of military power under American command.

But, as with the post-Vietnam military strategy, that does not mean simply a return to the military policies of the past. "Knowing the place for the first time" means using the past as prologue to build an effective military policy for the future.

To be effective, they must remain dynamic, for as Clausewitz said, such policies are influenced by events and their probable consequences. But, having said that, there are some fundamentals that remain constant. Based on the preceding analysis, ten such commandments must be taken into account when formulating military strategies for America's future.

I: Remember America's trinitarian roots

"Remember America's trinitarian roots" is the first commandment for one simple reason. If you do not do so, as President Clinton found with his abortive "peacekeeping" policies, the strategy will not endure. Sadder but wiser, he acknowledged that fact in his July 1994 policy paper, *A National Security Strategy of Engagement and Enlargement*:

> We can only engage actively abroad if the American people and the Congress are willing to bear the cost of that leadership—in dollars, in political energy and, at times, in lives. In a democracy, the foreign policy of the nation must serve the needs of the people. The preamble to the Constitution sets out the basic objectives: *to provide for the common defense, promote the general welfare, and secure the blessings of liberty to ourselves and to our posterity.* The end of the Cold War does not alter these fundamental purposes.

The founding fathers, most of whom were veterans of the Revolutionary War, discovered in that war what Clausewitz later discovered in the French Revolutionary War—that war was no longer a matter solely for kings or princes (or presidents), but was the province of the "remarkable trinity" of the people, the government, and the military.

That trinitarian principle was enshrined in the Constitution, first in the Preamble that made "We the People of the United States," not just the standing army, responsible for providing for the common defense; then in Article I, Section 8, which gave Congress the power to raise armies and navies, make rules for their regulation and governance, and commit them to war; and then in the Second Amendment to the Constitution, which states that "A well-regulated Militia, being necessary to the security of a free State, the right of the people to keep and bear Arms, shall not be infringed."

To that end, the Militia Act of May 8, 1792, required the enrollment "of every free, white, able-bodied male citizen between eighteen and forty-five years in the militia of his state. Each citizen was to equip himself within six months with a good musket or firelock, a sufficient bayonet and belt . . . and shall appear, so armed, accoutered, and provided, when called out to exercise, or into service."

Although it would remain the law of the land until passage of the so-called Dick Act of January 21, 1903 (after its sponsor, Congressman Charles W. Dick of Ohio), which laid the foundation for today's National Guard, the Militia Act had fallen into disuse, especially after the debacle of the War of 1812. But the principle of the citizen's responsibility to provide for the common defense did not diminish.

Beginning with the Civil War, the Congress, using its constitutional authority to "raise armies," passed laws requiring the involuntary conscription, or "draft," as it is better known, of young men for military service. Reinstituted in World War I and then again on the eve of World War II, the draft remains in effect until this day

Even though call-ups were suspended in January 1973 in the closing days of the Vietnam War, the citizen's responsibility to provide for the common defense remained. As recently as May 23, 1994, the House of Representatives voted 273–125 to continue registration of eighteen-year-olds for the draft.

Calling it a low-cost insurance policy against unforeseen threats, President Clinton acknowledged that "tangible military requirements alone do not currently make a mass call-up of American young men likely." But, he said in his recommendation to the Congress that draft registration be extended, ending it now "could send the wrong signal to our potential enemies who are watching for signs of U.S. resolve."

The trinitarian principle extends not only to the composition of the American military, but to its employment as well. In the National Security Act of 1947, as amended, the Congress charged the military with three primary missions. The least challenged is the task of safeguarding internal security. While some—notably the Israeli historian Martin Van Crefeld—have argued that safeguarding internal security will be a major future military mission, that is a most unlikely eventuality.

In America, internal security has traditionally been a matter primarily for state and local authorities. Rarely have federal troops been used to restore order, and then only as a last resort, most recently in the Los Angeles riots of 1992. While this mission cannot be totally disregarded, it does not play a major role in future military policy.

Historically, the most challenging task imposed by the Congress has been to uphold and advance America's worldwide interests. Throughout this century, that has been the primary reason for the commitment of U.S military forces. And in recent years it has also been the area where the trinitarian foundations of American military policy have most strongly come into play.

First in Vietnam, then in Somalia, and most recently in Bosnia, the American people and their elected congressional representatives have constrained and even reversed the direction of U.S. military operations. Any strategy that ignores the military's trinitarian roots is doomed to failure from the start.

II: Strengthen nuclear deterrence

The third congressionally mandated task, and the most important, is to protect and defend the American homeland. It is most important because if this mission is not accomplished, nothing else matters, for the nation will have ceased to exist.

The American military's primary purpose, said the renowned nuclear strategist Herman Kahn a quarter of a century ago, is not so much in its overt use, but in its value as a deterrent force-in-being. There are threats that never materialize, he said, simply because the military is "leaning against doors so that they cannot be opened."

To illustrate that fact, Kahn used the Spanish Land Grants in the southwestern United States as a case in point. When asked of their significance, a group of Mexican intellectuals had dismissed them as historical anachronisms that were of absolutely no value. But when Kahn posited a future where the United States had been severely weakened, especially vis-à-vis Mexico, as a result of a nuclear war with the Soviet Union, this same group of intellectuals then said unanimously that in that case they would have to reconsider the situation.

The criticality of deterring nuclear war cannot be overstated. As was true twenty-five years ago when those remarks were made, the only real external military threat to the American homeland is posed by the danger of a nuclear attack.

Protected by the broad reaches of the Atlantic and Pacific Oceans to our east and west, and by friendly—and militarily weak—neighbors to our north and south, the United States itself is virtually impregnable to a conventional military invasion.

With the end of the Cold War and the dissolution of the Soviet Union, the likelihood of a nuclear attack has decreased significantly. But it has not gone away. A fundamental tenet of a military policy for the new world order must be to ensure the survival of the nation by guarding against nuclear annihilation. One way to lessen this danger is through arms-control agreements such as the Strategic Arms Reduction Talks (START). As noted earlier, the START II agreements dramatically reduced the number of nuclear weapons in the arsenals of the United States and the several states of the former Soviet Union. But the bottom line cannot be zero, for nuclear weapons cannot be disinvented.

And as long as they exist, the United States must maintain a credible deterrent. During the Cold War confrontation with the Soviet Union, the basis of that deterrent was Mutually Assured Destruction or MAD. MAD rested on a simple premise: Each side had sufficient nuclear warheads and bomber or missile delivery systems that they could ride out a first attack by the other side and still have enough nuclear weapons left to annihilate the attacker. During the START drawdowns, that symmetry was deliberately preserved; it will survive as an essential part of U.S. military policy for the foreseeable future.

But arms control is not an end in itself, a fact some of its advocates and practitioners have tended to forget. Its basic purpose is to enhance the national security of the United States. While the START initiative should continue, what should not survive are the Cold War restrictions on the development of defensive systems to protect against nuclear attack.

At the time, the 1972 Antiballistic Missile Treaty served a useful purpose in stemming a nuclear arms race between the United States and the Soviet Union. If one side developed an effective ABM defensive system, it was argued, it would spur the other side to develop bigger and better offensive systems to counter that defensive advantage. Mutual vulnerability was an essential ingredient in the MAD strategy of nuclear deterrence.

But the Cold War is at an end, and so is the nuclear confrontation with the Soviet Union. The arms race is not only over, but with START it is moving in the opposite direction. The danger is no longer a mass exchange of nuclear weapons between the superpowers. The danger is nuclear proliferation and the potential for nuclear blackmail of the United States by such emerging nuclear states as Iran, Iraq, Libya, North Korea, and Syria. While MAD could and did deter the USSR, its underlying principle of mutual vulnerability now encourages rather than deters nuclear blackmail by these lesser states.

One would think that a nation like the United States with thousands of nuclear warheads and a number of highly sophisticated delivery systems in its inventory would not be concerned with nations like Iraq or North Korea, who are rumored to have only a few primitive nuclear devices at best. But such was not the case, and the United States has reacted with alarm and consternation to even the supposed existence of such weapons.

The Chinese strategist Wu Ch'i (440–361 B.C.) explains such a reaction: "Now if there is a murderous villain hidden in the woods, even though one thousand men pursue him they all look around like owls and glance about like wolves. Why? They are afraid that violence will erupt and harm them personally. Thus one man oblivious to life and death can frighten one thousand. . . . "

Wu Ch'i's "murderous villains" today are Third World leaders like Saddam Hussein and the late Kim Il Sung, whom some deemed "irrational and therefore undeterrable" because they stated publicly they would unleash a sea of nuclear fire against their adversaries and damn the consequences.

In 1994, at the wall of the new Holocaust Museum in Washington, D.C., President Clinton said that we "need an investment in a secure future against whatever insanity lurks ahead." On December 7, 1993, Defense Secretary Les Aspin had announced a counterproliferation proposal aimed at developing the strategic means of dealing with new nations that actually obtain weapons of mass destruction.

American nuclear negotiators do seem to have a kind of death wish. According to analyst Frank Gaffney,

the administration is exploring in the Standing Consultative Commission [a bilateral forum created by the 1972 ABM Treaty] new constraints on theater missile systems [such as the Army's THAAD—Theater High Altitude Air Defense system—and the Navy's Aegis system] out of fear that technological advances might produce weapons than can intercept not only shorter-range ballistic missiles [i.e., those aimed at overseas allies and troops in the field] but longer range ones as well [i.e., those aimed at the American homeland].

When U.S. nuclear negotiators "fear" the development of a purely defensive non-nuclear weapons system that will protect their own homeland and save the lives of their own fathers and mothers, husbands and wives, children and grandchildren, the "insanity" that "lurks ahead" referred to by Clinton in his remarks at the Holocaust Museum has already come home to roost.

"Foremost," says former Assistant Secretary of the Navy Seth Cropsey in a recent article in *Foreign Affairs*, "America must have a credible strategy—one that guarantees that the United States will inflict so much pain on an enemy that the certain disadvantages of firing a single nuclear weapon against America or its allies far outweighs the possible benefits." But that can't be done with nuclear weapons alone.

While "uncertainty about American nuclear retaliation still forces an enemy to think seriously," the United States is unlikely to launch a preemptive strike to forestall such an attack. As Cropsey correctly says, echoing the words of my North Vietnamese counterpart in Hanoi in 1975, it "falls beyond the pale of what America's public conscience will guarantee. . . .

"The objectives of U.S. policy," Cropsey goes on, "should be both to deter nuclear danger and defeat a possible aggressor. At a minimum, the United States needs an effective shield to defend itself and its allies from a rocket-borne nuclear or chemical weapon attack [and] an effective sword . . . that will discourage attack without using the nuclear forces that would turn an increasingly unstable world into a certifiably violent one."

Deployment of an effective ballistic missile defense of the American homeland has to be among the first requirements of a military policy for America's future. Without an ABM defense, the United States will remain vulnerable to nuclear blackmail at home and paralyzed in its ability to assure its allies abroad.

Significantly, the 1994 Republican "Contract with America" that laid out the priorities for the 104th Congress called for a renewal of the commitment to an effective national missile defense by requiring the deployment of anti-missile ballistic systems that are capable of defending the United States against ballistic missile attack.

In pursuit of that commitment, on January 4, 1995, House Majority Leader Newt Gingrich (R-GA) and National Security Committee Chairman Floyd Spence (R-SC) sent a letter to President Clinton asking that negotiations on the ABM Treaty be suspended until the new Congress had had an opportunity to examine the issue. "We also anticipate," they said, "that there will be considerable interest in reviewing the more fundamental issue whether a treaty that is intended to prohibit an effective defense of the United States against missile attack is consistent with our nation's vital security interests and emerging threats."

III: Maintain the nuclear shield abroad

And the two congressmen expressed concern about the U.S. position on negotiations on the demarcation issue for theater versus national missile defenses, an issue now standing in the way of providing anti-missile defenses for our allies.

That is a key deficiency, for it is not enough to safeguard the homeland from nuclear blackmail; the United States must safeguard its allies as well, not so much for their sake but for our own. The prospect that our allies could fall victim to nuclear attack from a regional adversary was one of the main reasons the United States became involved in the Gulf War in 1990, and the confrontation with North Korea in 1994.

During the Cold War, the U.S. nuclear shield protected our allies from nuclear threats. But that is no longer true. "The sad fact is that extended deterrence—the ability of U.S. nuclear forces to protect its allies—is dead," says Cropsey. And it is dead because its credibility has been undermined by "Washington's public hand-wringing about using nuclear weapons to defend states hosting U.S. forces. . . . This equivocation came both during Iraq's seizure of Kuwait and the events leading up to the current crisis with North Korea."

Cropsey's observations were validated by a May 1994 West

European Union (WEU) study. "The current debate in the United States on the role and utility of nuclear weapons is rather confusing to any European trying to relate it to European security," it said. "New nuclear threats may come from third-world countries whose leaders are called irrational and therefore undeterrable, because they may not follow the same logic as was applied by the United States and the Soviet Union in their nuclear deterrence relationship during the cold war."

But "the main reason why third world country leaders are considered to be undeterrable," the WEU report all too accurately notes, "may be that the threat to use nuclear weapons in a regional conflict has lost its credibility."

With the collapse of its nuclear credibility, points out Cropsey, "the entire weight of protecting allies and U.S. forces overseas [from nuclear blackmail or nuclear attack] thus falls on plans for a limited theater defense against ballistic missiles."

That new shield would be provided by anti-missile defense systems. In June 1994, the U.S. Ballistic Missile Defense Organization director, Lieutenant General Malcolm O'Neill, briefed Japanese officials on defense options to counter the perceived threat of a North Korean or Chinese nuclear ballistic missile attack on the Japanese homeland.

These options included the Japanese purchase of American-made Patriot PAC-2 and the follow-on PAC-3 ground-based anti-missile launchers, Aegis destroyers, E-767 AWACS (airborne early warning and control) aircraft, and Japanese participation in the U.S. THAAD (Theater High Altitude Air Defense) programs. Such deployments are now contingent on the ongoing ABM Treaty negotiations, which are attempting to differentiate theater anti-missile defenses from national anti-missile defenses.

If those differences cannot be resolved, the ABM Treaty ought to be abrogated. Just as it was questioned whether a treaty that prohibits an effective defense of the United States against missile attack is consistent with our nation's vital security interests, so the question arises as to whether a treaty that exposes our allies to nuclear blackmail and attack is consistent with our national security interests.

IV: Conventional forces are key

One of the defining features of the post–Cold War world is that while nuclear defenses are vital, U.S. non-nuclear conventional forces have become the true strategic forces of the United States, i.e., the forces capable of achieving U.S. goals and objectives. They are the primary instrument for deterring war, and, if deterrence fails, for fighting and winning on the battlefield. They are also the prime instrument for assuring allies of the certainty and the credibility of U.S. support.

It is also true that the United States is gradually cutting back on its overseas deployments. U.S. forces in Europe, for example, have been reduced from 326,000 troops prior to the Gulf War to some 100,000 today. Bases such as Clark Air Force Base and the naval base at Subic Bay in the Philippines have been closed. Reliance increasingly will be on U.S.-based forces capable of rapid movement to the crisis area, such as the deployments of Army and Marine ground forces to Kuwait in October 1994.

In geopolitical terms, the United States is a world island; therefore, strategic mobility is an absolute requirement for any future military policy. Where once Strategic Air Command with its nuclear bombers was the strategic military headquarters for the United States, now the true strategic headquarters is U.S. TRANSCOM at Scott Air Force Base in Illinois, responsible for the rapid airlift and sealift of U.S. military forces worldwide.

Candidate Bill Clinton acknowledged as much in a December 1991 campaign speech. "We need a force capable of projecting power quickly when and where it is needed," he said. "This means the Army must develop a more mobile mix of mechanized and armored forces. The Air Force should emphasize tactical air power and airlift. And the Navy and Marine Corps must maintain sufficient carrier and amphibious forces, as well as more sealift."

In a sense, Clinton was squaring the circle described by the famous naval strategist Alfred Thayer Mahan in 1890. When navies went from sail to steam, Mahan said, they gained a great tactical advantage because they were no longer dependent on the wind gauge for maneuver. But in so doing they surrendered the strategic advantage of sail, which when properly provisioned could operate independently at sea. Steam-powered warships, on the other hand, were dependent on coaling stations around the world.

Some of the first such U.S. coaling stations were the naval bases in the Philippines seized during the Spanish-American War in 1898. When the United States vacated those bases in 1992, it marked the beginning of a new strategic era. Nuclear propulsion, under-way replenishment, and aerial refueling enabled the United States to project military power around the world without being tied to overseas bases.

But total reliance on U.S.-based forces would be a strategic mistake, for a kind of "Catch-22" is involved. As in Joseph Heller's famous novel, there is an inherent contradiction involved in deploying forces overseas. You can only do it if they are not needed. If they are needed because of an ongoing crisis, such deployments cannot be made for fear they would exacerbate the problem. Thus, if the United States is to have influence in areas vital to its interests, it must have forces already on the ground. That fact is recognized in the 1993 Defense Department *Bottom-Up Review,* which points out that "U.S. forces deployed abroad protect and advance our interests and perform a wide range of functions that contribute to our security."

The Bottom-Up Review also noted that "a new concept is being developed that envisions using tailored joint forces to conduct overseas presence operations. These 'Adaptive Joint Force Packages,' under the control of the U.S. Atlantic Command (USACOM) which commands all U.S.-based military forces, could contain a mix of air, land, special operations and maritime forces tailored to meet a theater commander's needs."

Just how "adaptive" these force packages could be was shown during the 1994 Haitian crisis, when for the first time in history Army combat troops and helicopters were embarked on Navy aircraft carriers for deployment into the operational area.

The size of the conventional forces specified in *The Bottom-Up Review* remains controversial, but the main problem that has developed is not so much size as readiness. This is not new, for America has a long and disgraceful legacy of unpreparedness in peacetime, allowing combat readiness to suffer from a lack of sufficient funds for maintenance and training. Time after time those deficiencies were paid for in blood when war was thrust upon us. The challenge for the future is to ensure that we do not allow a "hollow army" to develop again.

V: Scare our enemies

The essence of deterrence, as Admiral of the Fleet Sir Peter Hill-Norton once put it, was "to raise the fearful doubt in the mind of any potential aggressor that any possible gain is not worth the inevitable risk." General Colin Powell put it more succinctly in 1992 when he said he wanted the world to be "scared to death" of U.S. military might.

And the way to do that, Confederate General Nathan Bedford Forrest was quoted as saying, was to "Git thar fustest with the mostest." TRANSCOM will guarantee the United States getting there "fustest," for as it proved most recently in 1994 in response to Iraq's buildup on the Kuwaiti border, the United States is the only nation in the world that can deploy substantial combat forces almost halfway around the world in a matter of hours.

Still, "mostest" is measured not only in numbers (which still count) but in warfighting capabilities, including arms, equipment, combat readiness, and training. There are legitimate concerns whether the force levels specified in the 1993 *Bottom-Up Review* are adequate to perform the missions they have been assigned, as we shall see.

But any realistic proposal for a military policy for the foreseeable future must take those force levels as a given. While additional readiness funds are likely, force levels themselves are not likely to be increased short of a major military emergency threatening vital U.S. interests. "Top Pentagon officials acknowledge that fulfilling the bottom-up review will be a stretch," reported *The Washington Post* in August 1994, "but they have no plans to back off it."

Following the Vietnam War, Army Chief of Staff General Creighton Abrams asked the Congress to give him the bottom line for the massive force reductions then under way. Once that figure was known, he said, he could build an Army for the future. And when Congress agreed, he did just that.

In January 1995, both the White House and the Congress recommended increased spending for defense, a sure sign that after ten straight years of defense budget cuts, the post–Cold War drawdown has bottomed out and the bottom line is once again known. Once again the services can begin to build a "balance of fear" that can scare our enemies without bankrupting the nation.

VI: Don't kid ourselves

But that "balance of fear" has to be based on real capabilities. The most dangerous thing the United States could do would be to attempt to bluff potential adversaries, for instead of deterring aggression it would encourage it. And that's precisely what's being done with *The Bottom-Up Review*'s claim that the force structure it recommended provides a capability to fight two major regional conflicts such as North Korea and Iraq near simultaneously. That simply is not true, for even one such contingency would put a severe strain on current force levels.

The Pentagon equivalent of the medieval Scholastics' arguments about how many angels could dance on the head of a pin, the two-wars' nonsense is a continuation of the two-and-a-half and one-and-a-half-war fandangos of the Cold War.

Not only is the United States kidding itself, with all the dangers that such delusions imply; much more dangerously, it fancies that it is kidding others as well. "Senior Pentagon officials," reported *The Washington Post* on August 8, 1994, "say whether the United States could fight two regional wars nearly simultaneously isn't as important as whether potential adversaries believe it could."

Any "enemy" who can count knows the two-war scenario is a fraud, and "senior Pentagon officials" who convince themselves otherwise are a menace. As the Chinese strategist Sun Tzu warned over two thousand years ago, "If ignorant both of your enemy and of yourself, you are certain in every battle to be in peril."

Unable for political reasons to back off from a declared strategy that is obviously deficient, there is a tendency to wish it away. In July 1994, Secretary of Defense William Perry told the *Navy Times* "that the United States now couldn't win two nearly simultaneous regional wars. But he said that weapons modernizations—known as 'force enhancers'—over the next few years will increase capability."

The truth of the matter is that, weapons modernizations notwithstanding, the forces provided by *The Bottom-Up Review* do not provide sufficient combat power for a "win-win" strategy where the United States could fight and win two major regional conflicts near simultaneously. At best they provide a "win-hold" strategy, where the United States could fight and win one such war, while holding the second conflict at bay until the first one was concluded.

Unless the United States faces up to those facts, it may find itself seriously overextended on two fronts with the prospects of a "lose-lose" strategy at hand.

VII: Don't fall into the technology trap

"Force enhancers" are an article of faith in what some have called a technologically driven "fourth generation" of warfare that, like the nuclear age before it, has rendered all past military theory, philosophy, and experience obsolete. Others label this new situation a "revolution in military affairs." As Michael J. Mazaar described it at an April 1994 Army War College strategy conference, it is "the revolution in information, sensing, and precision strike technologies." By whatever name, there is an element of truth in their descriptions, but there is an element of peril as well.

Mazaar accurately calls it "a post-nuclear revolution, a return to an emphasis on non-nuclear warfare, both conventional and unconventional," which stems, among other things, from "the dramatic effects of new military and civilian technologies." But a disturbing aspect of the revolution in military affairs concept is what he calls the "civilianization of war," where "the line between military and civilian endeavors is blurring."

"The substructure of war will be information dominance," Mazaar maintains, "and its primary building blocks are computers, communication systems, satellites and sensors. . . . When the instruments of war are no longer tanks and guns but computer viruses, microscopic robots and obscure germs, militaries, and indeed nation-states themselves, will lose even more of their monopoly on force."

The ultimate result he describes is "the disappearance of active-duty military force altogether. As the fabric of society is increasingly woven from fiber-optic cables, civilian technicians of the future could conduct all the deterrent threats and destructive actions that compromise what might be described as 'warfare' from a computer terminal." Shades of the electronic "McNamara Wall" of the Vietnam War, where computer-linked acoustic sensors and infrared intrusion detectors along the Demilitarized Zone were supposed to halt the flow of North Vietnamese infiltrators. It looked good on paper, but electronic gadgets proved no barrier to human ingenuity, and the wall was soon abandoned in favor of Marine riflemen on the ground.

As the military historian Sir Michael Howard noted

war at long range seems very sensible and civilized, but a troubling question remains. In spite of all the technology of the industrial and post-industrial age, does there not still lie at the core of all warfare a need to engage in the basic, primitive encounters of the agrarian age? And was not the lesson of Vietnam that, if the capacity to do so disappears, no amount of technology is going to help? To put it in brutish form, soldiers must not only know how to kill, but must also be prepared if necessary to die. More important, the societies that commit them to action must be prepared to see them die. . . . A readiness to engage in close combat in which there is a high degree of mortality remains the basic requirement, not only for the specialists in violence, but of every man and woman in uniform.

"While on one hand much will change in the conduct of war in the information age," says Army Chief of Staff General Gordon R. Sullivan in a recent essay, "the nature of war will change little. . . . Death and destruction will remain the coins of war's realm. And the value of these coins will not diminish, regardless of how much technology is available to the information-age army."

Over forty years ago Kurt Vonnegut made that same point in his 1952 classic, *Player Piano*, "a book not about what is, but a book about what could be," set somewhere in the future.

A superannuated first-sergeant, zebra-like under the symbols for patience, individual blood-letting, and separations from home, was telling tales of the last war . . . "there we was, and there they was. . . . The night before, a lucky shot knocked out the generator . . . there we were with no juice, eighteen of us facing five hundred of them. The microwave sentinels, the proximity mines, the electric fence, the fire-control system, the remote-control machine gun nests—pfft! No juice. . . . Well, boys, then the fun started. At seven hundred hours they tries a hundred man patrol on us, to see what we had. And we had nothin'! And communications was cut to hell, so we couldn't call for nothin'. . . . Snafu. So I sent Corporal Merganthaler back to battalion for help.

"So, over they come, screaming bloody murder, and us with nothing but our goddamn rifles and bayonets workin'. Looked like a tidal wave comin' over at us. . . . Just then up comes Merganthaler with a truck and generator he's moonlight-requisitioned. . . . We hooked her into our lines, cranked her up, and my God, I wish you could have seen it. The poor bastards fryin' on the electric fence, the proximity mines poppin' under 'em, the microwave sentinels openin' up with the remote-control machine gun nests, and the fire-control system swiveling the guns and flamethrowers around as long as anything was quiverin' within a mile of the place. And that's how I got the Silver Star."

As always in his morality tales disguised as science fiction, Vonnegut, who was a combat infantryman in World War II, is making a fundamental point. All the technology of the battle-field of the future is just so much useless junk without the Merganthalers who will risk their lives to make it work. "Even in the information age," notes General Sullivan, "the human heart and will govern action in war. Some person, as a member of a group, must still rush forward, drive forward, sail forward or fly forward in the face of possible death and maiming."

The idea that technological "force enhancers" can substitute for soldiers is not new. The inventor of the Gatling Gun, a nineteenth-century machine gun, thought the same thing. So did the atomic war theorists. And now, says the May 1994 *Defense News*, "The U.S. Army's recent demonstration of its newest warfighting capabilities is leading key members of the Congress to question whether advanced technology justifies further cuts in force structure."

"Can we make a trade-off between nine more-modern divisions and 10 less-modern divisions?" asked Senator Carl Levin (D-MI) during an April 3, 1994, Senate Armed Service Committee meeting. "You could start modernizing tomorrow if you lopped off another two or three divisions," responded Senator John Warner (R-VA).

"Ten divisions is as low as we should go," said General Sullivan in response to those comments. "Force structure counts. *Smaller is not better. Better is better.*"

VIII: Keep peacekeeping peripheral

An original tenet of the Clinton administration's military policy, spelled out in the Defense Department's 1993 *Bottom-Up Review,* was that peacekeeping should and would be a primary military mission for the future. As discussed earlier, that was an insidious and most dangerous mistake. It not only degrades the combat effectiveness of the armed forces but also has the potential to undermine civilian control of the military.

Its fatal fault, however, was that it soon lost the support of the American people and their elected representatives in the Congress. As *The Washington Post* editorialized on January 8, 1995, in support of Senator Robert Dole's Peace Powers Act, which would place severe limits on U.S. military participation in such operations:

> International peace-keeping covers a variety of functions from preventive diplomacy to actual combat. In a disorderly world it is an essential activity and as the Cold War ended, it became a popular idea. Now the wrecks—especially those in Bosnia and Somalia—have stirred a general disillusionment and a round of recriminations. The powerful United States has its own capacity to care for interests it deems vital, as in Iraq, and in that sense it can do better than most without international peace-keeping.

"But," the editorial went on to say, "as the lone global power, it also has a greater interest than any other country in improving and supporting a system which does not depend on American intervention alone to maintain world stability."

The first step should be to remove the military from its present role as the nation's primary peacekeeper and return it to its intended function. Former JCS Chairman General Colin Powell's observations bear repeating. Because the United States can handle "peacekeeping, humanitarian relief, disaster relief—you name it, we can do it . . . but we never want to do it in such a way that we lose sight of the focus of why you have armed forces—to fight and win the nation's wars."

The Vietnam War raised major questions as to the wisdom of tasking the military with nation building and similar other-than-war operations. But, ironically, that war may hold as well the answer to the military's legitimate peacekeeping role.

Much as with some of the extreme peacekeeping proponents today, the counterinsurgency doctrines of the time specified that the military's primary orientation was to be toward nation building and "winning hearts and minds" rather than warfighting.

Yet, although lip service was given to these non-military dimensions, it soon became obvious that U.S. military units were ill-suited by temperament and training for such operations. To correct that deficiency, in 1967 a new organization, CORDS (Civil Operations and Revolutionary Development Support) was created to deal with the Vietnam War's political, economic, and social dimensions. Headed initially by Ambassador Robert W. Komer, who was appointed as the deputy commander of MACV (Military Assistance Command Vietnam), the U.S. headquarters for the conduct of the war, CORDS was composed of personnel from the State Department, the Agency for International Development (AID), the U.S. Information Agency (USIA), and the Central Intelligence Agency (CIA).

Although primarily a civilian agency, it also had a military component to provide security and logistic support. CORDS was one of the most successful innovations of the war, ensuring that U.S. economic aid was properly distributed, and enormously improving the infrastructure of the South Vietnamese government. Overshadowed by the 1975 fall of South Vietnam to the cross-border North Vietnamese blitzkrieg, those successes were soon forgotten and the lessons of how to provide for the non-military aspects of conflict were never learned.

Today, those lessons need to be resurrected and reexamined. In order to "wage peace," we need to create a new and expanded Peace Corps under the auspices of the Department of State. Like CORDS, it should be headed be a civilian, an ambassadorial-level Foreign Service Officer, to emphasize its non-military character.

That's important. U.S. military intervention abroad, even in the name of peacekeeping and humanitarian aid, raises host nations' fears for their sovereignty and independence. A new Peace Corps would ease such misperceptions. Like CORDS, the majority of its permanent personnel should also be civilians, including political and economic experts from State, AID relief workers, USIA communications specialists, and other such "peacemakers."

And again like CORDS, the military involvement should be primarily to support peace operations by providing such backup assistance as might be required, including moving the relief teams and their supplies into position, and providing continuous logistical and other support.

As in Rwanda in 1994, this would involve mostly support personnel. Combat forces might also be involved, as in the initial stages of the Somalia operation, to provide security and guard against hostile attack. But, as with CORDS, the military would remain peripheral to what essentially should be a civilian responsibility. As Defense Secretary William Perry put it in November 1994, "We field an army, not a Salvation Army."

IX: Set the course

The Roman philosopher Lucius Annaeus Seneca observed almost two thousand years ago that "If a man does not know to what port he is steering, no wind is favorable." It is an apt description of post–Cold War foreign and military policy. The United States has yet to fully formulate policies that plot the course ahead and to mobilize the public support necessary for the journey.

In the aftermath of the Cold War, Clinton faced essentially the same problems President Harry Truman faced in the aftermath of World War II. Then as now there was a search for "peace dividends" after the enormous expenditures of the war. Then as now the military forces that won the war had largely been demobilized. Then as now a war weariness among the American people put a damper on U.S. foreign and military policies abroad.

Then as now the alliances that had won the war were becoming unglued. For over a century America had counted on Great Britain to maintain global stability. But that came to an end in 1947 with Britain's withdrawal from Greece.

President Truman's response was to instruct the Secretaries of State and Defense in January 1950 "to undertake a re-examination of our objectives and peace and war and of the effects of these objectives on our strategic plans." This instruction, observes Russell F. Weigley, "led to a landmark in the American government's recognition and definition of the revolution in strategy, the document known as NSC-68."

Paul Nitze, then chairman of the State Department's Policy Planning Staff, led an ad hoc State-Defense study group which formulated the policy that was approved by Truman in September 1950. It involved not only strengthening the armed forces but, equally important, a national campaign to convince the American people of the need for new foreign and military policies for the post–World War II world.

As Nitze recently commented in an article for *Strategic Review,* "The debate on purpose involved the question of the contemplated audience for the report [NSC-68]. Whom were we trying to influence? [Secretary of State Dean] Acheson later stated that the report was directed at the American people, that its purpose had been to convince the public of the significance of the Soviet threat and the need for increased defense funding in response."

While Nitze notes that NSC-68 was not publicly released until 1975, the Korean War that broke out in the interim between the report's completion in April 1950 and its approval by the President in September effectively convinced the American people and the Congress of NSC-68's findings. The same Congress that had difficulty finding $13 billion for defense in fiscal year 1950 found $22.3 billion, $44 billion, and $50.4 billion, respectively, in the next three fiscal years.

Much of this went to fight the Korean War, but, Weigley notes, "government and civilian leaders generally agreed that the growing funds for national security must be used to seek a larger security beyond the immediate demands of the war."

"The Grand Strategy of NSC-68 addressed threats to the U.S. and to the West which vanished with the end of the Cold War," says Paul Nitze in his article.

However, the idea behind NSC-68, the need for an organized approach to U.S. security policy, remains as valid today as it was after the war or at any other time.

A national security strategy requires an understanding of foreign and security policy objectives. . . . [But] There is less consensus today among Americans about the direction of U.S. foreign policy and security policy than there was at the end of World War II. . . . U.S. objectives and its world role seem unclear.

"In defining its security policy," Nitze concluded, "the United States must address some fundamental questions about how it deals with the world: (1) What should our role in foreign affairs be? (2) What objectives should our international efforts serve? (3) What sorts of means should we employ in seeking those objectives?"

President Clinton's July 1994 policy paper, *A National Security Strategy of Engagement and Enlargement,* was a major step in that direction, repudiating as it did his earlier focus on peace operations. "The primary mission of our Armed Forces," it states, "is not peace operations; it is to deter, and if necessary, to fight and win conflicts in which our most important interests are threatened." This public document reiterated the secret policies arrived at by the Pentagon two months earlier.

"Although espousing post–Cold War themes of world-wide engagement," says Eric Rosenberg in an analysis for *Defense Week* of unclassified excerpts from a secret May 1994 Pentagon document entitled *Defense Planning Guidance for Fiscal 1996–2001,*

the document lays out a broad agenda for U.S. involvement reminiscent of Cold War documents such as the famous 1950 National Security Council-68 directive.

Instead of countering Soviet "surrogates" in a world-wide crusade, the current Pentagon guidance lays out a new cast of villains and a twist on past containment policy. One policy goal is "isolating and containing 'backlash' states. U.S. strategy seeks to minimize the ability of states outside the circle of democracy and free markets to threaten the United States, its allies and friends."

While these secret plans are encouraging, they do not accomplish the task set by Secretary Acheson for NSC-68: to inform the American people of where we intend to go and to gain their support. The *Defense Planning Guidance*'s very secrecy hinders its usefulness outside Pentagon circles. As General Fred Weyand once said, "If you want support for your policies you must give Congress the rationale in clear, unambiguous and unclassified terms so they can convince their constituencies. If you don't, you'll never get their backing."

Unfortunately, the public articulation of those Pentagon policies, Clinton's July 1994 *National Security Strategy*, passed almost unnoticed, for the White House had mounted no public relations campaign to promote it. The reason for that lack of publicity was no doubt Clinton's sensitivity to charges of waffling, a charge that could well be leveled, given his abandonment of his earlier emphasis on peace operations.

Noting that the *National Security Strategy* had been issued "in the dead of night," William Safire, in an August 25, 1994, *New York Times* essay called Clinton's strategy paper "a serious articulation of the Administration's approach to the world [which] deserves academic dissemination and respectful or infuriated analysis by think tanks."

That's the last thing it needs, for it was the social science nostrums of the academics and the think tanks that led us into the counterinsurgency morass of the 1960s and into the peacekeeping swamps of the 1990s. What it needs first and foremost is the very public scrutiny the White House has avoided, the "respected or infuriated analysis" of the American people, the most important leg of the "remarkable trinity" upon which U.S. military policies must be based. Until that is done, U.S. military policy and strategy will remain adrift.

X: Above all, maintain escalation dominance

"Pax Britannica," it has been said, like "Pax Romana" before it, rested on the perception that if you crossed British interests or harmed a British citizen, maybe not tomorrow or maybe not next week or next month or even next year, but *inevitably* something bad was going to happen to you.

If America is to succeed in maintaining global stability in the post–Cold War world, adversaries must be convinced that they cannot flaunt the United States with impunity. To do that requires maintaining *escalation dominance*.

Defined as having the capability to escalate a conflict to the level where an adversary cannot respond, escalation dominance is syncretic, combining the tangible physical factors of military arms, equipment, and manpower with the intangible moral factors of leadership, battlefield bravery, and political will.

"If you want to overcome your enemy you must match your effort against his power of resistance," Clausewitz said, "which can be expressed as the product of two inseparable factors, viz. *the total means at his disposal and the strength of his will*." (p. 77) Over 160 years later, those words were validated in the Gulf War.

An Asian diplomat commented that before that war, "America was regarded as a paper tiger." Although aware of the enormous military capability of the United States, the perception was that "the United States lacked the will to fight."

Believing that because of the strength of his will he had moral "escalation dominance" over President George Bush, then being denigrated as "the wimp in the White House," Iraq's Saddam Hussein launched his 1990 attack on Kuwait. He soon found that he had grossly underestimated his adversary.

As President Nixon said of himself during the Vietnam War, George Bush had the will in spades. And so does Bill Clinton, as Saddam Hussein found out in 1994 when he again underestimated the will of the American President with his October massing of troops on the Kuwaiti border. President Clinton had both the will and the means to exercise escalation dominance.

Both dimensions are critical. Physical military strength without the political will to use it creates a "paper tiger," whose growls can be disregarded with impunity. But political will without the physical means to back it up can degenerate into bluffs and posturing that encourage rather than deter aggression.

That is what has happened with *The Bottom-Up Review*'s declared strategy that the United States can fight and win two major regional conflicts near simultaneously. If two such wars broke out at the same time, the United States does not in fact have the physical military to achieve escalation dominance over both simultaneously.

And that has potentially serious consequences. As Mark S. Watson noted forty-five years ago in his official history of World War II, "The facts of war are often in total opposition to the facts of peace. . . . The efficient commander does not seek to use just enough means but an excess of means. A military force that is just strong enough to take a position will suffer heavy casualties in doing so; a force vastly superior to the enemy's will do the job without serious loss of men."

"There is little doubt the United States could defeat any enemy," Army force planner Major General Jay Garner told *The Washington Post* in August 1994, "but reductions in preparedness mean more casualties than the nation's willing to accept." This raises the possibility that an enemy, by threatening to impose such casualties, can achieve moral escalation dominance. And this in turn leads to what the Congressional Research Service's Stanley R. Sloan calls "U.S. self-deterrence."

If the United States "is unwilling or unable to back up its professed international goals with the potential use of force," Sloan maintains in a recent report for Congress, "the international system will lack the leadership and means to deal effectively with many threats to the peace," and this way in the long term "lead to a progressively more chaotic international system."

But that trap is easily avoided. A simple equation is involved. As Clausewitz said, it is the value of your objective that determines the price to be paid for it, both in magnitude and duration. That's why it is so important for the President to set the objectives of U.S. military policy, for as he himself acknowledged in his *National Security Strategy,* "We can only engage actively abroad if the American people and the Congress are willing to pay the cost of that leadership—in dollars, in political energy and, at times, in lives."

Conclusion

When it comes to military policies for America's future, there will be no "revolution in military affairs," either in the narrow sense of that phrase as an information-age civilization of the battlefield, or in the broader sense of an upheaval in current military structure, organization, and doctrine. As a general rule, revolutions are sparked by catastrophic breakdowns of the existing system or by massive threats with which the existing system is unable to cope. Neither is true today.

Such a revolution in military affairs was set off two decades ago by the debacle in Vietnam, one that passed almost unnoticed outside of the military itself. Beginning at the Naval War College in 1972, it soon swept away the false academic prophets and their flawed doctrines of nuclear war and counterinsurgency in favor of a return to conventional operations and the traditional doctrines and philosophies of war.

Battle-tested in the Persian Gulf War and subjected to rigid scrutiny since, those warfighting doctrines survived post–Cold War attempts to overshadow them with neo-counterinsurgency notions of peacekeeping and other such operations other than war. Revalidated in July 1994 by President Clinton in his *National Security Strategy,* these warfighting doctrines will remain the basis for military policies well into the next century.

And no massive threats to America's security loom on the horizon either. "For the time being," JCS Chairman General Shalikashvili told the Congress in March 1994, "we are fortunate not to have a compelling danger that threatens our very existence." But that does not mean that no such dangers will arise; only seven months after those words were spoken, Saddam Hussein massed his forces on the Iraq-Kuwait border, prompting a major U.S. military deployment into the area.

What we are faced with is not so much a revolution as an evolution in military affairs, as military policies adapt to meet what Clausewitz called the course of events and their likely consequences. The ten commandments above are not so much prescriptions as they are cautions for the future.

We must not let the apocalyptic *fin de siècle* visions of the futurologists cause us to forget our trinitarian roots. And we must not let the current era of well-being with our former adversaries lull us into forgetting the criticality of protecting the American homeland, and America's allies, from nuclear attack.

While nuclear defenses are critical, conventional forces will remain the nation's true strategic force—the force capable of achieving America's national objectives in a dangerous and unpredictable world. That means we must pay the price in readiness, training, and modernization, and avoid the legacy of unpreparedness that has plagued us so many times in the past.

And we must not kid ourselves, either with the notion that we can avoid such costs by substituting technology for troops, or by declaratory strategies that promise more than we can deliver. Above all, we must maintain escalation dominance, having both the military means and the political will to raise any future challenges to our security to levels at which the adversary finds himself unable to respond.

Building an effective military policy for America's future is critical, not because we have a gun at our head, but, as General Shalikashvili told the Congress, "because we want to keep anyone from putting a gun at our heads, or ten years down the road, from doing so to our children."

‖ Notes on Sources

General

With the exception of background references catalogued separately in the Bibliography, the sources drawn upon for the book are listed by chapter below. Since the events discussed have mostly taken place since the fall of the Berlin Wall in 1989 and the dissolution of the Soviet Union in 1991, many of the references are drawn from newspapers and periodicals.

All quotations from Carl von Clausewitz's *On War* throughout this work are taken from the Michael Howard and Peter Paret translation, published by Princeton University Press in 1976. Texts of White House and Pentagon speeches are available through the Reuters Transcript Service.

References to my own analyses of the Vietnam and Gulf Wars are from *On Strategy: A Critical Analysis of the Vietnam War* (also titled *On Strategy: The Vietnam War in Context* in the 1981 Government Printing Office edition), which was published in hardback in 1982 by Presidio Press in Novato, California; as a mass market paperback by Dell Publishing in New York in 1984; and as a trade paperback by Presidio Press in 1995. *On Strategy II: A Critical Analysis of the Gulf War* was published in paperback by Dell Publishing in 1992.

Introduction

The text of President Bush's 1991 State of the Union address was published in the January 30, 1991, *Washington Post*. The implications of defensive operations were detailed in *The Conduct of War: A Brief Study of Its Most Important Principles,* by Baron von der

Goltz, translated by Lieutenant Joseph T. Dickman of the U.S. Army Infantry and Cavalry School (the forerunner of the Command and General Staff College), and published by the Franklin Hudson Publishing House in Kansas City, Missouri, in 1896.

Statistics on combat losses in Korea are from "Outpost Battles" in my *Korean War Almanac* (New York: Facts on File Publications, 1990). Professor Spector's post-Tet analysis is given in *After Tet: The Bloodiest Year in Vietnam* (New York: The Free Press, 1993). Commander Knox's remarks were originally published as "The Role of Doctrine in Naval Warfare" in the *U.S. Naval Institute Proceedings* (March–April 1915). They were reprinted in 1981 as "The Doctrine of War: Its Relation to Theory and Practice," with an annotation by myself and Colonel Wallace P. Franz, USAR, for the U.S. Army War College Art of War Colloquium. For a trenchant critique of the Vietnam-era limited-war theorists, including the comments of Robert Osgood, see Stephen Peter Rosen's "Vietnam and the American Theory of Limited War," *International Security* (Fall 1992).

Part I: Chapter 1

General Weyand's remarks quoted in the epigraph were in "American Myths and Vietnam Realities," *CDRS CALL* (July–August 1976), cited in my *On Strategy*. The "Weinberger Doctrine" was announced in an address to the National Press Club on November 28, 1984. A printed copy, entitled *The Uses of Military Force,* was published in News Release 609-84, Office of the Assistant Secretary of Defense (Public Affairs), Washington, D.C., November 28, 1984. William Safire's criticisms were in "Only the 'Fun' Wars," *New York Times,* December 3, 1984; and the *National Review* critique was in the December 28, 1984, issue.

The criticality of the failure to factor in public support for the Vietnam War is discussed at length in my *On Strategy*. McNamara's comment on arousing the public ire was quoted in Douglas H. Rosenberg, "Arms and the American Way: The Ideological Dimension of Military Growth," *Military Force and American Society,* edited by Bruce M. Russett and Alfred Stepan (New York: Harper & Row, 1973). Stephen Peter Rosen's limited-war critique is cited above. Colonel (later Lieutenant General) Dave Richard Palmer's analysis, *The Way of the Fox: America's Strategy in the War for America 1775–1783,* was published by Greenwood Press, Westport, Connecticut, in 1975. All references to *The Federalist* are taken from the James E. Cooke edition, published by Wesleyan University Press in Middletown, Connecticut, in 1961.

Among other places, the text of the Constitution of the United States is printed in *The World Almanac and Book of Facts* (New York: Pharos Books, 1994). Stanley Karnow's history, *In Our Image: America's Empire in the Philippines,* was published by Random House in 1989. The speeches of Woodrow Wilson, Franklin D. Roosevelt, and John F. Kennedy are reprinted in Vol. II of the Henry Steele Commager edition of *Documents of American History,* published by Appleton-Century-Crofts in 1963. The remarks on the immorality of the Korean War were published in *Military Situation in the Far East* (Washington, D.C.: Government Printing Office, 1951).

Rick Atkinson's comments are from his *Crusade: The Untold Story of the Persian Gulf War* (Boston: Houghton Mifflin, 1993). See also "Highway of Death," in my *Persian Gulf War Almanac* (New York: Facts on File, 1995). Senator John F. Kennedy's remarks made in a speech to the American Friends of Vietnam on June 1, 1956, are quoted in *The Experts,* edited by Clyde Edwin Pettit (Secaucus, NJ: Lyle Stuart, 1975). Hans Morgenthau's comments are from my notes of a 1968 seminar at the U.S. Army Command and General Staff College. John Mueller's comments are contained in his "Reflections on the Vietnam Antiwar Movement and on the Curious Calm at the War's End," in *Vietnam as History,* edited by Peter Braustrup (Washington, D.C.: The Wilson Center, Smithsonian Institution, 1984). Herbert Y. Schandler's analysis is in his *The Unmaking of a President: Lyndon Johnson and Vietnam,* published by Princeton University Press in 1977.

Secretary of Defense William J. Perry's remarks are from his November 4, 1994, speech, "The Rules of Engagement," reprinted in *Defense Issues,* vol. 9, no. 84 (1994). Washington's Farewell Address is reprinted in Vol. I of Henry Steele Commager's *Documents of American History,* cited above. John Quincy Adams's speech and the commentary by Norman A. Graebner, are contained in *Readings in the Intellectual Tradition of American Foreign Policy,* edited by Norman A. Graebner (New York: Oxford University Press, 1964), and in Bernard Brodie's *War and Politics* (New York: Macmillan, 1973). Robert Leckie's comments are from his *The Wars of America,* Vol. II (New York: HarperCollins, 1993), and General Weyand's comments were from my personal notes. I served on his personal staff in the Office of the Chief of Staff, U.S. Army, in 1975–76.

Dean Acheson's remarks are from *Present at the Creation: My Years in the State Department* (New York: W. W. Norton, 1969). Charles Krauthammer's article, "Isolationism, Left and Right," appeared in the March 4, 1985, issue of *The New Republic*. Secretary Perry's comments on Haiti are from "The Rules of Engagement" quoted above. Professor Stedman's remarks are from his article, "The New Interventionists," in *Foreign Affairs* (Winter 1993).

Chapter 2

An excellent appreciation of the influence of Clausewitz (and of the British anti-Clausewitzian bias) is Christopher Bassford's *Clausewitz in English*, published by Oxford University Press in 1994. Samuel Huntington's "The Clash of Civilizations?" originally appeared in *Foreign Affairs* (Summer 1993). John Keegan's *A History of Warfare* was published by Alfred A. Knopf in 1993, and Martin Van Creveld's *The Transformation of War* by The Free Press in 1991. General Dung's remarks are from his *Great Spring Victory* published by Monthly Review Press in 1977.

William Colby's observations are from his autobiographical *Lost Victories: A Firsthand Account of America's Sixteen-Year Involvement in Vietnam* (Chicago: Contemporary Books, 1989). Field Manual 100-5, *Operations of Army Forces in the Field,* was published by the Department of the Army in September 1968. Stuart Herrington was an Army adviser in South Vietnam's Hau Ngia province. *Silence Was a Weapon: The Vietnam War in the Villages* (Novato, CA: Presidio Press, 1982) is his account of that experience. Phil Goulding's remarks are from his *Confirm or Deny: Informing the People on National Security* (New York: Harper & Row, 1970). Archibald MacLeish's comments are from "A Time to Act," Office of War Information, 1943.

The White House debate on gaining congressional approval for the Persian Gulf War is recounted by Bob Woodward in *The Commanders* (New York: Simon & Schuster, 1991). General Palmer's comments on the Vietnam-era JCS are in his *The 25-Year War: America's Military Role in Vietnam* (New York: Touchstone/Simon & Schuster, 1985).

Hilton Kramer's remarks from the October 5, 1993, *New York Post* are recounted in *Defense Media Review* (October 1993). The Vietnam-era Case-Church Amendment was named after its sponsors, Senator Clifford Case (R-NJ) and Senator Frank Church (D-

ID); see "Case-Church Amendment" in my *Vietnam War Almanac,* cited above. The remarks of Senator Byrd and Senator Leahy were reported by Ann Devroy and R. Jeffrey Smith in "Clinton Reexamines a Foreign Policy Under Siege," *The Washington Post,* October 17, 1993.

Admiral Baker's comments on the news media are from "Last One in the Pool" in the August 1991 *U.S. Naval Institute Proceedings,* and General Funk's are from his "Accommodating the Wartime Media: A Commander's Task," in the April 1993 *Military Review.* Comments on the Mogadishu disaster, including quotes from Anthony Lake, Walter Goodman, Patrick Sloyan, Paul Watson, Ed Turner, and Bernard Kalb, are taken from Jacqueline Sharkey's article, "When Pictures Drive Foreign Policy," *American Journalism Review* (December 1993).

The *TV Guide* D-Day commentary is in their May 28, 1994, issue and the later comment on intervention in Somalia is in their January 16–22, 1993, issue. Dan Rather's Op-Ed article, "Don't Blame TV for Getting Us into Somalia," appeared in the October 14, 1993, *New York Times,* and David Broder's comments were noted by Richard Harwood in his May 28, 1994, *Washington Post* article, "Reporting On, By and For an Elite."

Alexis de Tocqueville's *Democracy in America* was republished by The New American Library in New York in 1956. *The Washington Post* editorial on Dole's Peace Powers Act of 1995, "The Future of Peacekeeping," was in its January 8, 1995, issue; the *Washington Times* editorial, "The Peace Powers Act," was in its January 9, 1995, issue. The Principles of War are laid out in JCS Joint Publication 0-1, "Basic National Defense Doctrine."

Chapter 3

President Clinton's remarks quoted in the epigraph were given to the graduating class of the U.S. Naval Academy on May 24, 1994, and quoted in Ann Devroy's "President Cautions Congress on 'Simplistic Ideas' in Foreign Policy," *The Washington Post,* May 26, 1994. *The Federalist* references are from the Cooke edition cited above. The National Security Act is contained in Title 10, U.S. Code, as implemented by Department of Defense Directive 5100.1, *Functions of the Department of Defense and Its Major Components,* January 10, 1986. The Tofflers' *War and Anti-war* was published by Little, Brown in Boston in 1993.

My unclassified version of the Abrams Study Group, "The Astarita Report: A Military Strategy for the Multipolar World," was reprinted as an Army War College Strategic Studies Group Occasional Paper in April 1981. Gulf War statistics are from my *Persian Gulf War Almanac* (New York: Facts on File, 1995). Krauthammer's remarks are from "Isolationism, Left and Right" cited above, and his "The Lonely Superpower" from *The New Republic,* July 29, 1991.

The change in the UN mission in Somalia is analyzed in Willie Curtis's "The Inevitable Slide into Coercive Peacemaking: The U.S. Role in the New World Order," *Defense Analysis* (December 1994). *The Washington Post* editorial, "The Future of Peace-Keeping," was in its January 8, 1995, issue.

General de Gaulle's remarks were reported in *Time* (July 12, 1963) and quoted in Jay M. Shafritz's *Words on War* (New York: Prentice Hall, 1990). Washington Irving's comment comes from his *Diedrich Knickerbocker's History of New York* (1809), also quoted in Shafritz. Findings of the Abrams Study Group are in my *The Astarita Report* (Carlisle Barracks, PA: Strategic Studies Gp. USAWC, 1981). Korean War statistics are from my *Korean War Almanac,* and NATO statistics from my "United States Armed Forces in Europe" in Lewis H. Gann's *The Defence of Western Europe* (London: Croom-Helms, 1987).

Colonel Kutter's remarks appear in his "European National Security Perspectives in the Era of Pax Democratia," *AUSA Landpower Series 93–2* (April 1993). Les Aspin's "The Partnership for Peace Proposal" is contained in a December 6, 1993, Office of the Secretary of Defense Memorandum.

Andrew Borowiec's comments come from his "Russia's Knock on NATO's Door Creates Problems," *Washington Times,* March 19, 1994. See also "The Evolution of NATO and Its Consequences for WEU," Document 1410, *Assembly of Western European Union,* March 23, 1994.

Defense Secretary Perry's comments on Russia joining the Partnership for Peace were made in a March 14, 1994, address, "United States Relations with Russia," at George Washington University (Reuters Transcript Report). His defense of the Nunn-Lugar program on nuclear disarmament was contained in his January 5, 1995, address to the National Press Club (Reuters Transcript Report).

Perry's May 1993 remarks about East Asia were made in a May 3, 1994, speech, "U.S. Security Policy in Asia," at the Asian Society in Washington, D.C. (Reuters Transcript Report); President Clinton's remarks were made in an address to the Korean National Assembly on July 10, 1993 (Reuters Transcript Report). For a discussion of geopolitical realities in East Asia, see Part I, "The Setting," in my *Korean War Almanac*. Professor Harding's remarks are from "Is China a Threat to the U.S.?", *Cosmos* (1994). For K'ang Yu-wei's *Ta T'ung Shu,* see Lawrence G. Thompson's *The One-World Philosophy of K'ang Yu-wei* (London: Allen & Unwin, 1958).

For background on the Middle East, see Part I, "The Setting" in my *Persian Gulf War Almanac*. The *New York Times* poll is discussed by Steven Greenhouse in "Poll Shows 4 Nations Differ on the Main Threat to Peace," on April 4, 1994. The Army War College study, *America in the Third World,* by Steven Metz, was published by the Strategic Studies Institute on May 20, 1994.

John F. Kennedy's remarks on "Wars of National Liberation" are quoted in *Autopsy on People's War,* by Chalmers Johnson (Berkeley, CA: University of California Press, 1973). The statistics on ongoing armed conflicts are from "No Time for Downsizing," by F. Andy Messing in *The World & I* (March 1994). Secretary Perry's remarks are from his "The Rules of Engagement" cited earlier.

Part II: Chapter 4

General Powell's comments quoted in the epigraph are from a September 1, 1993, Pentagon press conference on *The Bottom-Up Review*. The publication's full title is *The Bottom-Up Review: Forces for a New Era* (Washington, D.C.: OSD, September 1, 1993). Geoffrey Blainey's observations are from *The Causes of War* (New York: Free Press, 1973), and Rosemary Foot's from her *The Wrong War: American Policy and the Dimensions of the Korean Conflict 1950–1953* (Ithaca, NY: Cornell University Press, 1985). See also "Ike Was Ready to Use Nukes on China," *Washington Times,* December 13, 1994, which highlights a newly declassified April 12, 1954, JCS memo.

President Clinton's remarks on Korea were quoted in "U.S. Warns North Korea on Nuclear Weapons," *The Washington Post,* July 11, 1993; President Nixon's remarks on will were quoted by Henry Kissinger in *White House Years* (Boston: Little, Brown, 1979). The attack on Phuoc Long is recounted in my "Saigon's Last Days," *VIETNAM* (April 1995); John Foster Dulles's remarks were published in the January 12, 1954, *Department of State Bulletin*.

For a discussion on the dynamics of the Cold War, see "The Revision Thing" by Jacob Heilbrun in the August 15, 1994, issue of *The New Republic*. President Reagan's remarks are from the 1988 *National Security Strategy of the United States* (Government Printing Office, 1988). The strategy to bankrupt the Soviet economy is discussed in Peter Schweizer's *Victory* (New York: Atlantic Monthly Press, 1994). See also Vladimir K. Bukovsky's "Inside the Assault That Ended the Cold War," *Wall Street Journal*, August 8, 1994. Commentary on START is from the International Institute for Strategic Studies' *The Military Balance 1993–1994* (London: Brassey's, 1993). General Powell's warning on the Soviet nuclear threat was made in his April 25, 1993, testimony to the Defense Base Closure Commission. Pentagon comments on retargeting were reported by Bill Gertz, "Missiles No Longer Aimed at Soviets," *Washington Times*, June 1, 1994.

Bernard Brodie's comments on the "atomic age" come from his *The Absolute Weapon*, quoted in Barry H. Steiner, *Bernard Brodie and the Foundations of American Nuclear Strategy* (Lawrence, KS: University Press of Kansas, 1991). The 1949 edition of Field Manual 100-5, *Field Service Regulations: Operations*, was published by the Department of the Army in August 1949. Air Force Secretary Finletter's remarks are quoted by Earl H. Tilford, Jr., in *Setup: What the Air Force Did in Vietnam and Why* (Air University Press, 1991).

Russell Weigley's comments are from *The American Way of War: A History of the United States Military Strategy and Policy* (New York: Macmillan, 1973). The 1954 edition of Field Manual 100-5, *Field Service Regulations: Operations*, was published by the Department of the Army in September 1954. General Taylor's critique of Massive Retaliation, *The Uncertain Trumpet*, was published in 1959 by Harper & Row. An excellent overview of the nuclear debate is David MacIssac's "The Nuclear Weapons Debate and American Society," *Air University Review* (May–June 1984).

Dave Palmer's comments on limited war are from *Summons of the Trumpet: U.S.-Vietnam in Perspective* (Novato, CA: Presidio Press, 1978). Commentary from the "Great Debate" on the Korean War is excerpted from the U.S. Senate's *Military Situation in the Far East* (Government Printing Office, 1951) and is quoted earlier in my Vietnam War analysis, cited above. Dean Rusk's remarks are from his autobiography, *As I Saw It* (New York: W. W. Norton, 1990).

The 1986 edition of Field Manual 100-1, *The Army*, was published by the Department of the Army in June 1986, and the 1986 edition of Field Manual 100-5, *Operations*, in May 1986. The

Kennedy-Decker exchange was noted in Lloyd Norman and John Spore's "Big Push in Guerrilla War," *Army* (March 1992). Blaufarb's remarks are from *The Counter-Insurgency Era: U.S. Doctrine and Performance 1950 to the Present* (New York: Free Press, 1977).

The 1968 edition of Field Manual 100-5, *Operations of Army Forces in the Field,* was published by the Department of the Army in September 1968. J. Bower Bell's comments are from *The Myth of the Guerrilla: Revolutionary Theory and Malpractice* (New York: Alfred A. Knopf, 1971). Lin Piao's "Long Live the Victory of People's War" was published in Martin Ebon's *Lin Piao* (New York: Stein & Day, 1970).

Mark Lagon's comments are from *The Reagan Doctrine: Sources of American Conduct in the Cold War's Last Chapter* (Westport, CT: Greenwood Publishing Group, 1994). My discussion of conventional war as the model for the future is in "Mid-Intensity Conflict: The Korean War Paradigm," in Robert L. Pfaltzgraff, Jr., and Richard H. Schultz, Jr., eds., *The United States Army: Challenges and Missions for the 1990s* (Lexington, MA: D. C. Heath & Co.; Lexington Books, 1991).

Chapter 5

Commander Knox's 1915 article, "The Role of Doctrine in Naval Warfare," is cited above. The term "wizards of Armaggedon" was coined by the *Boston Globe*'s Fred Kaplan, in his book of the same name published by Simon & Schuster in 1983. Barry Steiner's *Bernard Brodie and the Foundations of American Nuclear Strategy* is cited above. General Thomas D. White is quoted by Bernard Brodie in *War and Politics* (New York: Macmillan, 1973). Dave Palmer's analysis of the Vietnam War, *Summons of the Trumpet,* is cited above.

President Roosevelt's February 26, 1942, letter is in the National Archives. Enthoven and Smith's comments are from their *How Much Is Enough: Shaping the Defense Program 1961–1969* (New York: Harper & Row, 1971). George Kennan's "Long Telegram" is contained in his *Memoirs: 1925–1950* (Boston: Little, Brown & Co., 1967). General MacArthur's complaint is recorded in the Senate's *Military Situation in the Far East,* cited above.

Ronald Spector's analysis, *After Tet: The Bloodiest Year in Vietnam,* was published by The Free Press in 1993. Admiral Turner is quoted in John B. Hattendorf, B. Mitchell Simpson III, and John W.

Wadleigh's *Sailors and Scholars* (Newport, RI: Naval War College Press, 1984). Romjue's comments are in his *From the Active Defense to AirLand Battle: The Development of Army Doctrine 1973–1983* (Ft. Monroe, VA: U.S. Army Training and Doctrine Command, 1984). The "SACumcize" quote is from USAF Colonel Jack Broughton's *Going Downtown: The War Against Hanoi and Washington* (New York: Orion Books, 1988). AFM 1-1, *Basic Aerospace Doctrine of the United States Air Force,* was published by the Air Force on March 16, 1984.

See my "Full Circle: World War II to the Persian Gulf" in the February 1992 *Military Review.* Kissinger's comment is from *White House Years,* cited above. General Schwarzkopf's remarks were reported in "A Tribute to the Navy/Marine Corps Team," *Naval Institute Proceedings* (August 1991). Gulf War statistics are from my *Persian Gulf War Almanac,* and President Bush's May 29, 1991, comments on airpower are quoted in "Chapter VI: The Air Campaign," in *Conduct of the Persian Gulf War: Final Report to the Congress* (Department of Defense, 1992).

Schwarzkopf's remarks on joint operations are from the *Proceedings* article cited above. Joint Pub 1, *Joint Warfare of the U.S. Armed Forces,* was published by the National Defense University Press on November 11, 1991. ". . . From the Sea: Preparing the Naval Services for the 21st Century" was republished in the November 1992 *Naval Institute Proceedings.*

Dr. Breemer's comments come from "The End of Naval Strategy: Revolutionary Change and the Future of American Naval Power," *Strategic Review* (Spring 1994). See also his "Naval Strategy Is Dead," in the February 1994 *Naval Institute Proceedings,* and Colonel Gary Anderson, USMC, *Beyond Mahan: A Proposal for a U.S. Naval Strategy for the Twenty-First Century* (Naval War College, 1993). Navy Secretary Dalton's remarks were reported in ". . . From the Sea: Views from the Top," *Defense Issues,* vol. 9, no. 53 (1994).

The U.S. Air Force White Paper, *Global Reach—Global Power,* was prepared in December 1989 but not formally published until June 1990. General McPeak's comments are from his address, "Does the Air Force Have a Mission?", given at Maxwell Air Force Base, Alabama, on June 19, 1992. The latest edition of AFM 1-1, *Basic Aerospace Doctrine of the United States Air Force,* was published by the Department of the Air Force in March 1992.

See also "The Air Force's New Doctrine" by Lieutenant Colonel Price T. Bingham, USAF (Ret), and "Reflections on The Air Force's New Manual" by Harold R. Winton, both in *Military Review* (November 1992), and "AirPower Thinking: Request Unrestricted Climb," by Lieutenant General Charles G. Boyd and Lieutenant Colonel Charles M. Westenhoff, USAF, in *Airpower Journal* (Fall 1991). General McPeak's October 1994 remarks were reported in Bradley Graham's "Air Force Chief on Attack," *The Washington Post*, October 24, 1994. General Wilkerson's remarks were also contained in the October 4, 1994, *Washington Post* article.

General Sullivan's remarks on jointness and the remarks on the strategic center of gravity were reported by Barton Gellman in "Army's New Doctrine Manual Sees High-Tech, Distant Battles," *The Washington Post*, June 15, 1993. The latest version of FM 100-5 was published by the Department of the Army in June 1993. General Franks was interviewed in *Jane's Defence Weekly*, February 20, 1993.

For a discussion of Force XXI, including the Louisiana Maneuver concept, Battle Labs, and digitalization, see General Sullivan's "The Army Is Leading the Way," *Army* (May 1994). See also Gordon Sullivan's *America's Army into the Twenty-First Century* (Institute for Foreign Policy Analysis, 1993); *Louisiana Maneuvers: The First Year*, Department of the Army, March 1, 1994; *Battle Labs: Maintaining the Edge* (U.S. Army Training and Doctrine Command [TRADOC], May 1994); and TRADOC Pamphlet 525-5, *Force XXI Operations: A Concept for the Evolution of Full-Dimensional Operations for the Strategic Army of the Early Twenty-First Century*, August 12, 1994.

Chapter 6

Secretary Aspin's remarks quoted in the epigraph were made at a September 1, 1993, Pentagon press conference on the Department of Defense's *Bottom-Up Review*. General Powell's remarks were to a Defense Writers' Group Breakfast Meeting on September 23, 1993. The *Nuclear Weapons Databook* is quoted in "Nuclear Leaders and Also-Rans," *The Washington Post*, March 24, 1994. START II nuclear force levels from *The Military Balance* were cited earlier. STRATCOM organization is detailed in James W. Caznan's "The New Order in Omaha," *Airforce* (March 1994). Presidential Review Directive 34 is analyzed in R. Jeffrey Smith's "Clinton Decides to Retain Bush Nuclear Arms Policy," *The Washington Post*, September

22, 1994. Admiral Miller's comments are from "Miller Helping Shape Military," by William W. McMichael, *Daily Press,* Norfolk, VA, May 23, 1994.

John Collins's observations are from his 1994 report to the Congress, "Military Preparedness: Principles Compared with U.S. Practices," *CRS Report for Congress,* January 21, 1994.

Statistics on women in the Persian Gulf War are from my *Persian Gulf War Almanac.* The Defense Department assessment is from *Conduct of the Persian Gulf War: A Final Report to the Congress* (Department of Defense, 1992). Aspin's announcement on changes in the rules for women were made in a January 13, 1994, Special Defense Department briefing, "New Ground Combat Rules." See also Rowan Scarborough's "Aspin Announces Rules for Women in Ground Combat," *Washington Times,* January 14, 1994. Statistics on women in the military were furnished by Department of the Army Public Affairs on March 10, 1994, and recruiting statistics were reported in Rowan Scarborough's "Military Recruiters Increasingly Rely on Women to Fill Ranks," *Washington Times,* February 28, 1994. NATO statistics are from "The Role of Women in the Armed Forces," Document 1267, *Assembly of Western European Union,* May 13, 1994.

The official Defense Department report on Reserve forces in Operation Desert Shield/Desert Storm, *Conduct of the Persian Gulf War,* is cited above. Statistics on Reserve forces come from my *Persian Gulf War Almanac.* For General Burba's remarks, see "1,000 Forms of Duty," U.S. Army Forces Command, Ft. McPherson, GA, April 1992.

George C. Marshall's comments on unpreparedness were contained in his "The Effect of School Histories on National Defense," *Report of the Tenth Annual Conference of The Association of Military Colleges and Schools of the United States,* March 7 and 8, 1923, Washington, D.C. President Bush's remarks are from his *National Security Strategy of the United States,* August 1991.

Base force analysis comes from John M. Collins's "National Military Strategy, The DOD Base Force, and U.S. Unified Command Plan," *CRS Report to Congress,* June 11, 1992. "Bottom-Up Review" commentary is from a September 1, 1993, Pentagon press conference. See also *The Bottom-Up Review,* cited above.

The degradation of military readiness was reported in "Readiness Problems Graver Than DOD Admitted—Thurmond," *Defense Daily,* October 5, 1994; Bradley Graham and John F. Harris's "Army

Readiness Lower Than Reported, Perry Says," *The Washington Post,* November 16, 1994; "Spence Challenges DOD Claim of Improved Military Readiness" (November 15, 1994) and "Spence Releases Readiness Report" (December 5, 1994), *Press Releases, Congressman Floyd Spence;* and Bill Gertz's "2 Republicans Seek Big Boost in Defense Budget," *Washington Times,* January 19, 1995. The Roles and Missions Commission is discussed in "Pentagon's Roles and Missions Commission Narrows List of Issues to 25," *Inside the Army,* October 3, 1994, and in Art Pine's "Hope Dims for Ending U.S. Military's Turf Wars," *Los Angeles Times,* November 22, 1994.

Chapter 7

Bottom-Up Review references are cited above. Gulf War statistics are from my *Persian Gulf War Almanac.* For Reserve restructuring, see "Defense Department Special Briefing on Restructuring the Army Reserve and Army National Guard," December 10, 1993. See also Robert L. Goldich, "Army Reserve Component Reforms and the Bottom-Up Review: Issues for Congress," *CRS Report to Congress,* January 4, 1994; "Enhanced Combat Brigades Named," *AUSA Washington Update* (September 1994); and "National Guard Strategic Reserve Combat Forces Named," *AUSA Washington Update* (October 1994).

Part III: Chapter 8

President Clinton's remarks quoted in the epigraph are from the May 3, 1994, Executive Summary of Presidential Decision Directive 25, "The Clinton Administration's Policy on Reforming Multilateral Peace Operations." Field Manual 100-23, *Peace Operations,* was published by the Department of the Army in December 1994. The multiplicity of Vietnam War objectives was noted by Hugh M. Arnold in "Official Justifications for America's Role in Indochina, 1949–67," *Asian Affairs* (September–October 1975). General Kinnard's remarks are from *The War Managers* (Hanover, NH: University Press of New England, 1977). Lin Piao's "Long Live the Victory of People's War" is cited above.

The South Vietnamese staff officer is quoted in Stephen T. Hosmer, et al., *The Fall of South Vietnam: Statements by Vietnamese Military and Civilian Leaders* (RAND, December 1978). Neil Sheehan's *The Bright Shining Lie: John Paul Vann and America in Viet-*

nam was published by Random House in 1988. For statistics on the CAP program, see my *Vietnam War Almanac*. An inside look is provided by Al Hemingway's *Our War Was Different* (Annapolis, MD: Naval Institute Press, 1994). For discussion of the 1915–34 U.S. intervention in Haiti, see Hugh DeSantis and Kenneth J. Dillon's "When We Last Invaded Haiti . . .", *The Washington Post*, July 10, 1994.

President Clinton's remarks on Haiti were made at his September 18 and September 20 White House briefings (Reuters Transcript Service). Secretary Perry's remarks are from his November 3, 1994, "Rules of Engagement" speech quoted earlier.

The comments at the Naval Institute conference where I served as a panel moderator are from my personal notes. Andrew S. Natsios's "Food Through Force: Humanitarian Intervention and U.S. Policy," was published in *The Washington Quarterly* (Winter 1994). Comments of Generals Wilkerson and Shalikashvili and others on humanitarian operations were reported by Eric Schmitt in "Military's Growing Role in Relief Missions Prompts Concerns," *The New York Times*, July 31, 1994. Criticism of U.S. efforts in Rwanda comes from R. Jeffrey Smith's "U.S. Mission to Rwanda Criticized," *The Washington Post*, September 5, 1994. See also Ivo H. Daalder's Op-Ed piece, "We Aren't Doing Much to Keep the Peace," *The Washington Post*, September 6, 1994.

For Secretary Perry's remarks on humanitarian aid, see his "The Rules of Engagement" quoted earlier. James Ngobi's comments were published in *Economic Sanctions and International Relations* (Notre Dame, IN: University of Notre Dame, 1993). The Military Academy study by Colonel Robert A. Doughty and Major Harold E. Raugh, Jr., "Embargoes in Historical Perspective," was published in *Parameters* (Spring 1991). See also "Sanctions: The Pluses and Minuses," *U.S. News & World Report*, October 31, 1994.

The comments of President Bush, Senator Nunn, and General Powell, and statistics on the Iraqi embargo are from my *Persian Gulf War Almanac*. *The New York Times* editorial, "Iraq Sanctions Cannot Be Forever," was published on August 1, 1994, and the *U.S. News & World Report* comment is from May 17, 1993. Colonel Barnett's comments are from "Exclusion as National Security Policy," *Parameters* (Spring 1994).

For background on sanctions, see Gary Clyde Hufbauer, et al., *Economic Sanctions Reconsidered* (2nd edn., Institute for International Economics, 1990); "Sanctions on Iraq," *The Economist*, April 2, 1993; Albert Wohlstetter, "Embargo the Aggressors, Not the Victims," *Wall Street Journal,* June 28, 1994; and R. C. Longworth, "Sanctions Sound Good, But Effect Is Minimal," *Chicago Tribune,* July 31, 1994.

For enlargement/engagement, including an analysis of the September 21, 1993, remarks of national security council director Anthony Lake which defined those concepts, see Mark M. Lowenthal, "The Clinton Foreign Policy: Emerging Themes," *CRS Report for Congress,* November 1, 1993. See also "Rules of Engagement," *The Economist,* October 2, 1993.

Chapter 9

President Clinton's remarks quoted in the epigraph are from his July 1994 *A National Security Strategy of Enlargement and Engagement,* cited above. General Douglas's remarks are from his paper presented at the Ira Eaker Lecture, "Peacekeeping, Peacemaking and Peace Enforcement," U.S. Air Force Academy, April 14, 1994. John F. Hillen's comments are from "UN Collective Security: Chapter Six and a Half," *Parameters* (Spring 1994). Sir Brian Urquart's remarks are taken from his testimony before the Subcommittee on International Security, International Organizations and Human Rights, House Committee on Foreign Affairs, on September 21, 1993. Mark Lowenthal's analysis is contained in "Peacekeeping in Future U.S. Foreign Policy," *CRS Report for Congress,* March 21, 1994. General Shalikashvili's remarks were made at an April 5, 1994, Pentagon press conference.

The best source for the Beirut debacle is Eric Hammel's *The Root: The Marines in Beirut* (New York: Harcourt Brace Jovanovich, 1985). Smith Hempstone's warning on Somalia is recounted in "A Vietnam Lesson to Consider for Somalia," *Boston Globe,* July 5, 1993. The text of President Bush's December 4, 1992, "Address to the Nation on the United States' Military Role in Somalia" was furnished by NBC News. Warren Christopher's remarks at his confirmation hearings are contained in the *Congressional Record.* The comments of Mohammed Sahnoun and Frank Carlucci were reported by Robin Wright, "Somalia Casts a Shadow on U.S. Policy," *Los Angeles Times,* March 4, 1994. *The Washington Post* editorial, "Shadow of a Doubt," was published on July 29, 1994.

The New Republic editorial, "Rescue Bosnia," appeared in its August 17 and 24, 1992, issue. Martin Sieff's *Washington Times* article, "Bosnia Is 'Top Priority,'" appeared on January 28, 1993.

Richard Cohen's "It's Not a Holocaust: Rhetoric and Reality in Bosnia," was in the February 28, 1993, *Washington Post*. For the debate on PDD 13, see Barton Gellman, "U.S. Reconsiders Putting GIs Under UN," *The Washington Post*, September 22, 1993; Paul Lewis, "Reluctant Warriors: U.N. Member States Retreat from Peacekeeping Roles," *The New York Times*, December 13, 1993; and Bill Gertz, "White House Retreats on Idea of UN Army," *Washington Times*, March 8, 1994.

For U.S. airdrops, see "Air Drop on Bosnia" and "America Drops In," *The Economist*, February 27, 1993. President Clinton's address, "Ending the Conflict in Bosnia," was reported in *Department of State Dispatch*, February 28, 1994. General Shalikashvili's comments are from an April 5, 1994, Pentagon news conference. Secretary Perry's remarks are from "United States Military Objectives," *Vital Speeches of the Day*, April 1, 1994. The executive summary of PDD 25, *The Clinton Administration's Policy on Reforming Multilateral Peace Operations*, was released by the White House on May 5, 1994. Commentary by UN Ambassador Madeleine K. Albright, NSC director Anthony Lake, and others is contained in the *Department of State Dispatch*, May 16, 1994. The November 28, 1984, "Weinberger Doctrine" was cited above.

For "the Somalia Syndrome," see Keith B. Richburg's "Somali Memory Lingers as GIs Head for Rwanda," *The Washington Post*, July 31, 1994. For the U.S. retreat on "peacekeeping," see Ann Devroy and John F. Harris's "U.S. Moves on Plan for Rwanda Troops," *The Washington Post*, July 28, 1994. See also my "Assertive Multilateralism," *Washington Times*, August 5, 1994. Republican attempts to cut UN peacekeeping operations are reported by R. Jeffrey Smith in "Republicans Seek to Curb U.N. Funding," *The Washington Post*, January 23, 1995.

Chapter 10

Colonel Dunlap's remarks are from his "The Origins of the American Military Coup of 2012," *Parameters* (Winter 1992–93). Those remarks were amplified in his "The Last American Warrior: Non-Traditional Missions and the Decline of the U.S. Armed Forces," *The Fletcher Forum of World Affairs* (Winter–Spring 1994). Representative Skelton's remarks were made in an October 4, 1993, special order speech to the House of Representatives.

Colonel English's *The Canadian Army and the Normandy Cam-*

paign: A Study in Failure of High Command was published by Praeger in 1991. T. R. Fehrenbach's *This Kind of War: A Study in Unpreparedness* was published by Macmillan in 1963. General Powell's comments were made at the Pentagon news conference on *The Bottom-Up Review,* cited earlier.

Colonel Dunlap's "Welcome to the Junta: The Erosion of Civilian Control of the U.S. Military" appeared in the Summer 1994 *Wake Forest Review,* and Admiral Crowe's remarks are from his *The Line of Fire: From Washington to the Gulf, the Politics and Battles of the New Military* (New York: Simon & Schuster, 1993). My analysis of the Vietnam War, *On Strategy,* is cited earlier. For the Admiral Boorda affair, see my "Wielding Harassment as a Weapon," *Washington Times,* June 23, 1994, and "Leadership Lemmings," *Washington Times,* July 23, 1994.

A. E. Bacevich's comments are from "Clinton's Military Problem—And Ours," *National Review,* December 13, 1993. Richard Kohn's article, "Out of Control: The Crisis in Civil-Military Relations," was published in the Spring 1994 issue of *The National Interest* and was summarized in a March 1994 *New York Times* Op-Ed article. See also "An Exchange on Civil-Military Relations" with articles by General Powell, former Navy Secretary John Lehman, former national security agency director William Odom, and Harvard Professor Samuel Huntington, with a reply by Kohn in the Summer 1994 issue of *The National Interest.*

For further commentary on civil-military relations, see Constantine Theodoropulo's "Smooth Operator," *Defense Media Review* (May 1994), and Angelo M. Codevilla's "Mis-leading the Military" in the June 1994 issue. Adam Yarmolinsky's remarks are from his "Civilian Control: New Perspectives for New Problems," *Indiana Law Journal,* vol. 49 (1974). Samuel Huntington's *The Soldier and the State: The Theory and Politics of Civil-Military Relations* was published by the Belknap Press of Harvard University Press in 1967.

Part IV: Chapter 11

President Clinton's remarks are from *A National Security Strategy of Engagement and Enlargement,* The White House, July 1994. General Weyand's quote from T. S. Eliot's "Little Gidding" is contained in the introduction to my occasional paper, "The Astarita Report: A Military Strategy for the Multipolar World," *Strategic Studies Group, U.S. Army War College,* April 30, 1981.

For history of the militia, see Russell F. Weigley's *History of the United States Army* (New York: Macmillan, 1967). See also "The New National Guard," *Century Illustrated Monthly Magazine* (February 1892). For draft renewal and Clinton's remarks, see Walter Mears, "Keeping the Draft in Place," *Washington Times,* May 28, 1994. See also Doug Bandow, "Draft Registration: The Politics of Institutional Immorality," *Policy Analysis,* August 15, 1994.

Missions of the armed forces are specified in Title 10: U.S. Code, and in Department of Defense Directive 5100.1, *Functions of the Department of Defense and Its Major Components,* January 10, 1986. Herman Kahn's remarks are taken from my notes of a seminar at the Hudson Institute in 1970. Wu Ch'i's works are translated by Ralph D. Sawyer in *The Seven Military Classics of Ancient China* (Boulder, CO: Westview Press, 1993).

Clinton's words at the Holocaust Museum are quoted in Stephen J. McCormick's "The Meaning of the Words," *The Shield* (July–August 1994). Charles Krauthammer's essay, "Time for a Little Panic," appears in the July 25, 1994, issue of *Time.*

For a detailed discussion of future nuclear strategy, see "The Role of Nuclear Weapons," *Document 1420,* Western European Union (WEU), May 19, 1994. For arguments of the arms-control advocates, see Mark Sommer's "Can Military Strategies Ban the Bomb?", *Christian Science Monitor,* April 29, 1994, and Spurgeon M. Kenny, Jr.'s, "Inventing an Enemy," *New York Times,* June 18, 1994. Ambassador Cooper's remarks are in his "Clinton's SDI Cuts Imperil America," *Empower America Issue Briefing* (Spring 1994). The ABM Standing Consultative Commission's meetings were reported in Frank Gafney's "Clinton Must Approach Missile Defense as D-Day of the '90s," *Defense News,* June 6–12, 1994.

Seth Cropsey's remarks are from "The Only Credible Deterrent," *Foreign Affairs* (March–April 1994). See also John M. Collins, et al.'s "Nuclear, Biological, and Chemical Weapons Proliferation: Potential Military Countermeasures," *CRS Report for Congress,* June 28, 1994. Japan's ABM defenses are discussed in "Japan Weighs Up Missile Defense Options," *Jane's Defence Weekly,* August 13, 1994. For West European views, see the WEU document, "The Role of Nuclear Weapons," cited above.

Clinton's 1991 campaign speech is quoted in David Morrison's "Over Here," *National Journal,* February 6, 1993. Alfred Thayer Mahan's *The Influence of Sea Power Upon History, 1660–1783* was republished by Presidio Press in Novato, California, in 1987. The DOD *Bottom-Up Review* is cited above.

For a critical look at the AJFP concept, see Margo MacFarland's "JCS Taps CINCs' Views of Controversial Joint Force Package Concept," *Inside the Pentagon,* February 17, 1954.

According to Colonel Robert Debs Heinl, Jr.'s, *Dictionary of Military and Naval Quotations* (Naval Institute Press, 1966), General Forrest actually said, "I make it a rule to get there first with the most men," but the more colorful words survive. General Powell was quoted in a *Houston Chronicle* editorial, "No Swagger," on February 8, 1992. The commentary on the two-wars scenario, including Secretary Perry's remarks, is from Bradley Graham and John F. Harris's "Skepticism Besets Plans for Military," *The Washington Post,* August 8, 1994.

The most recent translation of Sun Tzu's *The Art of War* is in Sawyer's *The Seven Military Classics of Ancient China,* cited above. The term "fourth generation warfare" was coined by Bill Lind, et al., in "The Changing Face of War: Into the Fourth Generation," *Military Review* (October 1989). For the Revolution in Military Affairs Conference, see the series of pamphlets from the Strategic Studies Institute, U.S. Army War College (Carlisle, PA), especially Michael J. Mazaar's *The Revolution in Military Affairs: A Framework for Defense Planning,* and Sir Michael Howard's "How Much Can Technology Change Warfare" in Sir Michael Howard and John F. Guilmartin, Jr.'s, *Two Historians in Technology and War.* For McNamara's Wall, see my *Vietnam War Almanac.* See also Thomas E. Ricks's "How Wars Are Fought Will Change Radically, Pentagon Planner Says," *Wall Street Journal,* July 15, 1994. For General Sullivan's remarks, see "War in the Information Age," by General Gordon R. Sullivan and Colonel James M. Dubik, *AUSA Landpower Essay Series 94-4,* May 1994. For the exchange among Senators Levin, Warner, and General Sullivan, see Lisa Burgess's "Congress Wrestles with Technology, Force Cuts," *Defense News,* May 9–15, 1994.

Comments on a new "Peace Corps" were initially made during my September 21, 1993, testimony before a subcommittee of the House Committee on Foreign Affairs, which was reprinted in *Strategic Review* (Fall 1993).

Seneca is quoted in Heinl's *Dictionary of Military and Naval Quotations,* cited earlier. Weigley's observations are from *The American Way of War: A History of United States Military Strategy and Policy,* cited earlier. Nitze's comments are from "Grand Strategy Then and Now: NSC-68 and Its Lessons for the Future," *Strategic Review* (Winter 1994). For Eric Rosenberg's comments see *Defense Week,* September 12, 1994. Weyand's comments are from my personal notes.

Mark Watson's words are from the Center of Military History's U.S. Army in World War II series, *Chief of Staff: Pre-War Plans and Preparations* (Government Printing Office, 1950). General Garner's warning was reported by Graham and Harris in their "Skepticism Besets Plans for Military," cited earlier.

Stanley R. Sloan's "The United States and the Use of Force in the Post–Cold War World: Toward Self-Deterrence?" appeared in the *CRS Report for Congress,* July 20, 1994. General Shalikashvili's remarks are from his testimony before the Defense Subcommittee of the Senate Appropriations Committee on March 8, 1994.

Bibliography

This bibliography is limited to those works not specifically cited in the text which provide useful background on military policy formulation. The majority of reference materials, however, are listed in the Notes on Sources.

Books and Pamphlets

Blackwill, Robert D., and Sergei A. Karaganov, eds. *Damage Limitation or Crisis: Russia and the Outside World.* Washington, D.C.: Brassey's, 1994.

Blechman, Barry M., et al. *The American Military in the Twenty-First Century.* New York: St. Martin's Press, 1993.

Brzezinski, Zbigniew. *Out of Control: Global Turmoil on the Eve of the Twenty-First Century.* New York: Charles Scribner, 1993.

Bundy, McGeorge, William J. Crowe, Jr., and Sidney D. Drell. *Reducing Nuclear Danger: The Road Away from the Brink.* New York: Council on Foreign Relations Press, 1993.

Burrows, William E., and Robert Windrem. *Critical Mass: The Dangerous Race for Superweapons in a Fragmenting World.* New York: Simon & Schuster, 1994.

Curtis, Gerald L., ed. *The United States, Japan and Asia: Challenges for U.S. Policy.* New York: W. W. Norton & Company, 1994.

Damrosch, Lori Fisher, ed. *Enforcing Restraint: Collective Intervention in Internal Conflicts.* New York: Council on Foreign Relations Press, 1994.

Dawson, Joseph G. III, ed. *Commanders in Chief: Presidential Leadership in Modern Wars.* Lawrence, KS: University Press of Kansas, 1993.

Guertner, Gary L., ed. *The Search for Strategy: Politics and Strategic Vision.* Westport, CT: Greenwood Press, 1993.

Hahn, Walter, and H. Joachim Maitre, eds. *Paying the Premium: A Military Insurance Policy for Peace and Freedom.* Westport, CT: Greenwood Press, 1993.

Hiro, Dilip. *Between Marx and Muhammad: The Changing Face of Central Asia.* New York: HarperCollins, 1994.

Ion, A. Hamish, and E. J. Errington, eds. *Great Powers and Little Wars: The Limits of Power.* New York: Praeger, 1993.

Jablonsky, David. *Why Is Strategy Difficult?* Carlisle, PA: Strategic Studies Institute, U.S. Army War College, June 1, 1992.

———. *Paradigm Lost? Transitions and the Search for a New World Order.* Carlisle, PA: Strategic Studies Institute, U.S. Army War College, July 1, 1993.

Lincoln, Edward J. *Japan's New Global Role.* Washington, D.C.: The Brookings Institution, 1993.

Mandelbaum, Michael. *The Strategic Quadrangle: Japan, China, Russia and the United States in East Asia.* New York: Council on Foreign Relations Press, 1994.

Manwaring, Max, ed., *Gray Area Phenomena: Confronting the New World Disorder.* Boulder, CO: Westview Press, 1993.

Martel, W. C., and W. T. Pendley. *Nuclear Proliferation: Rethinking U.S. Policy to Promote Stability in an Era of Proliferation.* Maxwell AFB, AL: Air War College, 1994.

Mazaar, Michael J. *The Revolution in Military Affairs: A Framework for Defense Planning.* Carlisle, PA: Strategic Studies Institute, U.S. Army, June 10, 1994.

Muravchik, Joshua. *Exporting Democracy: Fulfilling America's Destiny.* Washington, D.C.: AEI Press, 1991.

Odom, William E. *America's Military Revolution: Strategy and Structure After the Cold War.* Washington, D.C.: American University Press, 1993.

O'Very, David P., et al., eds. *Controlling the Atom in the 21st Century.* Boulder, CO: Westview Press, 1994.

Romm, Joseph J. *Defining National Security: The Nonmilitary Aspects.* New York: Council on Foreign Relations Press, 1993.

Roper, John, et al. *Keeping the Peace in the Post–Cold War Era.* Washington, D.C.: The Brookings Institution, 1993.

Rostow, Eugene V. *Toward Managed Peace.* Binghamton, NY: Vail-Ballou Press, 1993.

Sarkesian, Sam C. *Unconventional Conflicts in a New Security Era:*

Lessons from Malaysia and Vietnam. Westport, CT: Greenwood Press, 1993.

Shawcross, William. *Cambodia's New Deal.* Washington, D.C.: Carnegie Endowment Publication, 1994.

Smith, Gaddis. *The Last Years of the Monroe Doctrine: 1945–1993.* New York: Hill & Wang, 1994.

Stofft, William A., and Gary L. Guertner. *Ethnic Conflict: Implications for the Army of the Future.* Carlisle, PA: Strategic Studies Institute, U.S. Army War College, March 14, 1994.

Sturgill, Claude C. *Low Intensity Conflict in American History.* New York: Praeger, 1993.

Sullivan, Gordon. *America's Army into the Twenty-First Century.* Cambridge, MA: Institute for Foreign Policy Analysis, 1993.

———. *War in the Information Age.* Carlisle, PA: Strategic Studies Institute, U.S. Army War College, June 6, 1994.

———, and James M. Dubik. *Land Warfare in the 21st Century.* Carlisle, PA: Strategic Studies Institute, U.S. Army War College, February 1993.

Taylor, Charles W. *Alternative World Scenarios for a New Order of Nations.* Carlisle, PA: Strategic Studies Institute, 1993.

Toffler, Alvin and Heidi. *War and Anti-War: Survival at the Dawn of the 21st Century.* Boston: Little, Brown & Company, 1993.

Tucker, Robert W., and David C. Hendrickson. *The Imperial Temptation: The New World Order and America's Purpose.* New York: Council on Foreign Relations Press, 1992.

Van Ham, Peter. *Managing Non-Proliferation Regimes in the 1990s.* New York: Council on Foreign Relations Press, 1994.

Young, Peter R., ed. *Defence and the Media in Time of Limited War.* London: Frank Cass, 1992.

Articles

Ayittey, George B. N. "The Somalia Crisis: Time for an African Solution," *Policy Analysis,* March 28, 1994.

Berdal, Mats R. "Fateful Encounter: The United States and UN Peacekeeping," *Survival* (Spring 1994).

Brzezinski, Zbigniew. "Selected Global Commitment," *Foreign Affairs* (Fall 1991).

———. "The Cold War and Its Aftermath," *Foreign Affairs* (Fall 1992).

Bullard, Monte. "U.S.-China Relations: The Strategic Calculus," *Parameters* (Summer 1993).

Burbach, David T. "Presidential Approval and the Use of Force," *MIT Defense and Arms Control Studies Program* (May 1994).

Clark, Mark T. "The Future of Clinton's Foreign and Defense Policy: Multilateral Security," *Comparative Strategy*, no. 1 (1994).

Cohen, Eliot A. "What to Do About National Defense," *Commentary* (November 1994).

Collins, John M. "Korea Crisis 1994: Military Geography, Military Balance, Military Options," *CRS Report for Congress*, April 11, 1994.

Conroy, Barbara. "The Futility of U.S. Intervention in Regional Conflicts," *Policy Analysis*, May 19, 1994.

Higgins, William S. "Deterrence After the Cold War: Conventional Arms and the Prevention of War," *Airpower Journal* (Summer 1993).

Jablonsky, David. "Strategic Vision and Presidential Authority in the post–Cold War Era," *Parameters* (Winter 1991–92).

Mandelbaum, Michael. "The Reluctance to Intervene," *Foreign Policy* (Summer 1994).

Oksenberg, Michael. "The China Problem," *Foreign Affairs* (Summer 1991).

Rosenstiel, Thomas B. "Television's Emotional Effect on U.S. Foreign Policy," *Los Angeles Times*, July 22, 1994.

Silkett, Wayne A. "Alliance and Coalition Warfare," *Parameters* (Summer 1993).

Sullivan, Gordon R. "Doctrine: A Guide to the Future," *Military Review* (February 1992).

Thies, Wallace J. "A Twenty-First Century Army," *Parameters* (Spring 1991).

Vasquez, Ian. "Washington's Dubious Crusade for Hemispheric Democracy," *Policy Analysis*, January 12, 1994.

Vuono, Carl E. "The Strategic Value of Conventional Forces," *Parameters* (September 1990).

———. "Desert Storm and the Future of Conventional Forces," *Foreign Affairs* (Spring 1991).

Index

‖ About the Author

Colonel Harry G. Summers is a veteran of the Korean and Vietnam Wars, twice decorated for valor and twice wounded in action. His award-winning critique of the Vietnam War, *On Strategy*, is used as a text by the war and staff colleges and by many civilian universities. *The New York Times Book Review* called his *On Strategy II* "the best of any gulf war book to date."

The military analyst for NBC News during the Gulf War, Colonel Summers has been a frequent guest on radio talk shows nationwide. He is an award-winning journalist, a syndicated columnist for the *Los Angeles Times*, editor of *Vietnam* magazine, and was formerly *U.S. News & World Report's* chief military correspondent and a contributing editor of *Defense and Diplomacy* magazine. He has written for *American Heritage, The Atlantic Monthly, Harper's,* and *The New Republic* among other publications.

He is a member of the Council on Foreign Relations and the International Institute for Strategic Studies and has testified before Congress and lectured at the White House. An Army War College Distinguished Fellow who has held the War College's General Douglas MacArthur Chair and the Marine Corps University's 1993–94 Brigadier General H. L. Oppenheimer Chair of Warfighting Strategy and the 1994–95 Chair of Military Affairs, he has been named the 1996 holder of the fleet Admiral Chester W. Nimitiz Memorial Lectureship at the University of California, Berkley. A graduate of the Army War College, he holds a bachelor's degree in Military Science from the University of Maryland, and a Master of Military Arts and Science from the Army Command and General Staff College.

Married since 1951 to the former Eloise Cunningham, their two sons are serving Army officers and their daughter-in-law is a Gulf War veteran.